SOMETHING IS ALWAYS ON FIRE

Something Is Always on Fire

MY LIFE SO FAR

Measha Brueggergosman

HARPER**AVENUE**

AN IMPRINT OF HARPERCOLLINS*PUBLISHERS*LTD

Something Is Always on Fire
Copyright © 2017 by Measha Brueggergosman.
All rights reserved.

Published by Harper Avenue, an imprint of HarperCollins Publishers Ltd

First edition

*This work was created with the support of the Paul D Fleck Fellowship
residency at Banff Centre for Arts and Creativity.*

HarperCollins books may be purchased for educational, business,
or sales promotional use through our Special Markets Department.

HarperCollins Publishers Ltd
2 Bloor Street East, 20th Floor
Toronto, Ontario, Canada
M4W 1A8

www.harpercollins.ca

Library and Archives Canada Cataloguing in Publication
information is available upon request.

ISBN 978-1-44343-883-4

Printed and bound in the United States
LSC/H 9 8 7 6 5 4 3 2 1

To my parents, my siblings, my elders, my family,
my besties and my offspring

But the one who did not know and did things deserving of blows will be beaten lightly. But much will be required from everyone to whom much has been given.
But even more will be demanded from the one to whom much has been entrusted.

—LUKE 12:48

CONTENTS

PROLOGUE

As I was wheeled into the operating room for emergency open-heart surgery, I didn't know I had only a 13 percent chance of living to see my thirty-second birthday.

Just two days before—on June 8, 2009—I was at the Black Hoof restaurant in Toronto, when I suddenly felt a sharp pressure at the base of my throat and a strange numbness in my extremities. *Am I getting a cold?* I would be starting rehearsals for my concerts of Richard Strauss's *Vier letzte Lieder* with the Toronto Symphony Orchestra the next day, but I was still anticipating a hearty dinner when I realized my arms felt tingly. I eyed my red wine: *Am I having an allergic reaction? Dear God, please don't let me be allergic to wine!*

I was concerned enough to cancel my charcuterie plate (and I love a good *charcute*) but sure-footed enough to climb into my car and drive myself home. By the time I arrived, my legs were also feeling tingly. My husband, Markus, called 911 and an ambulance rushed me to the hospital. I was given medication for hypertension, then kept overnight. I was released the next morning, with an MRI scheduled for later in the week.

After a day and a half of me lying on the couch, woozy and just not quite myself, a friend drove me to my family doctor, who sent me back to the hospital with a strongly worded note requesting an MRI immediately. Three hours later I was in surgery. My blood pressure was so high it had ripped a hole in my aorta, the largest blood vessel branching from the heart. The blood was escaping from my aorta instead of circulating through my limbs—hence the numbness and the tingling. This condition—a dissected aorta—is extremely rare in people not of retirement age, let alone a young woman who has never had any children. It is usually diagnosed in an autopsy after sudden death from internal bleeding.

My surgeon opened my sternum, then repaired the tear in my aorta with a stent. When I regained consciousness, my parents were at my bedside, having flown in from Nova Scotia. As much as I do not fear death, the terror in their eyes told me how unbearable losing me would have been for them. Though my father, a man who himself had had a quadruple bypass, had constantly warned me to watch my health, I cockily believed I was too full of life to die. I now have a nifty scar—just like my dad's—running like a zipper down my breastbone, to remind me otherwise.

I knew that I would have to cancel some key engagements I'd been looking forward to. I had been invited to Cape Canaveral to watch the launch of the space shuttle *Endeavour* in which Canadian astronaut Julie Payette would carry my album *Surprise!* into space. My Strauss concerts with Peter Oundjian conducting the Toronto Symphony at Roy Thomson Hall and my debut in *Porgy and Bess* at the prestigious Styriarte Festival in Graz, Austria, with Nikolaus Harnoncourt conducting, were both casualties of my emergency open-heart surgery.

But pulling through my operation spurred me forward: *Okay, I've survived. Now, get me out of this hospital.* My own impatience elevated my blood pressure and delayed my hospital release for a couple of days. When I finally did escape, it was with five medications to take daily, including a beta blocker and a diuretic. This didn't stop me from resuming my schedule. Less than two weeks after my surgery, I appeared on the national morning show *Canada AM* to let the public know I was recovering well. Two weeks later, I performed one song at a dear friend's wedding in my hometown. Then, a little over two months after my sternum had been opened, I travelled to Prince Edward Island for my first concert: Berlioz's *Les nuits d'été* at the Indian River Festival. After the Berlioz, I had arranged for a two-week vacation for my family and my long-time voice teacher and mentor Mary Morrison, in an old farmhouse on the ocean.

From the outside looking in, my life seemed on an upswing. But it would soon be in shambles. There's nothing like an encounter with mortality to force you to look from the inside out, to examine your world with a hard eye and see what's working, what's missing, what may need changing. And sometimes you come to the wrong conclusions . . .

Adding to the confusion and instability growing inside me was the fact that I wasn't taking responsibility for much of anything in my life at this point. When you're a child prodigy, the focused nature of your training goes a long way to convincing you your needs are the only ones that matter. I came to believe the rules didn't apply to me. Over the years, I'd grown very comfortable with (and proficient at) lying to pretty much everyone: my parents, my husband, my management, myself. Until I was twenty-eight, I hovered around 350 pounds, and you can't be that fat without telling yourself a few big ones.

In October—four months after my surgery—I temporarily separated from my high school sweetheart and husband of ten years. Our dissolution wasn't dramatic. There wasn't any yelling or screaming. I felt adrift and unreachable. I knew I was in a prison of my own making, but I didn't know how I'd even gotten there, or why.

Arguably, my separation had been coming for a while, even if my reasons weren't entirely clear. I just let it happen. I didn't fight it. My career always affords me an exit strategy: getting on a plane and "escaping" somewhere is the nature of my job. Anyone can use a career to swallow up a relationship. Any job can make it possible to abandon anything stressful without having to deal with the consequences. I used my job as an excuse and I left.

My husband moved out of our Toronto home because he didn't want to be surrounded by all that was ours. I sank into the steady stream of ever-changing countries and repertoire. I certainly had nights when I choked on the grief of it all, suffocating on the personal failure and shame. I didn't know what would happen or how I would end up, but I had the merciful sanctuary of distracting myself with the changing scenery my job afforded me.

I also had my Bikram yoga practice to help me maintain some semblance of accountability. I've been an avid hot-yoga practitioner since 2006. I would enrol in a daunting nine-week teacher training course in the spring of 2010, but in the months leading up to that, my calendar would take me to Seoul, New York, Berlin, Vienna, Brussels, Oslo, Luxembourg, London, even to christen a ship in the Netherlands. Becoming a hot-yoga teacher would turn out to be a transformative experience. At the end of each of the nine gruelling weeks, I wrote a detailed dispatch from the trenches of teacher training to my "nearests and dearests"—the circle of friends closest to me who were supporting me and praying me through what I knew would be the hardest thing I'd ever done. Excerpts from these emails are included in this memoir because I believe they provide insight into the consistencies of who I am, while also revealing who I've become and how I've changed.

While I might have been trying to squeeze more out of life after nearly dying ten months before I went to Las Vegas for my yoga course, I was also miserable and numb. I was trying to find words that wouldn't come. Trying to find answers that weren't ready to be found. I didn't know what I believed anymore. I was unable to authentically engage in the most instinctual of pleasures. I had no reliable connection to anything but my job, and sometimes I didn't even like that very much.

My parents were worried. My friends were worried. My husband was worried. I was worried. This moral confusion was new to me after having been born and raised in a loving home with a strong Christian faith. Faith was the spine that had held my life upright and given it meaning. With no clue how to fix it and no will to do so, my vision blurred by guilt and shame, by the fall of 2009 I had developed a kind of comfort with this searching sense of confusion. It had become my new reality.

In the times when I add cheese to my whining, I remind myself that I've won the cosmic lottery by being born in Canada. I reaffirm that God has blessed me on a scale almost ridiculous in its rewards. I also believe that my life has been balanced by genuine heartache, not all of it self-imposed through what I like to call my own "emotional splurging." Everything in my life—good, bad, sad, triumphant, tragic—has served its specific function in steering me to where I'm supposed to go (or not go), and after some conspicuous faltering, I now find myself at a place of relatively consistent contentment, slowly inching toward peace. I can begin to understand the trajectory of my life as being divided (so far) into seven-year periods separated by some pivotal life change.

At thirty-nine, I've attempted to take stock, to examine the questions that have bubbled to the surface over the last few "sets of seven" and steer myself purposefully forward through the next seven years. Because if not now, then when? Why put it off any longer? I mean, it's never a perfect time. *Something* is always on fire. No matter who you are or how much you do or do not have. *Some* part of your life is always going to be in flames. If it's not your finances, it's your relationship, or your work, or your house, or your play, or your kids, or your mind, or your parents, or your car, or your health, or your taxes.

I'm sure there *must* be a study somewhere that examines the cosmic, undeniable shift that enters the reality of all sentient humans every seven years or so. The fork in the road where you ask yourself, *Am I really where I want to be?* and *Am I feeling how I want to feel?* Because one thing I know for sure: Nothing has turned out how I thought it would. And it's in those periods in my life where I feel something percolating, a groundswell putting into question every decision I've made, that I ask myself, *Who am I and why?* I search for an answer I can live with but try to find a hypothesis that will keep me hungrily moving toward a destiny of greater purpose. If I don't, I run the risk of becoming bitter or, worse, apathetic.

I also ask myself, *How do I get what I want?* Because I believe you can have it all, with the right timing, heaps of patience and the core veracity of what it is you actually want. Asking the question all on its own is a huge part of the equation for me. However, unless I ask myself *What's holding me back?* I'll never fully examine the obstacles and the openings that come into my life to guide, teach and, ultimately, maneuver me toward getting what I want. Because really, we're only here to pinpoint, or even clarify, the existential prognosis that results from answering the age-old question, *Why am I here?*

This memoir will contain some universal truths because we're all in this together, but you, dear reader, will decide for yourself what parts of the book are inspirational and what parts are a cautionary tale. I have the words SELF-CONTROL, WISDOM, LAUGHTER, TRUTH, FORGIVENESS tattooed on the inside of my left forearm. It's my cheat sheet. I have yet to experience any of them to their fullest and have never achieved them simultaneously. They represent the gifts I most want present in myself and in the people who surround me. And not one of us has it all figured out. But like getting pregnant, the fun part is in the trying.

Part 1

WHO AM I AND WHY?

~~~~~

~~~~~~~

Date: Saturday, April 17, 2010, 9:37 pm

From: Measha Brueggergosman

To: Nearests and Dearests

Subject: Life on the Strip

To my Nearests and Dearests,

I'm literally on my last leg. And it's taken me forever to get here. I have mixed feelings about how quickly the time has gone by, but the irony is I almost didn't come. A hefty mix of fatigue and fear provided ample reason for me to drag my feet with my application. I think because I put this yoga course in my calendar over 3 years ago, it somehow took on an objectivity that made its actual arrival somewhat of a surprise. I certainly didn't think that I'd feel like a whole other person than the one who started this practice over 3 years ago. As you all know, in June 2009 I almost died. I never indulged in the so-called me time that's supposed to help the dust settle. I just jumped right back in, and I've been focusing on getting better, getting back to work and getting back in shape. But I haven't been to a yoga class in 3 weeks and I'm about to start an intensive

26-posture course that sees me practising twice a day in 42-degree (Celsius) heat for ninety minutes—in addition to learning all the anatomy, the history and the class dialogue in three languages (my choice).

I'm trying to stay positive, but I keep wondering if I've made a horrible mistake. I owe so much to this practice. I've lost a ton of weight; it's strengthened my spine (literally and figuratively); it's connected my mind and body, strengthened my singing technique. I'm also convinced that it's the reason I healed so quickly and completely after my open-heart surgery. I make my living as an opera singer, but I've been often asked if I'm looking to start a new profession as a yoga teacher. I know many of the yogis at this course will be future studio owners, but I'm not sure that's my end game. I've never been very good at staying in one spot. I'm mostly looking to accomplish something truly daunting, and it would be nice to be able to teach while I travel for work. Which is why I plan to learn the series' dialogue in English, French and German. But I don't know if that's a realistic goal, since I'll be grateful to just make it to the end of these 9 weeks. For now, I've been given very insightful advice to focus on me, be open and approach each class like it's my very first one.

I've never been to Vegas. I'm ready for something new and intimidating and good for me. I hope this is it. To avoid wasting time and energy on hair elastics and wet hair, I chopped off all my Afro this morning, so I'm newly shorn and good to go. We've started our descent into Las Vegas. I'm sitting on the aisle, but I'm catching intermittent glances of lightly snow-dusted peaks and the Nevada desert. This vista is undoubtedly more calming than what awaits me on the strip.

Much love to you all,

Measha

Interviewers often ask me when I first decided to become an opera singer. I usually wonder if that means when did I first decide I could sing, or when did I first discover what opera was and that it was something for me? (I do know that these journalists aren't likely to be interested in the semantics of their question.) The question itself implies that they don't know that a singer is its own species. Not a profession. I decide to assume that they are asking me when I decided I was, Singer. When I became conscious of whatever genetic cocktail formed the ingredients needed to make up that rarest of breeds called Singer, and the ultra-specialized subcategory Opera Singer, that has made my friendly freak show complete. But in the way you can neither decide nor influence your own DNA, I can best describe my animal as always having been one possessing the compelling predisposition to be, Singer.

This doesn't mean by any stretch that people who are in love with the sound of themselves singing, or beguiled with the process of singing, are not good singers. Not at all. However, to be the animal that is Singer, there has to be a hunger that cannot be sated by anything but singing. You feel most alive by the process of creating evocative sound. Now, sometimes the people who claim to feel this way are not good. They're actually quite bad. Sometimes those people are delusional. They may have very strong portions of their souls that believe with great intensity that they should sing, even though they should not. Everyone knows someone who fits this description. But, mercifully, that's not the kind of person I'm talking about here. I'm talking about the person who honestly could not be anything else. I'm talking about the planets aligning and knitting together in my mother's womb a human who, seemingly without any free will, and subjected to a force stronger than gravity or the tides, neither "comes to a realization" nor "decides to be" but instead simply knows she is fulfilling her responsibilities to herself and to mankind by pledging her allegiance to, and pooling all her energies and resources to become, Singer.

I couldn't tell you when that happened. It just always was.

But since this is a memoir, I should tell you that I was seven years old when I took my first voice lesson. I don't think I truly knew what I was doing there. To learn piano was what I really wanted, because my sister had lessons and I wanted everything my older sister had. I went to these voice lessons, and because I was raised to respect authority, I did what I was told. I have never been an (overtly) subversive person. It is of no interest to me to stage a mutiny or do any overthrowing nonsense. I like to think composers such as James Rolfe and Michael Tilson Thomas have written pieces for me because I'm willing to fully commit to trying just about anything, since I'm confident that I can usually give or get people what they want.

To be good at a skill as specialized as singing, something that so many people love and cherish, is a huge responsibility, and I take it very seriously. I've had over thirty years to have that calling take root and grow within me. I remain passionate about, and committed to, knowing everything there is to know about singing because . . . well, it genuinely interests me.

I honestly can't imagine myself doing anything else. That is not to say I don't have any other interests or skills, but all my greatest joys can be linked to the life that singing has gifted to me. All my greatest agonies have been made bearable because of the outlet singing has afforded me. Becoming a mom was made sweeter by the bonding time with my babies that I was able to build into my schedule because I had built enough of an infrastructure within my small business that, to a certain extent, it could gift to me the closest thing I would ever get to "maternity leave."

But the singing itself is constantly kicking me in the tuchus. While some composers and styles seem to be an extension of my truest self, other music makes me feel stupid and slow, like I've never read a note in my life or taken a single voice lesson. There remain passages I'll never get right, operas I'll never sing and conductors and artistic directors who'll never like me. I'm in a pretty consistent state of dissatisfaction stemming from how much needs to be done. I will die leaving behind untapped repertoire, remuneration, distinction and artistry.

So why do it? In her book *Big Magic*, Elizabeth Gilbert writes that "holding yourself together through all the phases of creation is where the real work lies." The phases of my creative process include every ounce of the daily grind of emails, paperwork, diaper changes, guilt, translations, delayed flights, jerks, budgeting, fevers, lost wallets, stolen passports, arguments, sinus infections, taxes and massive cell phone bills. I am tired pretty much all the time. I have zero job security and no unemployment insurance or retirement savings. Granted, I should probably do something about a lot of those things, but I'm too busy doing what I love to let all the garbage I have to eat in order to do it get in the way of me actually doing it. In other words, I know how committed I am to singing because I'm willing to put up with just about anything to do it. I have crossed an ocean to sing for one job, journeyed to remote parts of the world for the right diction coach, Skyped with directors who didn't want me, stayed up all night doing translations, written countless emails to keep my career alive, travelled crazy distances to listen to those singers who really do it for me. I will fight for anything that feels expansive, restorative or strengthening, just so I can turn around and infuse that rejuvenation into my art.

I try to keep my blinders on and run my own race, but I sometimes find myself blind with jealousy and envy, coveting the careers of my peers—and I don't even narrow it down to classical singers! People have described me as happy and funny, perhaps even acquiescent, but the truth is, I want everything, all the time. I rarely live in the moment and am constantly looking for the off-ramp to something better. The different parts of me that push me in one direction for this pull me to another for that. I mean, I am an opera singer, not yet forty, writing a memoir. What could I possibly have to say and why in the world would anyone give me a platform to say it? I maintain that every life, no matter its current length, is "to be continued." There's no perfect time for anything, since everyone, regardless of age, is on borrowed time. I am entitled to nothing but my dreams. And I choose to dream big and go from there.

Early in my career I was in a city that didn't matter to me, in daily rehearsals to sing music that means nothing to me anymore. I hadn't seen my parents for a long time and I was feeling homesick. While wandering during a rare afternoon off, I came by a Tiffany's jewellery boutique, and I went inside to cheer myself up. After gravitating toward the perfume counter (the only thing in the store I could afford), I smelled one bottle, then another. Suddenly, I became this crazy lady, standing in front of the Tiffany's jewellery display, sobbing, "Mom . . . Mom . . . "

For me as a kid, my mother had a special scent—a combination of her moisturizer, her hair products and her makeup—

that infused her clothes no matter how many times they got washed. This combination of fragrances, in a row of innocuous, unoriginal scents in a shop I couldn't afford to be in, smelled just like my mother.

My olfactory system has always triggered memories of my childhood.

My maternal grandmother smelled like food and roses. I spent a lot of time with her until she died when I was five. My mind's eye pictures her smooth face in a bedroom filled with clutter. I remember wanting to rummage through it all because it was sure to unlock the secrets of the Matriarch. I had a keen sense of her prominence in the family hierarchy, but I mostly remember how warm she felt. Her comforting smell. Nanny once gave me a pair of white sandals with a picture of little bunnies on top of each foot. When she put them on my feet, I knew they were special. I was too young to remember how Nanny's death affected me, but I do remember being at my Grampy's funeral a few years later. I cried and cried and cried right along with the adults. My child's mind had convinced itself that we would be at this funeral for all eternity and that the sadness would never ever end. But then we went home. The adults were eating and laughing. It was over. I thought, *Oh! I guess dying's not so bad.*

Since my father's parents were both dead by his early teens, these are the only memories I have of the elder states-people of my family. We have always been open about such earthly things, but I didn't grow up with any grandparents. Consequently, seeing now how my parents and my in-laws interact with my children—and the transformative abandon with which they generously cast their loving net of joy and indulgence over them—has me clinging to all the memories I have of the generations that preceded my own. I know that my reactions to the major touchstones of life—death, love, intimacy, loss—are in some way informed by these grasping, transient, multi-sensory memories from my early childhood.

I was born on June 28, 1977, in Fredericton, New Brunswick, the youngest of Ann Eatmon and Sterling Gosman's three children. We lived in a bungalow with a damp, carpeted basement, on Oak Avenue, on the less affluent north side—the dark side. My tiny room was decorated with *Sesame Street* wallpaper and rainbow curtains. Since it was next to my parents' bedroom, I often heard my father snore. Today, I either sleep like a baby to the sound of snoring or I can't sleep at all. Later, when I became morbidly obese, it was me who snored. (I would wake myself up and think, *Who is making all that noise?*)

Oak Avenue was a short street with about twenty houses—the kind of place where everybody knew each other. The family who lived across the street from us, the Cronins, had, like, a million kids—all contemporaries of my older siblings. I would often drop by after school to say hi, and Mrs. Cronin, one of the few adults I was permitted to visit on my own, would give me either a pickle or a chocolate chip cookie, both homemade, as an after-school snack. To this day I love those two flavours in equal amounts, though never at the same time.

My own mother is an effortlessly graceful woman. Like all of us, she is not without her faults, but she has loved me flawlessly. She is our family's nurturer, who cooks with fluent intuition and sews like a champ. She had a full-time government job and I went to daycare after school until my parents picked me up.

My father is majestic and steadfast. He worked for the CBC for thirty-three years, first as a cameraman, then as a radio technician. He was an athlete, who has been twice inducted into the New Brunswick Sports Hall of Fame for his athletic accomplishments. He ran every morning when we were kids. He would be out by 5:30 a.m., and Fredericton commuters could set their watches to his crossing of the Westmorland Street Bridge. He wouldn't call it a meditation, but that's what it was: time alone to focus his mind and keep his body fit as a fiddle. Throughout his life my father has been shrouded by his own difficult upbringing in a family plagued by poverty, alcoholism and unemployment. As he's grown older, healed by God and time, he has mellowed, creating peace in his home and in his community.

My brother, Neville, ten years older than me, turned fifty this year and is one of the wisest people I know. Oddly enough, when he was in elementary school, one of his teachers told my parents, "Your son is a joy to have in the classroom, but he's stupid. We'd like to hold him back for a year."

"You put him through, and we'll get him through," my father said, and that's exactly what happened. Neville is so much more than a pastor, with a PhD and more degrees than you can shake a stick at. He's too over to be overqualified. He is inventive, ambitious and uncompromising in the standards he sets for himself and for his family.

My sister, Teah, who is five years older than me, is our family's pioneer. After competing internationally as a gymnast, she retired at the ripe age of sixteen (typical for gymnasts), and in so doing experienced her first crisis of identity. She transitioned into a track and field star, then studied international development. After living with her Kenyan husband in Africa for a few years, she returned to the Maritimes with one daughter and another on the way. Like my father, Teah has, with aplomb and razor-sharp wit, played the hand dealt to her. She is loving, complicated and protective.

As the baby of the Gosman family, I have always given the impression of being extremely obedient. My shift was pretty light overall, because, like all babies of a family, I learned our family dynamic by observing interactions between my parents and my siblings. In many ways, all three of us were "only" children because we were born five years apart. I'm emotionally closer to my brother, but my personality is more like my sister's. Though we each have our own distinctive look, we all share that Gosman vibe. I have proof that that is an actual thing because I now see it in my own boys. As I was growing up on the streets of

Fredericton, it wouldn't have been unusual for me to hear someone remark, "There goes a Gosman." Thankfully, it was always
said in a good way.

My first crush was a boy named Mark Leblanc. He lived next
door to us on Oak Avenue. With my bestie at the time,
Sarah Mahoney—who to this day remains a kindred spirit and
close friend—we made up a chaste threesome. She was Mark's
girlfriend number one, and I was Mark's girlfriend number two.
One day in kindergarten I saved a swing for Mark on the playground and Sarah didn't. That's when I was promoted to girlfriend number one and Sarah was demoted to girlfriend number
two. To say nothing of what this interaction says about childhood gender dynamics, it was an early taste of what it felt like to
win, and I liked it.

Brunswick Street United Baptist Church in downtown
Fredericton, with its congregation of about three hundred, was
the cornerstone of my family's social and spiritual life. The state
of Christianity being what it is, I'm always quick to point out
that this church was not one of those weirdo, Bible-thumpin',
close-minded, extremist nightmares but, instead, a community-
driven place of mentoring from which the teachings of Jesus
radiated into our lives in practical, sustainable, challenging and
joyful ways. Though the non-white representation in our congregation consisted of us plus one East Indian family (with

some good-natured folks naturally assuming we were related), racial prejudice was never an issue, because Christ (unlike us earthbound humans) does not discriminate. Now, I know it might make for a juicier memoir for me to tell a coming-of-age story about a scrappy black opera singer pulling herself up by the bootstraps in the face of small-town racism, but that just wouldn't be my story. The first time I realized my skin might be slightly darker than what I saw as average was when I was ten years old, running toward the pool at Green Hill Lake Camp. Suddenly, I noticed the other kids at our church's summer camp looked lighter. I thought, *If they're not gonna make a big deal of it, then neither am I.* And that was that.

I know from seeing the parts of town where my parents grew up that racial issues were a very real struggle for them. I can only imagine what they endured in that black-and-First Nations, poverty-stricken quarter, where the cycle of low expectations, no education, no funding, crumbling infrastructure and no prospects was destined to repeat itself in my generation. It bred in my father the need to bring up his children in a neighbour- hood where they would have a better chance—whether he could afford it or not.

Though people in my father's generation weren't hung up on the luxury of liking or not liking their work, I think my father would say that he had a good job at the CBC when he needed to have a good job. Early retirement allowed my father to enrol in university for the first time. He graduated from Acadia Divinity

College and became a Baptist pastor, exactly as my brother had done a decade and a half before him.

My mother's approach to our upbringing was to subtly instill pride in her children's identity. She never let her daughters play with Barbie dolls, or even Cabbage Patch dolls, because they reflected an unsustainable image she was not willing to endorse. Instead, she had dolls made for us in our own image. My sister's doll wore a little gymnast outfit, while mine was dressed as a majorette, since I was a baton twirler at that time. I don't remember being particularly attached to this doll (I wasn't much for play), but I knew that it was me and that it was different from the other kids' dolls, so I guess my mother accomplished what she'd hoped. My actual favourite toy was an Easy-Bake Oven, and I still prefer to eat what I cook myself.

High on my family's list of values are unconditional love and a good sense of humour. We laughed a lot, often over things no one else would find funny. Once, while driving home one Sunday after the evening service, one of us said, "Hey, Dad, if you go down Main Street, some of the stores will still be open," hinting, of course, that it would be nice to stop for a treat. My dad replied, "It's not a question of the stores being open but of my wallet being closed." He had every right to be pleased with himself. My father is not generally one to crack jokes on the fly and this one had us all laughing to tears.

The flip side of family love (or perhaps the same side) was discipline. It was predictable, not erratic, and I now recognize it for its comfort and stability, and I endeavour to create the same parameters of safety for my own sons. In the household I grew up in, we knew the meaning of "just wait till your father gets home." My parents never indulged in empty threats, and their consistency in all things is something I respect. As a child, if I acted up at a Sunday evening service, my mother would give me that look, and I knew full well what it meant.

During the last spanking I ever got, my father was devastated into weary silence. I'd never seen him that way before, and haven't since. I'd likely lied about something and been caught. My father was waiting for me in my room, with tears in his eyes. He said, "I want you to know how much this hurts me. I'm very disappointed in you, because you're old enough to know better, so I'm never going to spank you again." I started to cry and to apologize. I couldn't believe that my behaviour had finally exasperated this huge beast of a man. To this day, he remains my moral barometer.

After that pivotal experience, I was either more obedient or more cunning. Most likely, a mix of the two.

It's a wonder that my parents managed to create such a sense of security in our home while chronic conflict plagued their own relationship. My parents fought. A lot. I heard them fight over everything and nothing: the kids, fear of abandonment, the weather, the car, independence, jealousy, bitterness, the finances. Married people always know what buttons to push, and though my parents stayed together, I often prayed that they would put us all out of their misery and just get a divorce already. Both my parents had come from nothing, which created a lot of fear. My father's parents were dead by the time he was thirteen. The loss of his mother was especially profound, and everything in their rickety house fell apart after that.

I reveal all this to illustrate that in a Christian home, strife is accompanied by the love of Christ, without exception. That may sound weird to a non-Believer, but the fact that Jesus was so present in our lives created an underlying sense of genuine peace. Like we were all of us held in the palm of the Father, come what may. Perhaps part of the reason my parents stayed married was out of an unhealthy sense of habit. But with forgiveness and perspective, I choose to believe that they stayed married because through their relationship to each other, the God we serve is faithfully continuing the good work He started in them. They stayed married because they both accept the respective flaws and strengths that each brought to the partnership. They stayed married because of unconditional loyalty, support and fidelity. They stayed married because they are in love. Today I can think of no better witnesses to their sacrifice and humility than each other.

I sang my first solo in grade two. "Petit enfant Jésu" for the Christmas concert at Park Street Elementary School in my hometown. I remember our school's intrepid music educator, Mrs. Dianne Wilkins, on the Friday before our Monday concert, naming another little girl in my class as an "understudy" should I happen to get sick. Just as a precaution.

"Oh, I never get sick," I bragged, so of course after church the Sunday before my big debut I started vomiting. God's karmic joke, showing me who was in charge. Fortunately, I recovered by Monday. The concert was in the gymnasium, with all the other students, the staff and our parents in attendance. I remember being excited about the opportunity to finally reveal my true self in front of so many people. I understood their applause was a way of showing appreciation, but my sense of accomplishment was born of a desire to make my parents proud and to do a great job for Mrs. Wilkins.

I've always understood how damaging the addiction to outside approval can be. It's an inevitable downward spiral to self-doubt when that unreliable praise is absent. I was raised to a higher calling, a purpose. My gift, which I must nurture and develop, will be taken from me if I don't see it to its fullest potential, and to this day I have to keep my blinders on and make sure I let only the most trusted voices hold sway.

Apart from the contribution I made as a budding singer, Park Street Elementary School was a nightmare. I was bullied mercilessly.

Most of my friends from Brunswick Street United Baptist Church lived on the south side of Fredericton, whereas Park Street Elementary was on the north side. I didn't know many of my classmates, and my parents generally didn't allow me to go to the homes of families who didn't attend our church. Though the boys were the most aggressive, the girls—no shocker here—were especially creative in their cruelty. Having come from such a loving home, I discovered how ingeniously mean people could be without reason or cause. Purely for sport. I was uncertain how to deal with the new horrors that would greet me daily.

I had one (supposed) friend who was quite popular but who acknowledged me only when it served her purposes. In other words, when others weren't around so there would be no witnesses to our alleged friendship. She was so fickle I've bleached her name from my memory. The lesson I learned from her is the hemorrhaging bruise of betrayal. Although I was never physically tormented—I don't think I would have allowed that—the psychological games were just as damaging. The most painful part of the bullying from this girl and the others was the horrible, horrible name they called me. To steal its power, I refuse to say it, but the memories of children chanting it still take my breath away. It imprinted on me the idea that I was fat and ugly. I now know I wasn't obese as a kid, simply bigger and taller and darker than the others. Different. I would one day discover that you eventually become what you believe you already are.

My parents knew I was being bullied—I never had any trouble telling them—and I never thought the bullying was my fault, because my parents' love taught me that I was worthy of being respected. They would eventually descend on the home of one of the boys who was particularly cruel, and since the northside neighbourhood was quite small, other parents likely saw my parents' car roll up to their house. Word spread among the adults, and I believe they were ashamed enough to speak to their kids, and the problem decreased.

While I felt isolated at school, my church provided a sanctuary with its empowering ministries. One such program was called Pioneer Girls. It had a kind of mentoring-buddy program and my partner was Lois Bolden, who lived on the south side. Once, I was invited to Bolden's Diner, which was like a kitchen, except it had all these extra people sitting around and you picked what food you wanted from a list! I was seven or eight years old so I could read, but I had never seen a menu before. That diner flabbergasted me! So did Lois's rambling Victorian house—the largest house I'd ever been in—for only one family. What do you do with all those rooms? One contained only a washing machine and dryer. And where do these stairs go? Wait. There's another level with bedrooms?

It was so mammoth and exotic that I couldn't wrap my head around it.

Please bear in mind my family hardly lived in squalor. It's just that there was a room for every couple and child, with no extra space for superfluous things like entertaining or lounging. We didn't have an "upstairs" or a pantry. We had the den and the big cupboard or the cold room. We didn't have hardwood floors. We had wall-to-wall. We had a backyard and a piano that actually got used.

My mother takes great pride in her home. Even if she had the money to spend, I think her design choices would be guided by her ingenuity, creativity and her commitment to not spend money needlessly when she could just make it work with her own hands. I have known her to hand-paint this, glue that back together, resurface a good find and repurpose something else. She taught me that a good eye is priceless and that no amount of money can take your taste out of your mouth if you haven't got a sense of style.

If my church provided sanctuary, so too did my voice lessons. The reason I began taking lessons was that Mrs. Wilkins singled me out. She told my parents that I had good pitch relation, along with a kind of fearlessness that could be good onstage, and that if they put me in voice lessons, I was to also take piano lessons so I'd be able to read and play the music I had to learn. My parents had made it their mandate to discover and cultivate the gifts of their children. They asked David Steeves, the music director of our church, to become my voice and piano teacher. He was a very patient, loving and nurturing teacher, a teacher for whom mentoring was an act of service. He remains my musical role model, and I am still very proud and touched that he played at my wedding.

I also sang in Mrs. Wilkins's Huggy Choir, a chorale ensemble for gifted children. Receiving this musical mentoring at such a young age was critical in encouraging me to believe that becoming a classical musician wasn't some risky undertaking but a viable career option. I put all my eggs in one basket and developed no other marketable skills, and I'm glad I did. I have always forged forward in the confidence that my contribution to this world was always going to be first and foremost as Singer.

When I was around nine, I endured a brief stint with the violin that ended badly. My piano lessons had taught my brain that both hands should be doing essentially the same thing, and that proved a pattern difficult to break. With the piano, sound is created by mechanical motions from inside the instrument, whereas with the violin, notes are the result of exterior mechanics. I didn't understand how such a contrary instrument could create beautiful music, since the sounds I was making bore a striking resemblance to a dying bird. My violin gave up on me halfway through our first year, though I stubbornly clung to its unresponsive corpse till year's end.

Today the way skilled violinists seem to effortlessly create grandiosity through the precision of microscopic movements is still a miracle to me. I can admire the athleticism of their technique without loving the technique of the instrument; plus, violinists spend their careers trying to create sound that mimics the human voice. Both require pristine intonation and exactitude of movement to achieve a (seemingly) effortless result, so I've never felt like I missed out.

The best instrumentalists are their own species, just like the best singers. Singing came naturally to me, unlike playing the violin or the piano, so I didn't necessarily have to muster the courage to stand in front of an audience. Mrs. Wilkins became a hugely important influence, both as my teacher and as the founder of the District 18 Girls' Choir, which provided me on-the-job experience, as it were, from elementary through high school.

Despite my parents' attention to nurturing my talent, the Gosman house was never bursting with music. My whole family is musical, but as we kids were growing up, it was usually just me singing or playing. Our family didn't listen to any secular music unless it was on CBC Radio. Music and faith were a reflection and edification of the other. I see that now as a subtle underlining of my parents' faith and philosophy: What goes into a child's head at an early age—especially if it's set to music—will have a huge, long-term influence over the child's inner narrative. I believe my father loved to hear any singing in our house because he carries fond memories of his own mother's singing voice, so *Saturday Afternoon at the Opera* on CBC, with Howard Dyck presenting, was a real favourite.

My mom was also on board with all my musical goals. As a reward for passing one of my Royal Conservatory exams, she created "Measha's Special Music Book," which was held together with colourful twisted pipe cleaners and had a hand-drawn cover. It contained secular music (gasp!), like the theme from *Cheers*, the theme from *Fame*, Debbie Gibson's "Electric Youth," Richard Marx's "Right Here Waiting." Many eighties gems.

Knowing at such an early age what I wanted to do with my life played a role in isolating me from the other kids, which in a lot of ways wasn't so bad. My loneliness and my insecurity encouraged me to value my individuality—to develop my solo mentality. My focus on music also meant that I was never academically committed to subjects like math or the sciences. I sort of experienced my French-immersion elementary-school teachers as one-dimensional cartoons. In grade one I was taught by a large, maternal, cushy woman. In grade two my teacher was thin, angular and severe. My grade three teacher was beautiful, with wavy white-blond hair so different from mine—I don't remember her personality. My grade four teacher seemed like a tyrannical overlord, always angry and screaming—both my brother and sister had warned me about this harridan; yet when I met her as an adult, she was delightful and was likely never the gargoyle we thought she was.

By grade five I and my classmates had a reputation for being the worst hellions ever to haunt the halls of Park Street Elementary School. One day when our teacher came into the room with a dab of ink on his face, we laughed at him so hard that he turned pale, walked stiffly to the door, slowly opened it, shut it calmly behind him and never ever came back.

Nashwaaksis Junior High, which I attended from grades seven to nine, was a transitional time for me. Yes, the bullying continued, but changes were also taking place inside me.

Not all good.

I, the bullied, became a bully.

When a girl at Na'sis called me the N-word, I punched her in the face and left her crying with a bloody nose. I assume she weighed what she'd done to me against what I'd done to her and decided not to tell, because she never bothered me again. I did the same. Even though I (technically) got away with it, I still feel really, really bad that I resorted to physical violence.

Another payback involved a boy I really liked. He had auburn hair and very blue eyes and a great Harlequin-romance name—something like Carrington Steele, although I can't remember his name exactly. But you know the type. He turned up in our school from somewhere else, then became a king-pin in a group that bullied me, or tried to bully me (because I didn't care as much as they'd hoped I would). One day after school I saw him walking toward me by himself, so I said, "Why are you such a jerk?" He pretended that he had no idea what I was talking about. This was beyond rich, so I pushed him. He pushed me back and we ended up kind of wrestling. I didn't want to hurt him and I didn't want him to go away, so I just kept punching him to keep him close! I've since learned subtler strategies for flirting . . . I don't remember what happened to Bartholomew Harrisford, Esq. (or whatever his name was) after that. Needless to say, we never dated. And that was the last time I ever hit anyone.

My parents, ever observant, could see my survivor's instincts had me choosing fight over flight. They funnelled my abundance of negative energy into another solo pursuit: speed-skating. I took to it immediately. It's such an elegant sport and I really loved it, although I wasn't much of a competitor.

I think I just enjoyed the cool wind in my face. I've never considered myself much of an outdoorsy type, but I loved how the cold air would intensify the faster I skated, filling my lungs with frosty, neutralizing air and cooling me from the inside out. I can see how I was cleansed through the process, and though I was never emotionally close to the other skaters, they provided a different pool of kids, in which I felt safer. It still brings tears to my eyes when I think of how the simplicity of circling a frozen surface on long blades brought me genuine physical empowerment, and thus fortified the dikes of my inner island so to speak. For this reason, I understand the power that sport can have in the lives of children.

Throughout my childhood I always felt like I carried a secret. Even in moments of unaffected closeness—sitting with my family, everyone smiling in comfortable contentedness—I felt that I had this rich inner life that somehow made me unknowable.

In my debut album on CBC Records with the Manitoba Chamber Orchestra conducted by Roy Goodman, ironically titled *So Much to Tell* (released in 2007), I sang Samuel Barber's "Knoxville: Summer of 1915," set to a poem by James Agee. It speaks of a time when Agee lived "disguised to myself as a child." Listening to the gentle sounds of the evening, when his mother, his father, his uncle and his aunt would spread their quilts "on the rough, wet grass of the backyard" under the stars and talk of nothing in particular. He goes on to say all of them were "larger bodies than mine," all of them were good to him. They treated him as one beloved, but he was certain they did not, and never would, know who he was.

I have sung this epic wordscape the whole of my career because I still feel that way—that events happen outside me, involving me with people I love but to whom I'm not really connected in the deepest sense. I'm much closer to some than to others, but no one can make it in all the way. I remain autonomous. An alien. I often wonder if this is how everyone feels. I don't feel sorry about it, because it just is; I share what I can articulate and consciously do my best to not be withholding or withdrawn, but in the end, I've never felt wholly known by another living soul.

~~~~~

DATE: FRIDAY, APRIL 23, 2010, 7:43 PM
FROM: MEASHA BRUEGGERGOSMAN
TO: NEARESTS AND DEAREST
SUBJECT: JUMPING INTO THE DEEP END

Hello Nearests and Dearests!

Greetings from Las Vegas. We've had our orientation and it's been very enlightening to watch it play out this week. I've been very naive about the purpose and impact this process has the potential to have on my mind and body. If you've gotten this email, then you know that my life hasn't been particularly smooth these past years, and up until the very last minute I didn't know if I'd have the strength, resolve, courage or resources to come. Well, I'm here, and now I need to make sure that I have the strength, resolve, courage and resources to stay.

At the opening orientation, a lot of advice gets thrown at you by a lot of people. These were some of the things I heard that really stuck:

"Trust the process."

"Don't get bogged down with what's not happening for you."

"Set aside everything you think you know."

"All injury and illness is a result of some imbalance in your life."

"This nine weeks is about spending time on yourself."

"It's a one-time deal. Unique, simple and powerful."

"Be present. Stay focused."

"You are meant to be here."

So, I'm re-evaluating my situation. I will turn off my phone starting tonight (April 23, 2010) and will turn it on again on June 19 after I graduate. We, the students, have been told that this course is just a tool to get us to the starting line to begin the marathon. That's what I was told, and what I chose to believe, about my bariatric surgery, and that process definitely changed my life for the better. So please support me by getting to me anything and everything you need from me over the next few days, because I've committed to shutting off my phone and keeping my computer turned off.

When I think of how much I have to do and how little time I have to do it, it's enough to make me repack my stuff and leave. It will be just as hard for me to NOT check email or turn on my phone as it will be for you all to not hear from me. But I've committed to this, refinanced my house and paid thousands of dollars to be here. I wasn't sure if shutting off all communication was really the best thing, until it got reiterated over and over and over in the orientation, in the course book and then in my heart. I deserve the chance to give myself the opportunity to be better and get to the source of, and work through, my sadness and frustration.

Please don't worry about me. As hard as I know it will be, I feel optimistic. I feel like I'm at least allowing myself to be open to some kind of a change in direction. I'm trying to keep myself free from all expectations and just let the next nine weeks happen to me and me to it.

Much love,

Measha

Who doesn't have a complicated relationship with his or her body? I think the eternal struggle for truth and acceptance with your physical self is a dialogue that lasts your whole life. At any given moment in my life I have caught myself obsessed with my body, or ignoring it, or doing some mixture of the two.

When I hit junior high, this dialogue was in full swing. My body began to feel foreign to me. When I had my first period, my mother carefully explained, "This means your body can make a baby."

"But I don't want a baby!" I gasped.

She became more specific. "This happens to your body so you can have babies if and when you decide you do want them."

My mother was a total champ in the delicate dance of making this female rite of passage meaningful without overly inflating it. I wasn't scared, but I would have preferred to not have had to deal with it. At first, I thought that if I sat on the toilet long enough, all the blood would just run out. The failure of this strategy called for further explanation from my mom.

How I felt about my developing body was already burdened by the nasty, bullying names I had been called, making my body the barrier between others and me. Another contributing factor: I was molested twice before my tenth birthday. I don't remember my exact ages, but by the time I was ten I understood what had happened, that it wasn't my fault and that it wasn't going to happen again.

The first time was an older man who lived alone. I was allowed to freely roam the streets surrounding my Oak Avenue home on Fredericton's north side, and he lived in the vicinity. I tried not to attach too much emotion to his touching of my private parts. I mean, I didn't really understand that they were private. I just knew they were parts. But I do remember that the salt of his sweaty fingers burned me, and what he did felt unpleasant. I told my mom, thinking it wasn't a big deal. After that I never saw that man again. In my mind, my father made him vanish. But it could have also been my mother. That's certainly what I would do, now that I have babies of my own. The person would simply be gone. My parents and I never really spoke about it, but I remember feeling safe and protected. I never fixated on it, because it got handled.

With my cousin I believe what happened was a childhood experiment, carried out by the corrupted on the innocent. It could have escalated far beyond what happened had an older female cousin not walked in and put a stop to it. Again we never really talked about it. My family just stopped going over there.

I harbour no ill-will toward the guilty parties. I will never publish their names or carry out some vendetta. There's no need. I've obviously won. But I do know that this early arousal of sensations appropriately reserved for adults did affect my body image and my outlook on trust and intimacy. I'm grown enough to also understand the impact of that early sexualization on my relationships. I take responsibility for my recurring challenges with fidelity, my complicated relationship to food and my problems with impatience and anger. I accept and acknowledge them as symptoms and consequences to a happening I can neither change or deny.

Of course these things are painful, and I only occasionally let them come to the forefront of my mind for examination. I see no reason to dwell on what is done. Still, if I had my life to do again, one of the big changes I would make would be to try to heal my confusion about my body. I would attempt at a younger age to make a distinction between what I see and feel versus what others want and feel entitled to. I don't think I understood the division between what I had to offer and my ability to choose not to give it. I was empowered in a way that was divorced from my physical self, so the two coexisted but rarely interacted.

This disconnect from my body no doubt factored in to my struggles with my weight. By age twenty-eight I was morbidly obese, hovering between a lofty 350 to 370 pounds. As a student living in Victoria College at the University of Toronto, I focused on my studies and those bottomless buffets offered by my meal plan. I would go on to live in Germany, where my "food as sport, not fuel" eating philosophy continued—not through self-hatred or displaced emotion but through denial, distraction and neglect.

With my elementary school nickname figuratively nipping at my heels, I thought I was fat even when I wasn't. I hardly even noticed the pounds creeping on. I was married to a man who loved me unconditionally, my career was humming along and I was enabled by a profession with a tradition in which big voices came in big packages: It ain't over till the fat lady sings. If I had been pursuing a career on the operatic stage specifically, I would have potentially been forced to be more athletic, requiring a pretty large suspension of disbelief; but with concerts it was just me—park and bark—in front of the audience. I routinely heard myself described as "larger than life," and in one review of the uproariously awful opera *Aeneas in Karthago*, I was described as "a bright, well-nourished soprano." Hilarious, because I chose to believe they were describing the quality of my voice, not the amount of physical space I took up.

I believe now that I was more tormented by my weight than I was willing to admit. In the early 2000s I could shop in only about three clothing stores. I sat on banquettes instead of chairs. I felt humiliated each time I had to ask a flight attendant for a seat belt extension, no matter how lighthearted I seemed when I made the request. When you're fat, you're always somehow apologizing for how big you are, in an effort to distract people from the obvious. Whenever my father broached the subject out of concern for my health, I became extremely defensive because, although his words were not off, I just wasn't ready to listen.

So many people suffer over their weight. For some the pressure point triggering change is an aesthetic one. For me it was practical. I saw obesity as a form of inefficiency, and I prefer efficiency. Even though I'm not what you would ever describe as a math whiz, the numbers just didn't add up. The amount of food I was eating wasn't balanced by the amount of exercise I was willing to do, so I had to get this situation under control. Beyond that, who I wanted to be and the places I wanted to go, coupled with the greatness to which I felt destined, were all in jeopardy if I didn't start telling myself the truth about my health and how big I was. I didn't want to be emotional about it. I wanted to lose weight as a good investment.

I started with the Atkins low-carb diet, combined with a running program. I lost fifty pounds. For someone with more than a hundred yet to lose, that didn't seem like a good enough payoff for the effort. What's worse, after this initial taste of success, I started to gain the weight back. I struggled through two Master Cleanses, subsisting for ten and then fourteen days on water flavoured with cayenne pepper, lemon juice and honey. This transformed me into a raging bitch. And I cheated the whole time.

From denial of my weight problem I switched to obsession.

A few sample journal entries from when I was living in Augsburg, Germany:

December 4, 2001
Well, how cliché! I've started a healthy-living journal. The key is moderation not torture. Does getting healthy include chocolate fondue? There was that fruit! Well, I'm determined to walk to school tomorrow . . . I will only weigh myself once a week. I read today about this diet where veggies and fruits don't count for anything, and you can get bonus points for the more exercise that you do.

December 5

Today I'm a little down, a little bored. I've always wanted to live life to the fullest without restraint. I guess that's how I got fat.

December 10

I'm about to weigh in, and I'm trying not to make a big deal of it, but by virtue of that thought, it must carry some weight in my mind. Here goes—317 pounds. Last week I was 323 pounds. I feel good . . . Measha, God is with you and He wants you to be happy.

December 13

Failed attempt at an all-liquid day.

December 16

315. Not a huge difference, but my doctor said I should lose 2 pounds a month and I've done more than that. Not gaining weight is going to be hard at Christmas . . . Do I really want to live in a state of perpetual unhappy motion toward a goal I don't believe I'll reach?

December 28

Didn't write—why? Ashamed? Futility? Lazy? All three? I'd like to think this is just a slight stumble.

January 6, 2002

319. Well, the holidays are over and I think I escaped quite well . . . This journal goes a long way toward keeping me honest.

May 19

320. You've got to be kidding me! I weigh the same as I did on February 3?

October 2

331 pounds. Where have I been? Eating, that's where. It's discouraging to be an official yo-yo dieter, but I'm not going to give up. I honestly don't know how to find a regimen that works on the road . . . I want to be able to walk into stores and buy whatever they have on their shelves. I hope to be a consistent size 18.

October 13

330. The good news is that I'm not gaining weight.

Ugh. Dieting is the worst. Not just because of all the reasons the doctors tell you about it being bad for your health to shock your system with an unsustainable life change but because your mind stays exactly where it was while you force your physical self to pretend it doesn't have a brain or a memory. Think about it. By forcing the body to act differently (and hoping the mind will follow), we revert to the childish, dismissive reactions of *I don' wanna!* or *This is sooo stupid!* and *Why am I even doing this?* At least, I did. The point is, after prolonged disappointment I was adamantly opposed to setting myself up for more weight-loss failure, because I had a feeling a steady diet of this (heh) could lead to a demoralized, deep-seated disbelief in myself. I didn't have time for that. I needed something effective enough that I would only have to do it once.

I began researching the option of gastric bypass, also known as bariatric surgery, which markedly reduces the functional volume of the stomach. I researched it thoroughly. This included attending informational seminars for bariatric patients, recommended by friends who had had the surgery. I liked the idea that I could be helped by something physical, by my body working with me while I dealt with whatever psychological factors perpetuate addiction. Of all the surgical solutions available in 2005, the mini-gastric bypass seemed the most minimally invasive, with the highest success rate. I put that together with research on doctors who had the most operating room hours, which led me to choose a medical centre in North Carolina specializing in bariatric surgery.

Since my body is my instrument, I had to ask myself if losing weight would affect my singing voice. But this was the wrong question. The right one is, *What would be the impact on my health ten years down the road if I didn't lose weight now? How could I expect to live my life to the fullest while every step and every* breath I took was weighed down by my extra 150 pounds of fat? Additionally, being morbidly obese was weighing me down psychologically. I just knew I had to be proactive.

I jumped through every hoop and loop and filled in every piece of required paperwork. My family doctor, the intrepid Dr. Edward Pomer, completed endless forms and wrote me a referral for a psych evaluation. The psychiatrist asked me about my childhood and what I thought surgery would do for me, looking to see if I expected realistic results or a miracle. I had no trouble convincing her my motives were sound.

Next I had to find a two-week break in my singing schedule for the operation. (This may have been the most challenging part.) My surgery was eventually set for February 10, 2006. No one outside my immediate family knew. They trusted me to do my due diligence and make the most informed decision. I didn't even tell my agent. I thought it was too private to share.

My mom, who had seen my dad through his quadruple bypass surgery, travelled with me to the hospital in North Carolina. The only pre-op hiccup was my blood pressure. It was so perilously high when I arrived that the medical staff considered refusing to operate. *I've come so far. Will the door be slammed in my face?*

They intravenously administered me medication for hypertension overnight and were successful in lowering my blood pressure, and I had my operation. Everything ran smoothly, and for the months that followed I steadily lost weight through portion control. It might be more accurate to say that my behaviour

toward food was sharply and immediately corrected by the punishing hand of a restrictive digestive system that would consistently (and sometimes painfully) reject any portion of food
that was too sugary, creamy, fatty or large. To say that certain
things "disagreed" with me would be to say that Superman has a
"slight aversion" to kryptonite. To this day I do not find it worth
the sprint to the privy to stray from the plan: I stick to eating
plenty of salad and meat or fish, and I drink tons of water.
This way my super powers aren't threatened and no air fresh-
ener is needed.

By September of 2006 I had lost fifty-six pounds, taking me
down to 297. I started to stress: Had I hit the dreaded weight-
loss plateau? The scale had yet to petrify to a number, but I knew
I wouldn't be able to continue to drop weight through portion
control alone. Many uninformed people mistakenly believe that
bariatric surgery is a quick fix. The easy way out. But if you don't
change your lifestyle forever, you will gain all the weight back. I
knew I would have to start exercising (damn it), and again, what
I was looking for was an efficient, one-stop solution: none of this
weight-lifting, cardio-jogging, spinning, music-blaring, annoying-
pep-talk business. I like to exercise in a group, but I don't want
anyone yelling at me.

As I was grappling with this problem, my mind travelled
back to a horrible experience I had had in September 2005
before my surgery, when I was still regaining the pounds I'd lost
on the Atkins diet. To motivate myself, I had gone power walking

while working in Ann Arbor, Michigan. I was there to sing in the newly renovated Hill Auditorium. Mid-stride I happened to see a sign for something called Bikram yoga. Since I was willing to do pretty much anything to end the hellish monotony of my walk, I went to investigate.

Bikram yoga, I soon learned, consisted of a ninety-minute series of exercises in a room heated to 42 degrees Celsius. And I walked in to the worst of all possible set-ups: I was late, I was wearing a track suit, I had a face cloth for a towel and only a small foam cup of water. I will never forget how flippin' hot it was. I would have cursed every half-naked person in that room to hell, but clearly, they were already there. It was sooo hard. I saw my life flash before my eyes, and I vowed that if I got out of there alive, I would never go back. Not for a gazillion dollars times infinity.

Well, never say never. I would come to understand that Bikram could be my solution for muscle development, flexibility, endurance, discipline, focus and detoxification. So . . . about nine months after my mini-gastric bypass, and a year after that first nightmare of a Bikram class, I found myself at Vancouver Opera singing Madame Lidoine, in Poulenc's *Les dialogues des Carmélites*, which meant I would be in one spot for six weeks. I had no excuse. I had to go back to that cursed yoga. It was the most efficient solution.

After my second class I knew I would become a Bikram teacher.

By the end of my contract in Vancouver I had most of the cast attending classes with me.

By February 2007, a year after my surgery, I had lost about 150 pounds, and the media had grown justifiably curious. That same month I was to appear onstage at the National Arts Centre for the Black and White Opera Soirée, held annually to raise money for the National Arts Centre Orchestra and the now defunct Opera Lyra Ottawa. When journalists questioned me about my transformation, I gave the credit entirely to Bikram yoga while keeping quiet about the bariatric surgery. I thought it was private (apparently, it wasn't). Plus, I didn't want to go through the same media and collegial "whispers" that opera singer Deborah Voigt had been subjected to after her surgery. I was trying to avoid all the judgment I would get for my decision to skip all the yo-yo dieting.

Well, I got away with that for about a year, despite some skeptical murmurings that grew even louder after a cover story for *Chatelaine*, published in early 2008, during which I stuck to my half-truths. Eventually, to end the controversy, I decided to "confess" in a letter that ran in the April 2008 issue:

Dear Chatelaine,

I try to walk a very thin line whenever the subject of my weight loss comes up in interviews. I cherish my right to privacy, while still understanding that by choosing to be in the public spotlight, I automatically release anonymity with regards to my personal life.

I do understand that extreme weight loss is a hot topic and I completely support the battle against the false public perception of the fat person being fat due to lack of willpower. It is not my intention to revive this stereotype . . . As a person who has lost a ton of weight, I hope to provide inspiration but want the public to understand that what those of us who are suffering from morbid obesity really need is a medically supervised plan based on our individual need . . . I would never want to use my position in the media to influence a decision that should be made under medical supervision.

For me, weight loss wasn't the transformative, hallelujah moment that some people experience—I'm too pragmatic to have had many of those. It was a housekeeping item offering many benefits, with health at the top of the list. It gave me a sense of empowerment; it freed up more energy that I could put to good use. It wasn't until after my loss that I realized how much being obese had affected my motivations. It didn't mean I suddenly became this super-efficient, incredibly confident person devoid of insecurities who liked to walk around naked without a care as to who saw me. It simply meant that I could check "lose weight" off my to-do list. Now I'm a manageable size, and I've maintained that weight. I don't eat everything I want when I want to. If I did that, I'd be in considerable discomfort and back to 350 pounds. On the other hand, it's hard to find me not eating—I like to graze and I choose snacks that allow me to satisfy my oral fixation but not balloon back to my old size. Raw almonds are my jam.

I don't obsess over my weight and I don't weigh myself—that number has nothing to do with my health, so my scales have gone dark. If my clothes didn't fit, that would be my red flag. Having less weight to push against when I sing has required me to find new, more efficient, ways to use the muscles supporting my diaphragm, and my Bikram yoga practice has more than adjusted for that.

When someone loses as many pounds as I did, I think it's necessary to adjust to a different body image. Although I believed that I now looked the way I was supposed to look, my mind's perception of being fat remained. It was a major learning curve for my mind to catch up to my body's new reality.

I'm still surprised to discover I take up less space. Though I know my dress size when entering a store, I'm still surprised when I try on something in that size and it actually fits. I'm still surprised when I catch a reflection of myself and she's not per-fectly round. I'm surprised at how my individual parts look; I used to have a big rack, but I don't anymore—didn't even when I was pregnant.

In my profession people see me before they hear me, and I believe my clothes can speak before I even make a sound. My stage persona and costume could best be described as "high-class drag queen." I love makeup and I love clothes. I always knew how to look my best, no matter my size, but having a more conventional shape has invited different designers to use me as their muse. I also feel more comfortable appearing on fashion shows like *Project Runway Canada*, as I did in 2007, with designers challenged to create a performance look for me. My weight loss inadvertently led me to the wonderful duo of Cathy McDayter and Angela Mann of Magpie Designs (now Call and Response Clothing) in Toronto. They design and hand-make the high-glamour, low-maintenance gear I sport onstage and off.

Losing weight has also helped me to understand the power of conventional beauty. Like it or not, we are all of us influenced by aesthetic. Don't get me wrong—I don't believe losing weight made me pretty. Pretty can be accomplished at ANY weight. What I mean is that by allowing myself to be unencumbered by fat, I liberated the part of my mind that busied itself with compensating for that. I was free to more wholly focus on whatever task was at hand. I also know that it has helped me professionally.

In the spring of 2008 I performed Elettra in Mozart's *Idomeneo* for Toronto's Opera Atelier. Set against the backdrop of the Trojan Wars, the opera is a love story, with Princess Elettra as a jealous rival. When Colin Eatock, writing for the national Canadian daily *The Globe and Mail*, asked Marshall Pynkoski, Opera Atelier's co-artistic director, if he would have hired me before I had lost weight, Pynkoski was quoted as saying: "No. I wouldn't have considered her capable of the role of Elettra when she was heavy. I don't have a cutoff point for weight, but I need people who are comfortable in their own skin." Sometimes the opinions of the "never-been-fat" can be annoying, but I understand where Marshall, a movement specialist, was coming from. Having been one and then the other, I know there is a marked difference between being confident in your own skin and being comfortable in it. I wore a mask of confidence, but now I comfortably inhabit a shell that is working with me, not against me. At least for now.

It's not every day that you have the chance to shed the weight of an entire adult from your own body, and the process of dramatic weight loss—160 pounds—is an experience I truly cherish. It did something to my self-confidence. It felt like I'd literally dug myself out of a hole, because there is something subterranean about being morbidly obese. In some respects, you feel swallowed up by yourself and have to methodically trust that all your efforts upward will in fact lead to daylight. I'm not saying forces at work don't do their part to make things harder, because they do. Any person who'd rather be even twenty pounds lighter knows that those pounds are essentially made of quicksand, weighing you down and taunting you at the same time—like your big brother sitting on your chest, spit dangling perilously from his mouth above your face. Multiply that sentiment by how much weight I lost and you'll have some idea of how good it felt for me to dodge the bullet of a lifetime of morbid obesity. I was literally set free.

I allowed my expectations as an artist (and even as a person) to explode in every direction I ever wanted to go in—formerly having lacked the energy, desire, confidence or breath control to do so. More than liberating myself from a personal demon, I had won the war over my potential limitations as an artist in a visual medium. It's not to say that I wasn't doing just fine profession-ally at the weight I was (I was more than stably employed); I was simply putting in front of myself an obstacle that didn't need to be there. I've said that I believe in an efficiency of movement, and as emotional as I was about my body image, it was the ineffi-ciency of obesity and its potential detriment to my aspirations of Total World Domination that ultimately made me want to lose the weight and keep it off. And I didn't stop there. I had new mountains to climb . . .

Throughout my life, the concept of "trusting the process" has been a recurring theme. However, about eight years into my piano lessons, it started to dawn on me that it took me five hours of hardcore practising to accomplish what an actual pianist could do in one. As my singing progressed, I also learned that I wanted to face the audience instead of facing stage left, as pianists were obliged to do. I wanted direct access to my people.

At age twelve, I was made Junior Star of the Fredericton Music Festival. This two-week-long competition consisted of perform-ance categories for instrumentalists, chamber ensembles, choirs and soloists. I loved being able to hear other musicians my age, but truth be told, I was in it to win it. At first only classical music was featured, but later musical theatre was added. Essentially, they were giving us an opportunity to act as well as sing.

In junior high I had also taken up the trombone. Unlike my nightmare with the violin, its low brass notes were generated by the breath, with a less confusing process for my hands, so we bonded for a time. How else was I going to get to band camp? I played the French horn, too, but as much as I loved its warm, cushy sound, I failed miserably. The size of these lips is much better suited to trombone than French horn. So that year I entered every festival category that I could, consistently losing my trombone categories to Jim Tranquilla, the town's best player, and my piano classes to Jessica Bailey, who I still count among my dearest friends.

I won every voice category I entered, singing classics like "Après un rêve" by Gabriel Fauré; "I Will Give My Love An Apple," an English folksong; Schubert's "Gretchen am Spinnrade" and Brahms's "Wiegenlied." The fact that the festival competition took place in Fredericton's most beautiful churches and cathedrals made me feel right at home.

For my performance in the junior concert of the festival where I hoped to be crowned Junior Star, my mother made me a black velvet bodice dress, with a matching black taffeta ruffle skirt and an embroidered white lace neckline "to frame my face." My hair was parted in the middle and pulled back so slick against my head that it gave me a headache. I loved everything about this night. I did win the prize on which I'd set my sights. There's a picture of me sitting on our piano bench, holding the huge trophy that came with the first prize for singing that I ever won. This competition also brought my first cash prize—$200. My mother took me straight to the Canadian Imperial Bank of Commerce on Queen Street in Fredericton to open my first bank account so I could deposit my earnings. (This was classic Ann Gosman. One of the first things she did after each child of hers was born was apply for our social insurance numbers and our passports. And I've done the same for both my babies.) Since I'd never been in a bank before, this cavernous marble mausoleum to money created an indelible impression. To this day I have that same CIBC account, and I can always remember the number. Since then every accountant has told me, "Don't ever close this account. It has no fees, no holds and no red tape." It's the unicorn of bank accounts. If I ever wanted to launder money (which I don't), this would be the way to go.

I learned how to hone and focus my ambitions as a singer through the musicianship of Mrs. Wilkins, who moonlighted as the director of two significant choirs while also teaching music to the students in my school district. She was tough and exacting. Borderline cruel—but never wrong. I have been blessed to be guided by intuitive mentors with high standards. When David Steeves felt the best course of action for my voice studies would be to study with a woman, he sent me to Mabel Doak, whose students typically won all the singing prizes at the festival. I had no idea that Mrs. Doak was Mrs. Wilkins's mom! I was young enough to assume my authority figures didn't have parents. Given Mrs. Wilkins's demanding standards, I was terrified to imagine how much tougher her mother might be. That Mrs. Doak would be teaching me at her house added to the intimacy, which also added to the pressure. I was about to be taught by the tree from which the apple had fallen.

It was already dark out when I arrived at the Doaks' burning porchlight for my first lesson. I was led down a hall, then around the corner into a living room where the piano awaited, all the while knowing Mrs. Doak's husband (Mrs. Wilkins's dad!) was also there in another room. I felt like I was being handed the keys to the kingdom while simultaneously being condemned to death. I was going to have to work harder than I had ever worked before.

Mrs. Doak was very methodical—no "basking in the results" with all that work yet to be done. She taught me how to separate method from emotion, which meant serving your instrument by being objective about it. Years later, when I received what would be my third honorary doctorate, from Fredericton's St. Thomas University, Mrs. Doak received hers in the same ceremony. I remember wondering, *Why am I onstage giving the commencement speech, when the one and only Mrs. Doak is sitting right here? Nothing I can offer could compare with her wealth of wisdom and experience. She is a huge part of the reason I'm standing here in the first place.*

In Fredericton I knew what was expected of me. By the time I got to the University of Toronto for my bachelor of music in vocal performance, I was afraid of not being as good as people had told me that I was. I was afraid of letting down those who had donated to the Friends of Measha Fund—a fund started in my hometown by Jerry McFarland, a retired schoolteacher who had also taught my siblings, and Dr. Sydney Grant, a dear friend to my family, to help me give concerts to raise money for university and all the accompanying expenses. Even as I entered the Edward Johnson Building at the University of Toronto for my first day of classes, I remember thinking, *If this doesn't work, then everything I believe to be true isn't true.*

It still brings tears to my eyes to remember all the people who have scrounged and sacrificed and believed I was destined for great things . . .

I knew I was to study voice with Mary Morrison. We had not laid eyes on each other before. She was, by reputation, a distinguished teacher and an accomplished singer. Wendy Nielsen, my Fredericton teacher, had been one of her students. I went to study with Wendy on the recommendation of Mabel Doak, who had been Wendy's first teacher. Wendy was from New Brunswick but had gone on to an illustrious career and had started taking students. Her teacher at the time was Mary Morrison. This would complete the circle of teachers that have been the trajectory of my tutelage. David Steeves, at my ripening, would pass me to Mabel Doak, who would elevate me to Wendy Nielsen, who would then ready me for Mary. I have been Mary's student now for twenty-one years.

Upon Wendy recommending me to Ms. Morrison, my parents had driven the eighteen hours from Fredericton to Toronto to meet Mary on my behalf. It occurs to me that this might not be a normal thing for the average parent to do, but my parents are not the average. I can't remember why I didn't go (I was likely in school at the time), but I have no memory of it being weird that my parents would go in my stead. They were my managers, after all. When they met Professor Morrison, they assured this teacher that if she committed to me, I would commit to her, and that they, as my parents, would guarantee that I would fulfill every requirement of my advancement.

My parents also arranged for me to live in Annesley Hall, an all-female residence across the street from the U of T music faculty. They expected me to roll out of bed, go to school, then return to my dorm each night, which I essentially did for two years.

In my first year I shared a tiny room with Inez Mahmoud, a science major, who was the most exotic creature I'd ever met. She had beautiful olive skin, a mane of straight, thick black hair and perfect eyebrows, which she worked on every night. Inez was a first-generation Canadian from a Palestinian Muslim family who lived in Mississauga, a Toronto suburb. She knew nothing about where I came from and I knew nothing about where she came from. It was an incredible cultural intersection, and I remember looking at her and sincerely pondering, *Who* are *you?*

Despite Toronto's growing reputation as a multinational city, I discovered that U of T was extremely white—some Asian students, some Middle Eastern and some East Indian, but not many, and only whites on faculty. My two BFs on campus were two Kevins, one white and one black. White Kevin Skelton became Whevin, and black Kevin Richardson became Blevin, eventually shortened to Whé and Blé. If Blé and I happened to see two black people together on campus, we'd check the date to make sure it wasn't February (Black History Month). All this whiteness made me feel right at home, just like in Fredericton.

Like a lot of people, I suspect, my university years were when I homed in on my personal style. It wasn't without trial and (massive) error. At one time or another my wardrobe could have included: a dress with an overalls top, an above-the-knees skirt (quite racy for me), jean shorts with brightly coloured nylons, penny loafers. You could throw in a pair of platform, neon-green, quasi-clown shoes that I was particularly proud of, but never sweatpants. I've never been able to understand how anyone could leave the house in those. And don't even get me started on the yoga pants bodies run around in these days.

I met Mary Morrison in her basement office when I turned up for my first vocal lesson. I was so bombarded with the intensity and confusion of university life I don't remember first impressions. While I would prioritize my weekly voice lessons, the courses that really scared me were Materials of Music, Harmonic Analysis and Dictation—the transcription of rhythm and harmony by ear. I considered these of value only for geeky instrumentalists and the odd jazzer. Even thinking now about the hours I spent trying to wrap my untethered brain around their elusive exactitude makes me bleed from the eyes. Dictation turned out to be the only course I ever failed in my life.

Generally, music students arrive at university with a couple of arias and a few art songs under their belt (and yes—sigh—singers are music students). In your first and second years a jury will adjudicate your progress based on three or four selections picked from a list you've submitted—the first of which is the performer's choice. In your fourth year you perform a full recital.

Thanks to my Friends of Measha fundraising concerts, I arrived at U of T with a full recital of Mozart, Handel, Brahms and Mendelssohn already under my belt. Every year after that I would learn enough repertoire to sing another full recital to raise more money.

A lot of students go on to a degree in music with the goal of being the next big international soloist. This goes double for the students enrolled in reputed institutions such as the University of Toronto Faculty of Music. We spend a lot of time listening, competing, practising, gossiping, researching, memorizing, translating, auditioning, writing, procrastinating and trying to stay awake in class. The instrumentalists congregate according to instrument or ensemble configurations. There isn't a lot of fraternizing between instrumentalist and singer. But pianists have it the worst, since they bridge both camps. You need a pianist whether you're a singer or an instrumentalist. Pianists are either composed for specifically, in the case of concerti, piano quintets or art song, or their parts are a reduction of the orchestral accompaniment. The pianists who are good enough to get into a music faculty are usually convinced they're going to be soloists. I find this preposterous given that you could throw a rock and hit several people who've taken piano lessons, yet the average person would be hard-pressed to name three famous classical pianists. (And no, Geoffrey Rush and Adrien Brody don't count.) Students are regularly playing with other students of a similar level for the first time once they get to university. They tend to treat any kind of chamber music with contempt, despite the fact that statistically speaking, none of them will become world-famous soloists. And there is absolutely nothing wrong with that.

There is way more music written for chamber ensemble or orchestra than there is for a soloist. Even the composers whose music has lasted hundreds of years were more inspired by the collective than the individual. If we taught instrumentalists much, much earlier that they weren't compromising their musicianship or dashing their dreams by "lowering themselves" to chamber music or (gasp!) collaborating with a singer, then they would be open to a richness of repertoire that would make them more attractive to potential agents, orchestras and arts organizations, not to mention they would get So. Much. More out of their experience as a working musician. However, the "soloist mentality" is perpetuated by the system that teaches them.

The emphasis that is placed on becoming a star soloist, not unlike becoming an elite athlete, sucks the joy out of becoming a better technician, artist or team player. Heralding people who have no lives, social skills or empathy is a horrible example to the humans among us who are flawed, impulsive and relaxed. This myopic view of what constitutes an accomplished instrumentalist has done us singers a world of harm. Why? Because we love instrumentalists. Deeply! With the heat of a thousand suns!

The term "accompanist" has gone out of fashion and been justifiably replaced by "collaborative pianist" because the pianist is a full partner to the process. As a young singer, you expend a tremendous amount of energy trying to figure out why you can't make it to the end of that phrase, or why it is you can't seem to find the pitch or come in at the right time, and a good collaborative pianist, invisible though this person may seem to the average listener, is there to get you through all this. Collaborative pianists usually throw in a few good therapy sessions along the way, as well.

Whether accompanist or collaborative pianist, this is a special person who decides to dedicate his or her life to creating the most fruitfully musical atmosphere and environment for the singer and the music. The best ones know that they make or break it all. The best singers know this, too. In university, you spend most of your time convincing the unconvinced pianists that they are not to "follow" but should, instead, anticipate your needs as a technician, communicator and ticket seller.

You decide, as a duo, where things are going to go and what the ultimate point of it all is. Are we going for four-bar phrases? Are we playing against the minor mode and opting for a lighter interpretation? Does it make sense for me to take this breath here? In any given moment, what part needs to speak louder, piano or voice? What is the text telling us to do? What is the composer saying without saying it? I like to think of it as two guitar strings playing separately but perfectly together, humming along with an intensity appropriate to each other's place within the chord.

Recitalists (those singers who perform with piano only), usually fall into two categories: the unglamorous, detached academics (*sigh* . . . "I just love the sound of my voice") and the consummate storyteller (*fist pump* . . . "I commit to making whatever sound the story demands of me"). To paint in broad strokes: one is boring, while the other is trying too hard. I'm going to take a further diplomatic stance here to also say that the jury remains out on whether there exists, in this specified subsection of the classical singer, a group that typically would have a hard time being heard over an orchestra. As in, they would not be described as having large voices.

And of the pianists who've made their bones in the Art of the Song Recital? Heartthrobs like Roger Vignoles, Julius Drake, Martin Katz, Simon Lepper, Margo Garrett and Graham Johnson, in my experience, tend to have the temperament for the job; to understate it by a mile: someone who has devoted his (and thanks to pioneers like Margo Garrett, increasingly her) life of musical service to a maîtrise that is an essential mix of strong woman and flamboyant man. There is a technique, methodology and intuition to the elevated art form of collaborative piano playing. It's hermaphroditic in its push and pull because classical singers are crazy, but they're also magnetic and charismatic. But the collaborative pianist, along with the singer, commits to creating a time zone that will generate an atmosphere most conducive to the success of your ultimate master: Art. When the singer selflessly engages in this pursuit along with her collaborative pianist, magic happens.

The selfless part is where we can run into problems. Pre-existing egos re-creating pre-existing works have to find a way to selflessly infuse themselves into the process without tainting or blurring the ultimate goal of entertaining the paying bums in the seats. I've never been the type of performer who clenches my fists and says, *You'll take what I give you.* I don't know what purpose that would serve beyond alienating a willing audience.

If there's one thing that makes me sad about young singers today, it's that they don't seem to understand the power they yield or the space they take up. They're weighed down by their course load, their hormones, the chatter, the emojis, and they forget that we singers have been given the keys to the kingdom in that we've been chosen to sing the best music in the entire world. It's hard to teach someone to "own it," but in the rare instances when I do teach, that's usually what it comes down to.

Pride of place. Convince yourself that Schubert wrote this for you just yesterday; turn to your audience and exude, *Here's a little ditty I'd like to sing for you.* Commit to the narrative you and your pianist have worked out in rehearsal and let it rip. It's a methodical abandon. Instead of taking everything so goddamn seriously. Forgive me, but our core classical composers are dead and long gone. Your passion is your testimony. By singing with this type of methodical abandon, the living ones will want to write for you because they know you can bring it. And having composers write things for you is an effective way for a muse to stay connected to the future.

What do I mean by "methodical" abandon? You don't just show up and take ownership of something you have no rights to. Dues must be paid. Research must be done. Technique must be mastered. Languages must be learned. Recitals must be programmed with an eye to the listener AND the interpreter. But. Fun must be had. No singer who has made it to a certain level of success ever sets aside his or her methodology. That would be folly. But our technique serves as an invisible off-ramp to Fun Town.

Some singers need to work at better covering up all that technical thinking. Paying audience members don't want to see it. That's not the "humanity" they're after. Other singers need to rein in the emotion and trust that focusing it will actually make things stronger. Clearer. It comes down to knowing what kind of artist you are, finding repertoire that supports that and then becoming the only singer anyone calls to sing it. Because you're the one who sings it with committed, focused, methodical abandon.

Young singers, take comfort in the fact that you're not likely to have a wealth of endless repertoire through which you feel both connected and liberated. It's rare that your technical strengths and personal preferences intersect perfectly, but when it does happen, it benefits soloist and listener alike. That repertoire for me is Wagner's *Wesendonck Lieder*, Messiaen's *Poèmes pour Mi*, Ravel's *Shéhérazade*, the role of Jenny in Weill's *Rise and Fall of the City of Mahagonny* and Madame Lidoine in Poulenc's *Les dialogues des Carmélites*. It's worth noting that I learned all but one of these works in university (but you'd have to torture me before I'd tell you which one).

Generally, singers think instrumentalists are awkward and bloodless, and instrumentalists think singers are self-centred and stupid. Both sides are a tiny bit right. But it helps no one to perpetuate these stereotypes, because the fact is, we need each other. Not just for support but also because we could be hiring—or not hiring—each other in the not-too-distant future and karma's a bitch. So play nice! Plus, in some form or another everyone's paying for something: an education, a performance, a lesson, a composition. So we really should be striving to get our money's worth out of whatever step on the ladder of (ongoing) music education we find ourselves, because the art is going to outlast us all anyway. We really should throw the biggest party we can while we can.

How do you know whether you're good enough to really pursue the life and career of a soloist? It's an interesting thing to contemplate, because at its worst the life of a successful soloist is isolating, unconventional and exhausting, while the career of a successful soloist is relentless, tedious and, ultimately, inconsequential. Lived as separate realities, you'd be staring down the barrel of a challenge, but marry the two? And you've just about put the nail in your own coffin. No one needs help surviving the high points of a career, because everything's humming along smoothly. But at some point (likely several points) the chips will inevitably be down, and not surprisingly, many do not have the stomach for it. Whether you go on to super-stardom or not (and you likely won't), my advice is to hold fast to what is happening now. Grab it by the balls and run as far as you can with it—wherever you are and in whatever capacity you find yourself making music or living your life.

We know now that the future economy will be built by creative minds. There will be decades of a different kind of innovative self-sufficiency, divorced from the "job market" in which our parents shopped and financed our lives. Though it may seem like a consolation prize, it's not. My prayer is that the social pendulum will swing away from a culture of people who go to the same workplace every day to generate the same rhetoric that's gotten us to where we are right now. Instead, let it swing toward the cultivation of minds that produce sustainable, innovative solutions for stability. A music education does a lot to set a person up on that trajectory.

Don't look to me as an example of what could happen. I'm the example that proves the rule. It is not normal that I knew already in elementary school that singing would be my life; or that my journey, as God would ordain it, would support that initial hypothesis, because—save for that singular kernel—nothing has turned out how I thought it would. However, by putting one belief-filled boot in front of the other and going to university to study and perform with other classical musicians my own age, I would get my long-awaited boot camp, my breeding ground and my safe space where I'd finally get to talk about music all the time.

It will come as a shock to no one when I confess to being a very competitive person. But Mary Morrison has never indulged any petty comparisons, and I began to understand that it was best to run my own race. In her studio we were encouraged to listen to our fellow singers in order to learn; to attend masterclasses; and to audit courses we weren't eligible for and for which we would receive no credit. To this day I am so grateful she endorsed my thirst for contact with people who were better than I was and who knew more than I did. In particular, she prescribed a high exposure to the teaching of Douglas Bodle and Greta Kraus. Professor Bodle taught the class focusing on repertoire from the oratorio genre—works for orchestra, choir and soloists, normally set to biblical texts or a Christian mass. He was an incredible pianist, but due to a childhood illness that had damaged his vocal chords, he could speak no louder than a stage whisper. No matter. He said everything he needed to say with the piano. When you're taught by someone who can't actually generate pitch, you learn that music is just as much about intention as it is about sound.

Mary was also keen for us to audit the great German Lied coach Greta Kraus. By the time I got to sit silently in her class, Professor Kraus was a frail, hunched woman with such a profound German accent that I could hardly understand her. But my ears eventually adjusted. She had coached Teresa Stratas, Douglas Bodle, Russell Braun and Mary Morrison—once again I was learning from the teacher of a teacher. Quite frankly, there was nothing about German Lieder this prophetess didn't know.

With both Professor Bodle and Professor Kraus I had the experience of being in the presence of people who oozed knowledge, expertise and experience. It was like oratorio and German Lied were, respectively, the marrow in their bones. I'm struck with gratitude for the guidance I received in an unbroken chain of musical tutelage stretching all the way back to age seven.

But Mary was always my destiny.

Our relationship is about the work. Though I knew that her husband, Harry Freedman, was a renowned composer, I was in my third year of school before I realized Mary had three daughters. Somehow I'd always imagined her and her husband gallivanting around Europe, attending concerts and performing;

never being weighed down by something as mundane and pedestrian as procreation.

Mary's classes began with a half-hour warm-up, which at first made me itch to get to the repertoire already. I still regarded my voice as a natural gift that would always be there. It has taken me over twenty years to see the benefit of this essential step, and thirty to understand its absolute necessity, because now if I don't warm up, my voice doesn't work. Today before going onstage I'll play a recording of one of my warm-ups with Mary and go through the warm-up note by note. I send Mary my recordings from all over the world to make sure I'm on track, and when I'm in Toronto, I make regular pilgrimages to her office in the basement of the U of T Faculty of Music, where she still teaches. Mary is my yardstick both for quality and for work ethic. Though she always encouraged me to collect "tools for the tool box" from other teachers, I always come back to her because I truly love and respect her.

As a teenager my singing was torso based, to the extent that I didn't connect my voice to my body at all. Now I understand that my legs, my knees, my feet and the soles of my feet are completely involved in what comes out of my throat.

I used to fidget while singing without knowing it, a nervous tick: rubbing my fingers together at my sides or playing with my dress in a way that was distracting. With Mary's tutelage I worked hard to streamline what I do onstage, to put all my focus into my voice—and on my face—and to take complete control of my body as my instrument. In fact, when I first sang opera and had to actually move, I felt like I was betraying Mary! Of course, in opera you have to get to that stupid candelabra or whatever. You have to get in or out of the bed. You have to get through the door. Ideally, you want each movement to have purpose and seem natural (and not be in slow motion!), but thanks to Mary I've always maintained a stillness within myself while taking care of these important housekeeping items onstage.

Mary has tried, without success, to change my talking voice, which sits quite low. She knows if I raised it a few notches, that would be easier on me as a soprano. I'd have a smaller distance to go when I warm up. Yet she also understands that I'm not a singing human but a human who sings. She is all about solutions and digs tirelessly, exploring new territory, until she finds what is needed. With Mary it is the pursuit and not the destination: the persistence and insistence to get things right. Mary has given her students wings, though she would never think that about herself because she isn't a romantic. Those of us who are worthy of her hang on to her every word, even though her actual goal is to equip us with tools that will make us independent. Those ears of Mary's were—and are—a wonder. She combines that gift with patience and a serving heart, though she's capable of kicking students out of her studio when necessary. She has now been teaching so long that she may be a hundred and twenty—but, Mary, you still got it!

One afternoon midway through my second university year, Mary had a surprise for me. "You've been chosen to workshop a new opera called *Beatrice Chancy*. I told the producers they could send the score," she said.

At the time I didn't understand what most of those words meant, but it didn't sound like I was auditioning or even making a choice. It sounded like it was happening and I was to board the train because it was leaving the station.

Beatrice Chancy, as I discovered, was being staged by the Queen of Puddings Music Theatre, founded by artistic co-directors Dáirine Ní Mheadhra and John Hess for the commissioning of original Canadian chamber opera. The composer was James Rolfe, the librettist George Elliott Clarke. It was a reinvention of *The Cenci*, a play by Percy Bysshe Shelley, based on a true story in sixteenth-century Italy. The Canadian production, transplanted to Nova Scotia in 1901, told the tragic tale of Beatrice Chancy, a slave who murders her abusive father and master for raping her and is then hanged with her co-conspirators.

John Hess had apparently asked Mary, a close professional friend, "Do you happen to have a young student from the Maritimes whom you could recommend for this? Oh, and maybe she could be of Afro-Canadian descent."

Beatrice Chancy, intended as a minimal production, was very much in the gestation stage when I came to it, necessitating the trial, or "workshop," process. Our first workshop was held at the historic Front Street rehearsal space of the Canadian Opera

Company. A few of us, including the African-American soprano Christina Clark and the (white) Canadian baritone Gregory Dahl, were to sing excerpts from the opera, to be recorded for potential investors and donators. Later we would move to a rehearsal studio in Toronto's Parkdale neighbourhood. As funds were raised, a small orchestral ensemble was added, with Dáirine Ní Mheadhra as conductor and John Hess on piano.

At first we performers sang the roles interchangeably. Sometimes I would be Lustra, Beatrice's stepmother; sometimes another slave; and sometimes Beatrice. I assumed the lead would be awarded to Christina Clark, a phenomenal singer perhaps ten years older than me, tiny like a gorgeous doll, with her hair pulled neatly back in a chignon. I remember listening to her perform Beatrice and thinking, *Wow, that is so hard. I'm so glad I'm not saddled with that!* I hoped I might be given the shadowy mezzo role of Lustra, the stepmother. But that part would eventually be sung by the lovely Lori Klassen.

It just goes to show that you never know when God will play a joke on you, because I was offered the role of Beatrice.

What? It seemed insane. Obviously, I was going to do it, because it was a huge opportunity, daunting though it seemed. With *Beatrice* I had the unique opportunity to see an opera built from the ground up. The creators, James and George, often attended workshops and made changes as they heard their words and music sung from actual mouths. We were also encouraged to suggest ways to clarify our parts and flesh out our characters—allowing us singers to feel like a valued part of the process. Since the experience of *Beatrice*, I've jumped at any opportunity to work with a living composer. (I am also amassing a pile of tough questions for Beethoven and Bach and Duparc.)

Director Michael Cavanagh gave all his performers a good reason for each piece of stage business instead of leaving us to overact the way opera singers so often do. In our defence, opera singing is hardly natural, and hyperbole is the engine of most operatic narratives—we're singing at the top of our range while taking forty minutes to die. I defy anyone to make *that* look natural. Consequently, I've learned to appreciate directors who extrapolate from this grandiose art form or even play against it in a way that highlights its believability and relatability. I am also grateful that Mary always stressed singing as communication rather than as performance. My favourite stage directors— Michael Cavanagh, Michael Albano, Johannes Erath, Leonard Foglia, James Darrah—all emphasize, in their way, that the secret to looking halfway natural onstage is to never add importance to the mundane by executing any action in slow motion, and to time your reactions for after the text has been spoken. That may sound simple enough, but when you're winding up for your big high C or singing a zillion notes per bar, remembering to shut the door behind you, place a prop for a colleague or to even act at all might be the furthest thing from your mind.

That said, no matter how high or low, fast or slow the score calls for you to sing, I still maintain that a large part of singing is glorified speech, an extension of who I am or whom I'm playing. As classical singers we get to have a soundtrack for our actions, with each nuance timed to music and every syllable put in its place. As I lean in to the uncertainty of life in general, it has actually become a huge relief to know—in my work, at least—precisely what is coming and when, so that I can craft the musical and dramatic moment for maximum impact.

With *Beatrice Chancy*, I also engaged with a physicality that forced me out of my head. Singing is a full-body experience; that's especially true of opera. Shifting your weight; locking your knees; how you angle your hips and head; the placement of your sternum; the tension in your shoulders, upper arms, jaw— they all affect your technique. If you're aware of this at an early stage, you're ahead of the game, though it's a continuing process because you have to adjust to the body you wake up with each new day. After thirty years I sometimes still have a shaky tongue, an issue connected to sympathetic tension in my jaw and larynx; but I'm aware of it, and I police it if it gets in my way. There's no shortage of fires to put out, but you have to know yourself, have a set of ears you can trust and pick your battles.

We were very fortunate in our rehearsal time—a year and a half, from workshop to premiere. *Beatrice*'s music, its narrative, its characters lodged themselves in my brain, where they continue to live. Though I wasn't raised in a black community and had never identified as black, the character of Beatrice allowed me to live inside a black skin as I soaked up the whole theatrical experience. When the director asked if I would braid my hair for the production, I thought I'd won the lottery. I'd always wanted braids, but they were extremely expensive and time-consuming. For people with "white" hair, it may be difficult to understand what a huge experience those braids became for me. For the first time I had hair that lay flat to my head and reached to my shoulders; hair that fell to either side of my face from a middle part; hair that I could toss or push behind my ears. Black hair can be very coarse and inflexible, with such thick shafts that it won't do any of that without the weight of braids. Ironically, though braid extensions are traditionally a hairstyle for black people, they made me feel as if I had long, flowy hair.

But braids aren't forever. They grow out. When I loosened my hair, I discovered the cornrows had been protecting it, allowing it to grow naturally without breaking off. I saw my new, natural growth and I vowed never again to straighten my hair—a decision viewed as radical or rebellious in some corners of the black community. We all straightened our hair. It was what black women did. In some circles it is still what black women do. Long, straight hair is a symbol of prosperity in the black community, whether anyone wants to admit it or not. After unbraiding my cornrows, I either had to live with hair that was curly at the roots and straight at the ends or I had to cut it very short.

I chose to cut off the chemically straightened hair, even though I had no idea what weird shape my head might be. And that's how I came to have my famous Afro, with all the political implications and cultural assumptions that came with it. But the world continued to rotate on its axis, and I was able to lead a freer life because of my choice. I could swim when I wanted. I could go out in the rain. I didn't have to tie up my hair when I went to bed to keep it from breaking off. When I stayed somewhere overnight, I didn't have to take a million styling products. And my scalp could finally breathe.

Though I've sometimes been cited as a champion for natural black hair, my choice was based on comfort and convenience. That's the choice I routinely make regarding personal style. I have a similar lack of interest in high heels, tight clothing and makeup, meaning that I put up with these only in the context of having fun and creating a style that's useful for me based on the impression I want to give. The big lesson I learned from my Beatrice braids is that black hair—like so much in life—is only as stressful as I allow it to be.

It's worth noting that during this time in the late nineties, though I was still putting on weight, I didn't create the kind of vibe, either onstage or off, that let anyone dismiss or judge me because of my size. If anything, my hidden insecurity might have injected an element of overcompensation, making me strive all the harder. I was hell-bent—as I always would be—to avoid the humiliation of being the weakest link in the production. For any reason. I prayed that everyone would have the performance of a lifetime, when I knew my real heart's desire was to be the best in the show, the standout, the person everyone remembers.

Beatrice Chancy premiered in June 1998 at Toronto's Music Gallery in the old Richmond Street location—a bare-bones theatre in no man's land for a bare-bones production. Though I was familiar with having my picture taken for newspapers, the publicity shoot for *Beatrice* was a big step up from any point-and-snap process I'd known. The photographer wanted my head to float out of a black background—a young girl, no makeup, with a neutral expression, who might be about to laugh or to cry. I remember how hard he worked, how he wanted me to breathe and exhale in time to the snap of the shutter, and how he asked me to place my tongue against the top of my mouth—all these tricks to create a certain striking effect. Do I ever wish I could remember the name of that photographer so that I could immortalize him here, because he was a true artist.

I felt nervously proud to be part of something so significant. I also felt ready. I knew the music; I knew where and when to move. My biggest problem was in making myself fully present so that I could fearlessly execute what everyone seemed to believe was within me. I wanted to be in the moment, enjoying it. I didn't want to be fretting about the audience's reaction, because there was nothing I could do about it anyway. The tickets—probably about 150 of them—sold out before they even went on sale. It was before Twitter or Facebook, so rumour and word of mouth sold that first round.

Our stage was a runway, with the audience seated on the cement floor to either side. If you looked right and left from that runway, you could see everybody. My parents knew *Beatrice Chancy* was about slavery and murder, but I doubt they were prepared for how deeply tragic it would be. In Michael Cavanagh's staging, the plantation house was at one end of the runway, with the community and the fields and the gallows where Beatrice (and everybody else) would be hanged at the other. When Beatrice's slave-owning father, played by Greg Dahl, intended to rape Beatrice, he dragged her all the way down the runway from the field to his house. Though I, as Beatrice, screamed, kicked and thrashed, there was an inevitability to how this one-sided power dance was going to end. At his house, the father forced Beatrice under a table, then stood up and unfastened his belt and undid his zipper before disappearing under the table to rape his daughter.

For me this whole scene was motion over emotion, because I had to get where I needed to go, sing what I needed to sing and be where I needed to be. When Greg slapped me for the first time, my head spun sharply right, with sweat flying off my face—right onto my mother! I could see tears streaming down her cheeks, and it was horrifying to know how she was suffering, while my father, beside her, had turned pale. During the rape, which was hidden as I've said under the table, I was focused on slowing my breathing after such a physical scene because eventually I had to stagger back into view, dishevelled, with clothes torn, to sing an anguished aria about what had just happened to my character.

By then my mother's hand was over her mouth and my dad's hands were clenched. Other people were equally shocked and motionless. But they weren't my parents.

Later in the opera, during my satisfaction of slitting my rapist's throat, my mother's shoulders were up around her ears, her brow was furrowed, and she did a tiny, single, inaudible clap of her hands: a vindictive exclamation of triumphant revenge.

After the play my mother had a hard time looking at Greg Dahl, my character's rapist, even though she knew him well. My dad said, "Son, you played that part . . . " which was all he could manage.

Greg, who's a Mennonite and a real teddy bear, was mortified. He kept apologizing to my parents. "I'm so, sooo sorry," he would say over and over.

Of course, after Mom and Dad had attended the production five more times they came to understand the larger purpose of *Beatrice Chancy*: that it dramatized our ancestral history as former slaves, and the history of Canadian society. They were genuinely proud of their youngest daughter and have always maintained a deep respect for my craft and the people who allow me to use it.

I can't remember the reviews for *Beatrice Chancy*, and since that was before I stopped reading reviews altogether, they must have been good, or I would have remembered them (since we only ever remember the bad ones). Most important, I was pleased with the process and I knew that Mary was pleased with my performance. Our production was a success and it had several incarnations—it was remounted the following year in Toronto, then in Edmonton and Halifax, and later it became a CBC-TV special.

Beatrice came along when I was trying to figure out how this whole opera thing might fit into my life, since I'd mostly been singing recital and chamber music and loving it. As the hardest material in my repertoire, it taught me that I was capable of more than I had imagined. It was also such a big, juicy, salacious role—jealousy, lust, slavery, power, gender, racism—that it gave me a career-long resentment of crappy opera (of which there is plenty). When you add the journey of discovery and growth that came with it, it encapsulated all that I could want then, and now.

I contextualize this early operatic experience as an intersection of so many versions of myself. It forced me to grapple with many parameters that were up in the air personally and professionally: being hand-picked for as-yet-to-be-written repertoire, giving over to the process of creation, having my input desired and valued, responding to direction with enthusiasm, changing my physical self for a character I'm playing, the pressure of embodying a title role, and having the people closest to me support me on the journey.

For me, nothing has changed. Whatever it is that we do for money, I think we have to be able to create experiences along the way where everything coalesces in the opportunity to explore our own living methodology. To examine who we want others to see when they look at us, the authenticity of our output, the superficial choices we make about appearance, how we're perceived by the meaningful people in our lives, and the power we have to change everything whenever we want. It's important to put into focus all the different roles we play, because no man or woman is one thing, and there is nothing wrong with acknowledging, or monetizing, that. In fact, I think it's essential. It's what makes a lifestyle a career instead of a means to an end. We play many roles and fuel countless desires that exist and coexist simultaneously. These roles nip at our heels, spur us on and jockey for supremacy in our lives. Simultaneously living and believing concurrent, coinciding and conflicting ideas at any given moment in our ever-changing lives and bodies is one of the most satisfying and challenging parts of being human. Every day we commit to the survival and/or nurture of these roles in us, whether we acknowledge it consciously or not. Distinguishing all that makes you "you" is an exacting exercise in self-reflection (it can also be fun). So, to get the ball rolling, allow me to introduce you to the starring cast of *MEASHA*:

Musician Measha: Dear God, let me be the best thing that has ever happened to these people. I've got this. You? Relax. Music IS the food of love, and if you unwrap that candy, I'm going to punch you square in the throat. Putting your child in the front row is always a bad idea. Lashes or no lashes? No time for lashes! Solid intonation, Brueggergosman, but next time, why don't we try actually singing the right vowel and having a bit of fun? Where's the humidifier? Whew! Made it. Let's eat.

Cosmo Measha: She who will not be tamed. I have platinum status on my frequent flyer card, and flying coach is my compromise. I can read a menu in several languages and don't shy away from ordering for the table. My illicit night about town is a *menu de dégustation* for one, with wine pairings, and I will be going to the after-party with the strangers at tables 6 through 10. I never go to the third location. I have an international taxi app and a XXXL rape whistle.

Female Measha: Mighty Aphrodite. She who is coaxed, cajoled and entertained by her own fearless femininity, as well as the likely, and unlikely, consequences born of it. She desires to relinquish the traditional trappings of the "power struggle" and give over to a partner who offers her an all-consuming, unwavering love while asking for nothing in return. If such a man exists, then please, come right this way. I have some land in Atlantis I'd like to sell you.

Male Measha: I'm not sure what you mean. I don't remember you saying that. I'm certain her name will come to me. Who said yes to this? I'm more of a lone wolf, actually. I'm willing to take the time to hear what you have to say, so long as we do what I want in the end. Are you sure this is a Ribera del Duero? I will not be going onstage until the money is in my account, like you promised it would be. No, please. Let me get it. Your money's no good here! It's not you—it's me.

Christian Measha: There are no mistakes. My sense of humour is God-breathed and born from tragedy. You don't need to rob me—I'll give you all I have. Pain is both fear leaving the body and proof of life. Apathy is the bedfellow of genocide. It is impossible to hate something you understand. It is impossible to die of embarrassment. When I get out of bed in the morning, the devil says, "Oh crap! She's up." I may not be right . . . but what if I am?

Mama Measha: If I say I'll be there, I'll be there. If I say it's not happening, it's not happening. If I say I'll pay for it, I'll pay for it. If I say you can do it, you can do it. I won't give up on you, even if you give up on me. I'm the adult; you're the child. You're the best decision I ever made. You're your own person, but you're my responsibility. I will lead by example and fail miserably. You're the best thing that ever happened to me.

Part 2

WHAT DO I WANT AND HOW DO I GET IT?

~~~~~~

Date: Sunday, May 16, 2010, 2:37 pm
From: Measha Brueggergosman
To: Nearests and Dearests
Subject: Humming Along

Hi Wonderful Peeps,

End of the fourth week and I'm feeling pretty okay. I'VE BEEN HERE FOR A MONTH! I can't believe that. As difficult as this experience has been for me, I honestly can't believe it's gone by so fast. I'm starting to think I might actually be enjoying myself . . . :-)) That's when time flies, isn't it? This week wasn't nearly as emotional for me as last week. The body is starting to tighten up—which is just what happens. We were told to expect it, so I think it just means that I'm building more muscle, and my joints and cartilage are getting tense from all the activity. So far, I've practised 44 classes. The first sign of that fact is my left hip, and sympathetic to that is my right lumbar. I just have to be patient. I've committed to getting massages every Saturday, but believe me, they're not relaxing. But it means I hit the reset button on the weekend and can actually continue to go deeper into my practice during the week—that's the idea anyway . . .

This week also saw the beginning of ramped-up posture clinics. Senior teachers volunteer their time and come to teacher training to help us aspiring teachers get through the class dialogue. We take turns reciting the dialogue (hopefully memorized verbatim) while our colleagues do the postures. Each posture is about half a page to a page of dialogue, and of course everything has to go in the right order and with the right words or else the posture doesn't make any sense to the students. This yoga IS the dialogue and how you deliver it. I think I'm getting progressively better, but it's a lot to cram in, and sometimes I'm a bit discouraged that there's not enough time to really get the presentation of the dialogue as good as I'd like it to be. I'm still very much concentrated on remembering the words. I spent most of the weekend memorizing dialogue, just trying to stay ahead so that I can get better. If I have a prayer request, it would be that over the next two weeks, I'll be able to get the dialogue solid enough in my head and in my mouth (verbatim) that I'll actually be able to work on its presentation so that I can take full advantage of the advice I get in posture clinic.

It's all part of the process. There was an amazing teacher this week who was so warm and strict and funny and disciplined. She ended the class by playing Bob Dylan's "Forever Young," and everyone who wasn't singing along at the top of their voice was getting a reeeally good cry.

So, when Bikram gets back, that also means the return of the late-night lecture and Chinese water torture–esque post-midnight Bollywood filmfests. This week we saw *circa* 1960s video footage of Bikram and his guru's amazing feats of yogic prowess, as captured by the TV show *That's Incredible* (do you remember that show?), along with other interviews. We also continued on with *Mahabharat*, the 92-episode low-budget Indian saga recounting the life of the young Krishna. I gotta say, although I'm not drinking the Kool-Aid, I do find these films quite entertaining in a kitschy kind of way. I mean, what alternative do I have? Heh. I know the whole idea of this "process" is to break us (or have us die to the self, so to speak) so that we can rebuild ourselves from scratch. The challenge is in trying not to plan and create expectations and/ or to think you know what's going to happen or how you're going to feel. But I think (and I'm not sure about anything, mind you) the key is to just hear the words, and move accordingly. Anything else and you're just going to frustrate yourself and poison those around you.

That's all you can do. You do your best and that's what leads to improvement. We're only human, but we're constantly underestimating ourselves—starting with our bodies. And it's the mind that tells the body it's not good enough . . . OR that it is. So is it the mind or the body that's most important? Without the body, there is no mind, but the mind controls the body. Or does it? Too deep. Moving on.

I am truly grateful to those of you who have sent me mail.

And regardless of whether you've been able to write, I know you continue to surround me with your thoughts and prayers, and it honestly helps me to focus my mind. I feel ALL of your thoughts and prayers, and my goal for this week is to let whatever is in store for us yogis in week 5 (!!!) just happen. Wow. Week 5. I mean, there are no guarantees that I won't let my "Zen and the art of yogic torture" philosophy fall by the wayside the minute that Bollywood film comes on the screen, or after my third day in a row on 3 hours of sleep. So please just think of me in those moments cuz I want to learn to do more than the "right thing."

Now I'm going to read a chapter from Proverbs and hopefully set my mind up right for the week.

Stay blessed and know you're constantly in my thoughts. As a wonderful, loyal and dear friend of mine wrote to me, "There's nothing more valuable than your peace of mind."

Namaste,

Measha

I do believe you can have it all. But it requires patience and forgiveness. Patience for the time it takes for your hard work to be made manifest; for the words to crystallize; for the action you've learned to become second nature, to recognize, organize and seize the opportunities that add to your village and skill set.

To wait for the gap in traffic before switching lanes. And forgiveness? Well, that's for yourself. For the times you didn't make it, you couldn't be there; when you missed this, or couldn't take advantage of that, or just plain needed to sleep or get over a cold or rebook a flight.

I've given up my dream of being cloned. But it was hard.

And because I want to dream big but also be patient enough to be thorough, and persistent enough to be successful (dear GOD, don't let me give up too soon!), I like to have a solid plan. This way, if people ask me what I'm up to, I can have an answer in case they have some insight into or influence over how I might get closer to my goal. From my early education on the East Coast of Canada to my studies at the University of Toronto to completing my voice studies in Germany, I've always had some kind of five-year plan. Not to be confused with the seven-year itch I mentioned earlier, a five-year-plan is a hypothesis with a time limit. Goals attached to a best-before date. A bet you make with yourself. I'm not sure why five years, exactly. But it worked for me in my younger years—likely a measurement from a junior high guidance counsellor. For the goals I'm talking about, four years seems unreasonably short and six years seems too long. It's always had a way of working out: I dated my husband for four years, married by five. I competed in international singing competitions over a very crucial five-year period in my early twenties, perhaps a bit longer. I lived and studied in Germany for four years and moved to Toronto in the fifth. It might be that a proclivity for five years runs in my family, as all the children are five years apart, but whatever the target, I believe it can be mastered in five years or less: weight loss, home ownership, a busy performance calendar, making or adopting a baby, or my current focus—debt freedom.

While it's all fine and good to attach a realistic time limit to pursuits, a crucial ingredient in the art of knowing what you want is facing up to your mistakes. I've learned this the hard way more often than I'd like to admit, but my first career-damaging mistake woke me up fast: I had one week between finishing my degree at U of T and singing my first Verdi *Requiem*. I decided that, during that week, in lieu of going to my graduation or practising for my performance I would get married, instead. So after four years of emails, international flights and scraping together every penny we had to see each other whenever we could, Markus and I had a perfect wedding and an enthusiastic wedding night. There was just this little *Requiem* for me to sing and then we could leave for Spain on our honeymoon.

The house we rented in Mojácar was nestled inside a compound of beautiful flowers. It also had a view of the ocean, which was within walking distance. While growing up, I had never experienced those destination vacations where the whole family climbs onto a plane, then tumbles out in, say, California to glamp around in a rental RV. With the Gosmans it was a trip up the road for a Baptist convention or to summer camp. I had always wanted a beach holiday, so Mojácar spelled luxury to me, and because Markus and I were together all the time, eating and being sassy newlyweds, it also felt like the best Christmas ever.

And then I called home.

Since our Spanish house didn't have a phone—and in 1999 neither Markus nor I had cell phones—I'd been out of touch with my parents for a couple of weeks. After a pleasant chat my mother asked, "How was Peterborough?" She had her Manager Voice on and her tone indicated something had gone awry. When she called my dad to the phone, I knew I was in serious trouble. An event I'd hoped to forget came rushing back in hideous detail.

After our perfect wedding Markus and I had travelled to Peterborough, Ontario, for me to sing my very first Verdi *Requiem*. It is a very demanding part (at any age), but in my mind at the time, I was thinking that this concert would position us nicely to fly out of Toronto to Europe—neither the first nor the last time I would use professional pursuits as a springboard for what I ultimately wanted to be doing with my own time. Frankly, I didn't know the music as well as I should have, so I was playing a recording of it on the drive from the airport. I was twenty-one and I knew what the standard was, but I was hoping—just this once, please!—to fly under the radar and coast through.

One of the indisputable tenets of getting what you want is putting in the work. There are no shortcuts, there are no drivebys and there are no small gigs. If there are ears present, it's up to me to deliver my highest standard. Does this always happen? No. But am I the one responsible for having enough under my belt and between my ears to maintain the illusion? Yes.

This would be my first real-world career experience in which I truly came up short. Because of poor preparation, I was unable to dazzle the audience with how much better I was than the pool of professionals with whom I was singing, which was my usual experience. Instead, I weighed everybody down. I had been given this wonderful opportunity, and I had squandered it because of a sense of entitlement or overconfidence or some other hubris. I had taken my eye off the ball and used my wedding as an excuse to not be good at my job. Of course I hoped no one had noticed and that I had escaped unscathed. Now my father, who was my co-manager with my mom, was telling me somebody had indeed noticed.

"Your conductor from Peterborough called me. He was very angry and he had some serious words about your performance." He told me this could do damage to my career if it got out, so we had to figure out how to go about responding.

Standing in the oceanfront phone booth, I could feel my face drain of blood as a proverbial fist punched me in the gut and the high-pitched whistle in my ear made it difficult to hear. I was so short of breath I was afraid I was going to faint. Was my career finished before it had started? I tried to explain why I had been so unprepared, even though the words rang hollow. Excuses are so lame! I could tell from the edge in my father's voice that he needed to know the truth, even as his paternal side was trying to protect me against the hurtful things the conductor had said. The truth was, I had blown it.

I hung up the phone in a panic. Who can help me? I decided to reach out to John Hess and Dáirine Ní Mheadhra, the producers of *Beatrice Chancy*. Ours was a small community, and I wanted some perspective on how this might damage me and how I could improve my situation. Though I tried hard not to cry, the tears spilled as I confessed everything to them.

As I wept into the pay phone on the beach in the south of Spain, John and Dáirine were wonderful and provided balanced, candid counsel. They told me that the conductor's assessment might not do a great deal of damage; however, it was important for me to accept responsibility for failing to live up to my own standards.

I was still devastated, still convinced that when I returned to Canada, the customs officer would snatch my passport: "We do not allow into this country those who have messed up their debuts in the great Verdi *Requiem*!" Thankfully, in the end, my reputation didn't suffer. But I knew how deeply I had failed myself. This was my first deep wound of humiliation, and because I was just twenty-one, it wouldn't be my last.

When I did return to Canada after my honeymoon, it was with new determination and dedication to my process. It was also without the groom. Even though Markus and I were now married, we weren't spending the summer on the same continent.

He needed money to continue his studies, which meant working as a security guard in Switzerland, while I was due in Toronto for rehearsals for a remounting of *Beatrice Chancy*.

At the end of the summer of 1999 I enrolled in the Goethe-Institut in Düsseldorf, billeted in a woman's home while I learned German. As well as wanting to speak my husband's mother tongue, I knew that German was a language I hoped to use the whole of my career. I also knew that being able to speak the language fluently would cut down my workload (efficiency or bust!), since I wouldn't be spending all my study time doing translations. It seemed easier and less time-consuming just to become fluent. Here is the first piece of advice I give to young singers: Learn your languages. Don't be satisfied with simply doing translations.

I think it's imperative to get the flavour of the language in your mouth so you will sound more authentic, because the devil is in the details and every language has its "tells." For German, foreigners tend to make the closed *e* too narrow, or roll the *r* at the end of the schwa. For English, a good non-native-speaker "tell" is whether someone has mastered our odd consonant and vowel clusters, like the voiced and unvoiced *th*, as in the difference between *through* or *though*, which includes knowing that those vowels are *u* and *o*, respectively. Any language will have its syntax, its own natural rhythm chained together with unimportant filler words and connectors. Mistakenly stressing what is inconsequential also gives you away as a non-speaker.

Markus and I would be reunited in Düsseldorf at the end of September when my German course finished. That's when I would begin my graduate studies with Edith Wiens at the Robert Schumann Musikhochschule, while Markus would study art history as a prelude to taking over as my manager from my parents. Turns out art history was not my husband's bag, and he would later switch to studying international business management.

Though Edith Wiens had already accepted me as a student, I needed a certificate guaranteeing proficiency in German before I could enter the Robert Schumann Musikhochschule. After that, all my classes would be conducted in German. I was nowhere near ready to have my entire world switch over to a language I'd only been "speaking" for a month. But I was determined, because I knew I wanted to understand what was going on and have access to a culture that was not my own. Language is the passport to other worlds. Sure, you can visit places, take in the scenery and eat the food, but you're not really there unless you can render yourself invisible. A culture's language reveals the character and regional divides of any country. Germany was no different and I wanted total access.

M arkus and I have always enjoyed an ease of being together. I'm generally annoyed by most people, but Markus has a very calming disposition. That's not to say he's a peaceful person. It just means he has a streamlined approach to things—

something I've always admired. He can also make people nervous with his silence. It's not his intention to make people nervous, of course, but over the years, I've learned to employ an "ears open, mouth closed" approach to any uncomfortable situation, if only to see how the situation evolves and resolves itself. Markus, perhaps in complement to me, has learned that "small talk" is just as much about making the other person feel comfortable—and showing that you have a genuine interest in having some sort of exchange—as it is about controlling the narrative and not letting tension set in where, were it not for the silence, there would be none. I've learned that the Swiss Germans are perfectly content to allow whole minutes to pass without so much as a peep, while us Maritime Canadians fill every millisecond with chatter. Markus and I each welcomed the other because we'd both been at either extreme for our whole lives.

We moved into our Düsseldorf apartment, our first home as a married couple, mere days before we both started school. As soon as I walked in the door, I asked Markus, who had found the apartment on a short break from his job in Switzerland, "Where's the kitchen?"

Markus replied, "In Germany you don't get kitchens with apartments."

"Wait. What?"

"You bring your own kitchen, and then you take it away with you when you move out."

News flash: Kitchens do not come standard in German apartments.

I also discovered that I still couldn't meander through German culture on broken English or what I'd learned at the Goethe-Institut. I needed Markus to open a bank account, figure out where to buy things, read our rental agreement and tell me what an *Immatrikulationsbescheinigung* was when my university asked for it. (It's a certificate of enrolment. Obvi!)

Having someone take over all the logistics that come with setting up your life away from your parents—in a new time zone, continent and language—was a big departure for me. In Fredericton Markus had been essentially living my life, in my culture, my language, my hometown. But in Düsseldorf we were in his linguistic and cultural wheelhouse. He was also more travelled than I was with all the vacations and adventures he'd had with his family while growing up. I came to trust him more as the head of the house and as a provider.

I also discovered how handy Markus was. Though we had been together four years before marrying, we had never lived together, so we didn't know each other's skill sets. I felt proud of how adeptly I had drilled an Ikea coat rack to the wall . . . until it ripped itself out of the wall when I tried to hang actual coats on it. Once Markus attached it, we could have both swung from it at the same time. If I assembled a piece of furniture with the raw side out, I artfully shoved that exposed section against the wall. No one could ever feel confident sitting on a chair I had put together.

After more trial and error (and badly assembled furniture), we learned that I was better at picking out and arranging the rugs, the art and the side tables, whereas Markus was better at executing their assemblage. I also took over the cooking because Markus eats for the fuel of it, whereas I eat for the fun of it.

During our four years in Germany, Markus and I lived on Canada Council and Chalmers performing arts grants, a New Brunswick Arts grant, a Sylva Gelber Music Foundation Award, plus income Markus earned during summers and money I made singing concerts and winning competitions. This amounted to about $30,000 annually, which seemed downright luxurious to me at the time.

I felt proud walking through the doors of the music school. Even though it was intimidating to know that if someone approached me and started rattling off in German, the chances of me understanding what was said (let alone being able to respond) were slim to none, I was still tickled that I was actually living in Europe. Germany! ME. The girl who grew up in Nashwaaksis was now walking through the doors of a German music school (where they spoke German!) to start not my first but my second degree as a classical singer. I remember my mind being completely blown.

Though Düsseldorf was an old industrial city, I liked what it taught me about German life. People walked instead of drove. The Germans were dependable. The bread tasted better. Düsseldorf had boutiques instead of big-box stores. The super-fancy Königsallee featured a landscaped canal lined with designer shops selling sophisticated European brands I'd never seen before. Since I've always possessed a supreme adoration for makeup—the skill required to apply it, its transformative powers—I was thrilled to discover a mega MAC Cosmetics store standing like a proud beacon to beauty in the heart of the Königsallee. A big moment for me was when I walked up to the counter to make my purchase with my MAC professional discount card—one of the originals from Canada.

Markus and I found a wonderful church, full of young people, offering many community programs, such as weekly ballroom dancing. Given my travel schedule, we probably made only one or two of those classes, but they were one of the only husband-wifey things we ever did as a couple, and it made me feel I might really have a chance at something resembling a normal life. And while I was away, Markus created such strong community that he was eventually asked by one of the new friends he made to be the best man at his wedding.

Life in Germany moved along swimmingly, but one very intimate event revealed an important difference in modus operandi between Markus and me.

Rewinding to the previous spring . . . Three weeks before our wedding, my dad had taken me to our family's pharmacy in Fredericton to pick up my birth control pills. I was going to be having sex for the first time, so I needed to be proactive about contraception. Or as my father put it, "Measha, you're a woman now, with a very busy schedule, and we need to make sure that you have everything in order."

Six months into my marriage, now living in Düsseldorf, I said to Markus, "This is odd. I have my period and it isn't in my one-week break."

Markus asked, "What do you mean, your 'one-week break'?"

I replied in a patronizing tone, "Well, let me explain the birth control pill to you. I take a pill for twenty-eight days, then I stop for a week."

In complementary opposition to my own approach, Markus wisely read the instructions on the box, which I'd never bothered to do. Now, in full possession of the manufacturer's point of view, he informed me, "Taking a week off doesn't mean going without pills. This box contains a week of sugar pills to keep you in the habit of dosing during the break in your cycle."

That's how I discovered that Markus and I had been having sex for six months with me taking sugar pills I thought were birth control pills, then skipping a week, then sometimes forgetting to take any pill at all. Hence, me getting my period smack dab in the middle of a cycle of pills. My body had no idea what was going on.

That first year was a bit of a blur. There was so much newness and discovery. So many firsts: first year married, first language from scratch, first apartment, first trip to Ikea, first power drill! I couldn't really keep track of the fact that time was even passing, because there were so many things to absorb and interpret.

The strongest voice in my head for four years running when it came to vocal technique had been Mary Morrison, and now I had a new mentoring voice in my head in the form of the voice teacher for whom I had made the decision to continue my studies in Germany: Edith Wiens. New terminology, the uncovering of technical shortcomings that I'd managed to squirrel away, exercising humility and exorcising bad habits. That first year was a bit of a diagnostic reconnaissance mission for both Edith and me, and it felt like I was starting all over. I was the first student to have come from such a distance to study with Edith, and she was getting her bearings as a mentor. I have distant memories of pangs of frustration and confusion as we both deciphered our bearings in our new lives, mixed with strong memories of breakthroughs and complete clarity.

After that first year in Düsseldorf, Edith accepted a teaching position in the south of Germany, so Markus and I packed up everything we owned and drove south to Augsburg, Bavaria. There was nothing for us in Düsseldorf, since I had moved to Germany to study with Edith. The possession I most remember bobbing along in the back of our van was our money tree—a generic houseplant with a braided trunk and big leaves that grows and grows and grows. We bought it at Ikea. Though it would flourish for three years in Augsburg, it did not survive our return to Canada. After its demise we bought another money tree, also from Ikea, which has since travelled in all our moving vans, dying and resurrecting as required. It's a great plant . . . and a loyal friend.

Though I had enjoyed Düsseldorf, it wasn't until we moved

to Augsburg—a university city with cobblestone streets and a history going back to the Roman Empire—that I discovered what Germany was supposed to look like to my Canadian eyes. Our apartment, a fourth-floor walk-up, was twice as big and half as expensive. Plus, Bavarians are super fun!

The reason for our move was a pragmatic one: I wanted more of what Edith had to teach, so I would have followed her wherever she went. The change also worked for Markus, who wished to switch from art history, which he hated, to international business management, which would prove handy, since he eventually became my manager.

Who was this Edith Wiens, the voice teacher who had lured me from Canada and now across Germany?

A very striking, very blond, very charismatic and very successful recitalist and soprano is the easy answer. Born in the Canadian Prairies in 1950, in Saskatoon, daughter of a Mennonite pastor, she sang her way up through church and beyond her small-town roots—very much as I have. Though Edith would tell you she didn't have the voice of the century, she carved out a career in which she was universally heralded and deservedly respected. She made her operatic debut at Covent Garden—no baby steps for my Edith! She performed her last public concert at age fifty, the soprano soloist in Mozart's *Requiem* with the New York Philharmonic in what was then known as Avery Fisher Hall (now David Geffen Hall). Out on an upswing and with a bang. That's my Edith.

I was there, and she was the absolute best. Kurt Masur conducted and I don't even remember who the other soloists were. That was what Edith brought to the stage. You couldn't look away from her and you didn't want to, because she was giving you everything you needed—musicianship, authenticity, presence, generosity.

I first met Edith when she gave a masterclass during my third year at the University of Toronto. I was thrilled I had the opportunity to sing for her, and more thrilled later when she accepted me as a master's student at the Robert Schumann Musikhochschule.

Edith was building her reputation (her tool chest, if you will) as a teacher, and I was the first of a wave of Canadians who travelled to Europe to study with her. (One of the reasons my German ended up improving so rapidly was that I was there with her at the beginning, before there were other English speakers to talk to.)

Understandably, Edith's knowledge of the repertoire was nowhere near as extensive as Mary's, but while developing her own style, she gathered knowledge like a foraging ant, visiting other teachers, discussing what I had learned from the people I'd studied with and importing experts for masterclasses at the Hochschule. We would discuss vocal technique for hours on end. I was in total heaven as we articulated the role of the hard palate in the generation of hard consonants, or whether the jaw should hinge or drop and if the motion depended on the physiology of the singer. These techy talks were interspersed with a healthy dose of career designs and strategies. The German word *schlau* connotes a mixture of clever and savvy. That was Edith.

When I first entered Edith's studio, my breath support was so screwed up that my abdomen shook. She knew that had to be the first thing to go. I also knew she wouldn't stop until a solution was found, which endeared her to me. Anyone who has met the force that is Frau Doktor Edith Wiens knows that you are better off aligning your desires and goals with hers, because chances are she will outwit, outlast and outplay you even with her dying breath. But more on that later . . .

Edith was and is an impeccable musician. She taught me to prioritize the text and use all that the voice has to offer, in order to paint a picture through the words. She always served the music and left her pride at the door, because sometimes the colour you need might not be the prettiest, but it is the most effective and appropriate. She was the first voice teacher I studied with who concerned herself with what the audience would see or feel because of what you, the singer-performer-communicator, had to share. And according to Edith, singing is an act of servitude. "People can see you!" she would declare. She would enjoin, "Tell me what Schumann heard and saw in you when he decided to write this song cycle for you." She used this image of a mama hippo pouring water into a baby hippo's mouth: a massive stream of water flowing into a much smaller space. She would say, "The audience wants the music you have to share, but you have to make the current big enough for it to flow into their mouths and hearts. Your musicianship must get past the footlights of the stage and to the very back row of the hall. You have to fill all the entire space with YOU."

She taught me how to choose music that spoke to me. Regardless of difficulty, the piece should feel like it was written for me. I was to be a muse—a vessel from which music flowed unobstructed. That meant I had to be in sync with a piece with regard to my vocal strengths, my brand of charisma and my technique. Edith also taught me that a performer's power is the ability to show his or her personality while paying homage to the accuracy of the composition. It's the cooperation between both that creates the synergistic electricity of the live classical performance. Otherwise, you might as well stay home and listen to the recording.

Today I don't have to hear a piece of music to know whether it's for me. I look at the tempo and the range and how many notes there are. Because frankly, at this point I know that singing fast is not my jam. This isn't to say that I avoid coloratura. I just think there are singers who do it much better than I do. Since my strengths are colour, range, risk, humour, diction and drama, I discard songs that are just pretty or pyrotechnical and opt for the good story and interesting soundscape. Ditto if I see a lot of sixteenth notes above the staff. There are singers just dying to get their hands on those high sixteenth notes. But not this one. Show me an adagio tempo marking with plenty of long, sad, slow, meaningful space into which I can expand and I'll look closer at the text and decide if I have anything to say about the subject matter. I can also do "funny"—something else I learned from Edith—which can mean creating a moment of unexpected irreverence, providing relief from all the sadness, releasing the pressure valve when you've elevated everything to a fever pitch.

Edith was the reason I became primarily a concert singer rather than an opera singer. I knew opera would be there when I felt ready but that the art of the song recital required a precision that I used my studies in Germany to explore, expand and embrace. I also knew I could never learn from a better source than Edith, because she also had the career I wanted. Her concerts were all about charisma, magnetism and energy-driven intimacy. She could have programmed the phone book and people would be on the edge of their seats, hanging on her every word. Like Edith, I wanted people to not only enjoy my singing but to also feel that when I stepped out on that stage, I was the only singer they wanted to hear . . . and see. That, by conveying my truest self and strengths as a singer, the audience is getting more than just the notes. They're witnessing where investment meets artistry and vulnerability meets risk.

While I have nothing but praise for Edith's skills, I also observed that she had a highly emotional dark side. Whereas I'd been trained by teachers who were all about the work, Edith was quite skilled in psychological warfare. Though she knew how to kill with kindness, she did not respond well to resistance. She could get inside people's heads and make them do her bidding. It reminded me of this quote from Goethe's "Der Erlkönig" that hung on the wall of a voice teacher I'd studied with at the Boston Conservatory: *Und bist du nicht willig so brauch ich Gewalt!* "And if you're not willing, I'll have to use force!" (It's what Goethe's *Erlkönig* says to the young child when he refuses his advances.)

I was sympathetic to the struggles a strong personality confronts when faced with the wilting flowers who sometimes walk into your studio. What does an ambitious career singer who has been to the mountaintop even say to an eighteen-year-old who's doing a singing degree "for fun"? Or to the mousy, sexually confused tenor who only wants to sing loud and high? I do believe that people who take up a space in a performance degree program should do so knowing that they're taking that space away from someone who's potentially a better worker, hungrier and shows up with fire in the belly. Early on, Edith had time for those people with fire and borderline contempt for anyone else. I did not get sucked into Edith's force field, because frankly, I agreed with her. I would say we were allies as much as anyone can be in a teacher-student relationship. I kept things professional because I saw our interaction as a means to an end, and I think she respected that. Plus, I wanted what she had and I acknowledge that we share a lot of the same characteristics.

Like Edith, I can get people to forgive me for all kinds of crimes because I'm loyal and they believe what I contribute is worth the price. Like Edith, I am goal-oriented and ambitious. Edith is a champion who knows how to win. She recognized that same animal instinct in me—a characteristic I had previously downplayed, perhaps to appear more humble. It's likely a Canadian thing. It's definitely a Maritimer thing. Through Edith, I learned that I could climb to the top using my own ladder. And I didn't need to look sideways to do it. I could keep my blinders on and just keep going up and up. Edith encouraged the champion in me and had little patience for students without that killer instinct. In those early days of her teaching career when I was with her, she left wreckage in her wake, though I know she evolved to have a broader empathy. She now teaches at the Juilliard School in New York City. The top of the mountain. Where she belongs.

It was because of my teacher Edith's encouragement that I entered and won so many international competitions while stationed in Germany. This included taking it all at the inaugural 2002 Jeunesses Musicales International Musical Competition held in Montreal; the second prize in the 2003 Queen Sonja International Music Competition held in Oslo, with a special prize for my interpretation of Edvard Grieg; the highest prize at the Wigmore Hall International Song Competition in London; and the highest prizes at the George London Foundation in New York, the Robert Schumann Wettbewerb in Germany, the ARD Music Competition in Munich and the International Vocal Competition in 's-Hertogenbosch in 2004.

From a young age, I have loved competition. It's connected to my respect of a formula for success: be charismatic, be precise, be good. And for goodness sakes, know who's on the jury! Don't pound your head against a brick wall, trying to prove someone wrong. The fact is, not everyone is going to like what you do. If you're a heavy voice, don't go compete for a jury lined with light-voiced Lieder singers and expect to be the first heavy voice the jury ever liked. No one is objective, least of all classical musicians. If you're a counter-tenor, don't go to a competition that has never given any prizes to a counter-tenor. I did not go to competitions to protest and fight or to prove a point. I went to competitions to get paid. We are all human, and often we want to see ourselves—or the selves we wish we were—walk away with the money. So pick your tribe, compete in front of them and then get yourself to the bank.

For the first round at these competitions, a contestant was usually asked to perform one piece from a particular era of classical music; for the second round, the jury might select the piece for the contestant; for the third round, the contestant might be given the opportunity to present a mini-program, with various components; and for the final, sometimes with orchestra, the contestant, in addition to core repertoire, might also be required to sing an imposed or commissioned work from a living composer. I never went into these competitions with anything but the safest of repertoire, within reason. Safe for me might be risky for you. Modern for me might be downright weird for you.

I might be John Cage, while you are Korngold. Your Schubert might be my Brahms.

Among my happy competition memories, I have one very unpleasant one. During a competition in Zwickau, in the former East Germany, I was competing in the Robert Schumann International Wettbewerb with Tobias Truniger, an all-round great guy and the pianist from Edith's studio, who now coaches at the opera in Munich. Zwickau also happened to be hosting a Trabant car convention. The attitude of some of those who'd come out to fawn over this Communist-produced vehicle was disgusting. I felt safe while at the competition, but fans of the Trabant were so rude to me as I walked from my apartment to the venue that I feared something dangerous might happen.

During a free afternoon, Markus and I attended a marathon of the horror movie franchise *Scream*. A group behind us began throwing popcorn at me, touching my hair and shouting insults in German: "Black garbage!" "How do you expect us to see through all that hair?"

I said to myself, *You know what? I deserve to be here.* Bolting up, I told them in perfect German, "I understand what you're saying to me and you should be ashamed of yourselves." My German was even good enough to add, "Stop being a bag of assholes and let everyone watch the movie!" (I had just learned the German word for bag—*Tüte*—and was pretty proud to have used it here.)

This incident was so hurtful because I had come to like the

Germans, and living in Germany, so much during my years of study. And I still do! But I had to go all the way to Zwickau to experience my first incident of overt racism, and it will always be associated with that culture and language, unfortunately.

My time in Germany also gave me the opportunity to get another kick at singing the Verdi *Requiem*—which I had messed up in Peterborough—this time conducted by Helmuth Rilling, in Bonn, Stuttgart and Berlin. Maestro Rilling had insisted that I replace the soprano originally contracted to sing the gig. The *Requiem* remains one of my favourite works, and you can bet that I know every part with my eyes closed, inside and out, forward and backward!

I am pleased to be able to look back on all the times that I failed or suffered some private embarrassment, because I know that these usually came down to not being prepared. It's liberating to put my finger on the problem instead of trying to convince myself that external factors were to blame. Whether it was the problems that would emerge in my marriage, getting my babies to kindergarten on time or showing up to the first piano rehearsal with the conductor, I know that the success of any given event in my life is directly linked to how much time and effort I put into being ready for it. And I share this not only to encourage you but also to illustrate the nature of forgiveness. If I hadn't forgiven myself for so royally screwing up my first Verdi *Requiem*, I would have never made room in my heart and mind for the promise of redemption with one of the world's most legendary conductors. I don't believe in luck, because it takes too much of my power away, in addition to robbing God of His sovereignty over my life. Luck leaves too much to chance. Through a series of missteps and bad judgments, I have come to believe in preparation leading to opportunity. And I have the receipts! I learned my languages, I used my summers for work not vacation, I put the granola bars that my babies eat for breakfast on the way to kindergarten in the car the night before, and I try to memorize useful Bible verses to keep me from losing my cool when push comes to shove. I have to be prepared for battle, ready for the fight and forging victoriously forward into the career for which I believed I had been groomed my whole life.

In December 2004, I made my recital debut at Carnegie Hall with Roger Vignoles. By then, I had concluded my studies with Edith Wiens, and Markus and I had moved from Augsburg to an apartment in Toronto's High Park neighbourhood. Markus was my manager and my career was our baby.

On the morning of my first recital at Carnegie, I knew enough to wake up terrified. No matter how much I tried to convince myself otherwise, this was not just another hall. I let myself feel that terror instead of pushing it down, then gave myself time to regroup and conquer. My art and my responsibility to an audience mattered too much to allow any unnecessary self-indulgence. It might seem strange to say this, because as an artist and storyteller, I'm meant to be conveying raw authenticity, but to do my job effectively, I have to shut off personal emotions. In classical singing the impression of emotion is what is most effective. Its actual manifestation is unhelpful because it impedes resonance and cripples breath control. The audience is meant to feel what I am conveying, while I, on the other hand, am not. I guess it's called acting. I am describing an emotion with my voice and my body, commenting on it in words. Being it, but not experiencing it. Even thinking I am sad will give me the posture and approach I need, the inflection that allows the audience to feel what I can't allow myself to feel. This was something I had to learn—that less is more. It came from realizing the strength of the music combined with my stage presence and how sucked into me people already are, allowing me to ration my output rather than stretch myself beyond the footlights. Economize. To always leave a comfortable 20 percent in the tank.

Before my Carnegie performance, Mary Morrison coached me into my comfort zone by warming me up on the Carnegie Hall stage just like when I was a teenager and we were in the bowels of the University of Toronto Faculty of Music. I was so happy to be sharing this moment with Mary. It was exactly how I'd hoped my Carnegie debut would go, because my respect for Mary Morrison is on par with my desire to please my parents.

This pivotal concert was also enormous because Jim Myles, my high school musical director, had organized a bus tour to travel to my New York debut from my hometown of Fredericton.

It was such a generous gesture that I still don't feel as though I've ever fully expressed my gratitude to him and all those New Brunswickers who invested the time and money to be in New York City for me. It remains one of the most singular moments of my career.

Jim died suddenly of a massive heart attack during the writing of this book. I was sitting in Westminster Abbey in London, England, waiting to sing for Her Majesty Queen Elizabeth II and members of the Royal Family for the mass celebrating International Commonwealth Day. Fifty-two countries—the member states of the Commonwealth—were represented and I was chosen to be the soloist to start the festivities. I was to sing an unaccompanied spiritual on the centre steps of the sanctuary, and as you can imagine, it was a highly pressurized atmosphere, so when I felt my phone vibrate with the news of Jim's passing, I didn't want to engage. I would deal with it later. I had to deal with the task at hand. This was not the time to get emotional. My performance was being broadcast worldwide by the BBC, live on television and online. But my phone kept buzzing. People wanting me to know about Jim, or wondering if I had heard, or offering their condolences. All I could think of was his family—his wife, Carmel, and their four boys, the youngest of whom, David, a singer-songwriter, I admired and had collaborated with. I couldn't think of how best to harness the grief that threatened to surface, and then I remembered how much Jim loved the Queen. I thought of how tickled he would have been

Raised in Fredericton, I was camera-ready before I could walk. This was the first of many pretty dresses.

My older brother and sister, Neville and Teah. They've always taken such good care of me.

The 1970s. That's my mom with us kids. Could she be any foxier?

Me on my nanny's bed. I spent a lot of time with my mom's mom in my early years and have always wanted the same for my boys.

Were there black pilgrims? Apparently my family thought so. 1986 was a good year and my family decided to celebrate by dressing up. Let no one say the Gosmans didn't have a sense of humour.

My parents on their wedding day in 1965 with my mom's parents (my father's parents were already deceased) and their wedding party. I think you'd agree the fashion choices here are significantly better.

My very first trophy: Junior Star of the Fredericton Music Festival. And what can I say about that dress? It was the '80s. That lace collar is EVERYTHING.

1994. To be clear: this is a costume. Pictured here as Evillene from *The Wiz* with my director and mentor, Jim Myles.

This photo just says everything that I am from high school to the present: in the centre, wearing a pretty dress and surrounded by boys. L to R: Kirk McInerney, Keith Loukes, Conrad Yavis and Tony LePage (a Fredericton native who became a Broadway big shot, with roles in *We Will Rock You* and *Come From Away*).

1995. Adorableness. Even at the time, I knew this photo was good enough to be my high school graduation photo. I love the "1920s bombshell" of it all.

My wedding day to Markus, my high school sweetheart! It was perfect, start to finish.

Me and my siblings. This is me at my most "abundant." The two of them make up one of me and it is nothing but love.

That's right. My family's a statistic. Fifty percent of these couples are still married.

Ottawa, 2012. The first few days of our first-born Shepherd's life. He has his daddy's perfectly shaped head, and I couldn't be happier about it.

Nanny and Papa with their seventh grandchild, Shepherd Peter.

Shepherd making his debut with Oscar Peterson. Ottawa, 2013.

Unlike my first-born, Sterling is perfectly content to sit in his crib and play while Mama gets ready in the morning. (So long as I leave the door open so he doesn't miss anything!)

Markus and I sold our Toronto Parkdale home for significantly more than we paid for it. We opted for a low-key celebration.

that not only had I made it to Carnegie Hall and he had witnessed it but also that I had been hand-picked to represent my country at Westminster Abbey and sing for the Queen and her family. I know Mr. Myles was there, too. He just had a better seat.

Just like in Westminster Abbey, thirteen years earlier at Carnegie Hall I experienced a nauseating mixture of pressure, glee, acceptance and singularity. The girl who grew up in the Maritimes and went away to do something strange that few people understand. I feel completely displaced most of the time and did then, but here were these familiar faces from my community, led by Jim Myles, cheering me on in this exotic and reputedly exclusive concert hall. I wonder if it was weird for them watching someone they had taught or babysat or spoonfed or directed or gotten plastered with walk on that stage. I wonder if it perplexed them or if it made perfect sense, like a circle completing itself.

My recital program was Maurice Ravel, Joseph Marx, Xavier Montsalvatge, Benjamin Britten, Aaron Copland, William Bolcom. At the end of the recital, the hometown crowd draped a New Brunswick flag over the first balcony of Weill Hall.

Fan-bloody-tastic.

I sang three encores, and afterwards a reception was held for me at a nearby restaurant, hosted by Pamela Wallin. Lorna MacDonald, head of voice studies at U of T and a fellow Maritimer, was there. I sometimes picture them all gathered together: Lorna, along with Edith Wiens, Wendy Nielsen,

Dianne Wilkins and Mabel Doak. My life's Royal Family. With Mary, of course, as the Queen Mother.

This is the monarchy that has governed my craft.

When I look back at my career during the first decade and a half of the 2000s, it's a haze of significant firsts and golden opportunities for which I worked extremely hard: repeated recitalist and soloist in London's Wigmore and Royal Albert Halls, the Palais des Beaux-Arts in Brussels, Spivey Hall in Atlanta, the Kennedy Center, Hill Auditorium in Ann Arbor, as well as halls in Oslo, Helsinki and Reykjavik, all over Europe, and eventually all the halls in Carnegie. I sang the major festivals of Edinburgh, Bergen, Tuscany and Verbier.

I would share the stage with Bill and Melinda Gates during the 2006 opening ceremonies of the XVI International AIDS Conference in Toronto, and in March 2006 an invitation to appear on Bravo TV's award-winning *Live at the Rehearsal Hall* allowed me to create a musical partnership with Aaron Davis, who would become the lynchpin in my non-classical career. For the televised collaboration, I split the program into a classical half, in which I collaborated with Jacques Israelievitch on violin (may he rest in peace) and Cameron Stowe on piano, followed by a non-classical half of hymns, jazz standards and selections from the Canadian Songbook, with Aaron Davis on piano, Marc Rogers on bass and John Johnson on woodwinds. For our live-to-tape performance before a studio audience, I wore a gorgeous black-and-white, all-feather bolero by Canadian designer Wayne Clarke and jewellery by Myles Mindham.

Aaron and I worked together once again, for the 2008 Junos, when I sang his arrangement of the Oscar Peterson–Elvis Costello song "When Summer Comes." The band was stacked. Through my musical relationship with Aaron, I have met and worked with so many of the gigging, studio-recording, go-to living legends because he knows them all and they love working with him. In addition to Johnny Johnson and Marc Rogers, I've breathed musical air with Rob Piltch, George Koller, Kevin Turcotte, Davide Direnzo, Carlos del Junco, Marty Melanson and Dave Burton, to name but a few. I love them all and I have Aaron to thank for meeting them all.

I have had what could best be described as an obsession with Aaron Davis since high school, when Geoff Cook and I would carpool home from the Sunday-evening service at Brunswick Street United Baptist Church, blasting the Holly Cole Trio's album *Don't Smoke in Bed*, with Aaron's solo on "I Can See Clearly Now" on repeat. That Aaron and I would go on to work together for over a decade is nothing short of a dream come true for me.

I wouldn't have explored to the artistic depths I have if I hadn't had Aaron underwriting my choices and taking for granted that I was simply qualified and deserving of these opportunities to expand myself vocally and compositionally. I honestly don't think my career would have even led me to writing this book if I hadn't first set my sights on making him like and respect me. I have revered his gentle genius since I was a teenager, and his uniquely warm but funky aesthetic has grown to inform so many of my own musical choices. Quite simply put, he gave me wings to dare to define myself as Artist, instead of caving to tradition and confining myself to Soprano.

Not long after starting to work with Aaron, I rang in New Year's 2007 by singing "Auld Lang Syne" for a crowd of forty thousand in Toronto's Nathan Phillips Square. At the composer's request, I sang Joni Mitchell's "Both Sides Now," as one in a group of three artists invited to induct her songs into the Canadian Songwriters Hall of Fame that year. I'd always admired Joni's passion and was deeply honoured to have been tasked with interpreting "Both Sides Now" for the televised CBC broadcast. I won my first Gemini for that performance. During the private hang afterwards in Joni's suite at Toronto's King Edward Hotel, I found myself sandwiched between Joni and Chaka Khan, who, along with James Taylor, had also been summoned to Toronto to sing for Joni's induction. Chaka had been accompanied by Herbie Hancock (this was where we met for the first time). I recall him sitting at the end of the suite's luxuriously long couch on which we all found ourselves laughing, drinking (except for Herbie, who is a Buddhist) and reminiscing. I did not contribute much in the way of conversation because I wanted to be sure to remember every millisecond of this privileged, fly-on-the-wall evening. Chaka was reciting lines from Joni's songs, and Joni was chain-smoking and laughing her lusty, smoky laugh. Herbie was grinning like he'd been given all the punchlines beforehand, and I remember thinking, *I hope I never think this is normal . . .*

In July of that year, I made my debut at the Royal Nova Scotia International Tattoo, singing "Con te partirò," the duet made famous by Andrea Bocelli and Sarah Brightman. The snobs among you might wrongfully judge this plebeian, but you sing anything with three full brass bands, hundreds of bagpipes and a full chorus to a sold-out arena and get back to me with how powerful that feels.

Later that July I debuted with the New York Philharmonic in Central Park. Sir Andrew Davis conducted. After pouring crazy amounts of rain, the sky cleared and sixty-five thousand people turned up. I remember being preoccupied about how to address my conductor: Sir Andrew? Sir Davis? Sir Andrew Davis? I settled on "Maestro." He could not have been kinder to me. I wore a hopeful purple-and-green dress (designed for me by Canadian designer Rosemarie Umetsu) and sang arias by Catalani, Massenet and Weber, along with "Summertime." My photo would be published in *The New York Times* with the newly announced chief conductor of the New York Philharmonic, Alan Gilbert, the successor to Lorin Maazel, and an old buddy from our times at the Verbier Festival in Switzerland.

Despite its international context, the classical world is pretty teensy. For my debut with the Chicago Symphony Orchestra,

I performed a program of songs from Mahler's *Des Knaben Wunderhorn* conducted by Jaap van Zweden, who would succeed Alan Gilbert as chief conductor at the New York Philharmonic.

The crowd in Central Park was breathtaking, but I think the most eyes had to have been on me when I sang the "Olympic Hymn" in the opening ceremonies for the 2010 Vancouver Winter Games to a stadium of sixty thousand people, plus a TV audience of 3.2 billion, I remember every second, every syllable, every emotion.

At almost forty, I feel blessed to be able to look backward and forward. I have had incredibly fond experiences singing Messiaen's *Poèmes pour Mi* with Daniel Harding, on tour with the London Symphony Orchestra, and Janáček's *Glagolitic Mass*, also with the LSO, with Michael Tilson Thomas—a loyal collaborator, visionary, maverick and pioneer; and a force I am privileged to call Friend, along with his beautiful husband, Joshua. With Franz Welser-Möst and the Cleveland Orchestra, I sang and recorded Beethoven's *Symphony No. 9* and, later, Wagner's *Wesendonck Lieder*, which would be nominated for a Grammy, which I would lose to Cecilia Bartoli (not that anyone "loses" to Cecilia Bartoli). I didn't go to the actual Grammys because I was giving a recital in Spivey Hall in Atlanta on the same day. I found out at the intermission that I didn't win but was grateful for the singular experience of being nominated—I simply hadn't expected to win.

When he exploded onto the international classical music scene, Gustavo Dudamel, whose conducting genius was groomed and nurtured by the incomparable El Sistema program in Venezuela, and I made our respective conducting and singing debuts with the Israel Philharmonic performing Mahler's *Lieder eines fahrenden Gesellen*. Gustavo and I would go on to collaborate at the Hollywood Bowl for his inaugural concert as music director of the Los Angeles Philharmonic. Here, I would be reunited with Herbie Hancock, who was also on the program!

I sang Mendelssohn's *Elijah* with the Orchestre Métropolitain de Montréal and Yannick Nézet-Séguin the night Barack Obama won his second term as POTUS, and I did an international tour with the Ensemble Intercontemporain and the composer and conductor Peter Eötvös, singing his *Snatches of a Conversation* and Luciano Berio's *Recital I for Cathy*, with Jeff Cohen on piano.

That's a bit of a highlight reel, and I'm grateful that on and on it continues to go.

During all my travels, I've learned to allow twenty-four hours to recover from jet lag, thanks to the in-flight air that is usually several decades old. It's honestly my Achilles' heel. I've lived with the knowledge of my singing voice from age seven, and I used to take its resilience for granted. When cigarettes were banned from bars, I honestly did a little jig because it meant I could finally spend time in them without fear of damaging my voice. Other kinds of vocal kryptonite for me include screaming (no theme-park roller coasters or overly outraged parenting), cold air (no long winter walks for me, thank you) and boisterous sex (a massive sacrifice).

Dryness for any voice is death. The voice loves to be wet, so a humidifier is essential. When none is available, I run the shower. An apple, orange, grapes or any juicy kind of fruit or plain salted chips are what I snack on while warming up because they activate the saliva and lube everything up. Some singers can't eat before they sing. I am not one of them. Nothing annoys me more than going onstage hungry. If I could eat and sing, I'd honestly have it made. Praise the Lord that I'm not cursed with acid reflux! I know opera singers whose careers have ended because of it, and others who are forced to sleep in an upright position to avoid it.

But let's be honest. No one would ever describe me as the Queen of Healthy Living. My attention to those details has fluctuated during my career. I've gone through periods where I've been resentful of the sacrifices I've had to make for the health of my instrument, and thus have let the pendulum swing a little too much in the other direction. This rebellion increases my prestage anxiety but expands my quality of life and keeps me connected to my humanity by helping me stay connected to things I really enjoy, like swimming in a public pool, drinking coffee, talking in a loud place, boisterous sex (because who wants to live without that) and the occasional smoke—a pretty common practice among opera singers, believe it or not.

I love singing, and I love making my living as a singer, but sometimes I feel like I spend so much time working against my baser inclinations, which are to procrastinate, drink lots of wine and smoke weed all day. I know I can't be the only human—let alone classical singer, woman, parent or Christian—who feels this way. My desire to make my life all about my job has ebbed and flowed throughout the years, and as I get older, I understand that the strength of character that fuels the artistry is just as crucial as the art itself. You can't possibly hope for the audience to believe your humanity if you don't in fact live as a bona fide human. There is a kind of exchange of empathy between me and my audience that has come to influence me more than anything the so-called music industry has to say. It might have something to do with being on the brink of forty, having thirty-three singing years under my belt—and very few f***s left to give.

P art of the magic of feeling free in this job is making sure you have the right representation. I get asked a lot about how to secure artistic management. The answer isn't easy, because a classical singer should be looking for a general manager with whom he or she can envision clear long-term goals. You are to audition them as much as they are to court you. Never pay a retainer, under any circumstances, and take your time until you find someone who gets you. I've switched agencies once in my whole career and I wouldn't have switched if I hadn't been forced to. The larger agencies offer name recognition to get your foot in the door, while the boutique agencies have the strength of personally pounding the pavement for you and building customized brands. I went from the first one to the second one, and after a brief period of panic at the prospect of being adrift with no one to represent my professional interests, I found the glorious Alan Coates of Keynote Artist Management in London to spearhead my classical music interests worldwide.

To tell it from the beginning, my journey to management started in 2003. Shortly before I left Germany, I auditioned and was accepted into the Steans Music Institute, the Ravinia Festival's summer young-artist program. For three weeks we received masterclasses by musical luminaries and private coaching from an internationally renowned faculty. I chose to feel excited rather than threatened that I was in a group of peers who forced me to raise my own game. Such a choice required almost daily reinforcement.

Ravinia—a young-adult summer camp for the exceptionally talented—proved to be a crucial touchstone in my career. Most notably, Bill Palant, then working for IMG Artists—one of the largest agencies—heard all of Ravinia's young artists and chose me and one other Canadian, Joseph Kaiser, as potential artists for his roster. Bill and I courted each other for about a year before he heard me sing Liù in Puccini's *Turandot* with Cincinnati Opera. After that he became my loyal agent for all things classical, someone invested in proactively building a career rather than expecting it to just happen. The preceding professional hit parade was brought to you courtesy of Bill Palant's belief in my artistry.

Bill Palant also connected me to Deutsche Grammophon, the Holy Grail of classical recording companies. In 2007 I released my first DG album, *Surprise!*, featuring cabaret songs by William Bolcom, Arnold Schoenberg and Erik Satie, sung in English, German and French, respectively. I preferred this personality-driven overture to the international classical recording scene over the more traditional debut album of "opera hits." *Surprise!* won more than a few awards, but I have a soft spot for it winning the 2008 Juno Award for Classical Album of the Year.

Bill would eventually leave IMG and start his own boutique agency. Despite many conversations and the hope that what we'd built together would be enough to sustain his transition to a smaller collection of artists, he chose to not take me with him. I was shocked and devastated. I am fiercely loyal and had expected the same in return. But sometimes our destiny is presented to us through a process of elimination. As it turned out, Bill's dropping me from his roster forced me to reacquaint myself with an industry with which I'd had to have very limited contact on a managerial level because I'd always believed where I was had roots deep enough to weather the storm of a changing industry. In fending for myself, I became aware of the remodelling of the classical landscape. Plus, it was a little over ten years since I'd been "on the market," and big agencies were taking on more artists but not more managers. It had gotten to the point where people who had been interns for less than a year were suddenly in charge of entire artists' calendars and careers. Cost-saving measures were overriding the traditional, impresario-like priorities of the old-school classical agent. I know more than a few managers who left their large conglomerates to start up outfits that allowed them to add the personal touch that had attracted them to classical management in the first place but that had all but disappeared from their workplaces. This shift in the industry has provided a bastion for the reputably unique, nonconformist classical artist or ensemble. It has also forced some pretty big fish into smaller, more personalized, pools where, believe it or not, they're able to actually swim more freely. I am one such artist.

My agent Alan Coates and his colleagues at Keynote Artist Management could be the poster children for the wave to quench the thirst in the industry for managers who will cultivate a roster of artists from various disciplines at various points in their careers, invest in their long- and short-term goals and stick by them to facilitate their artistic objectives. Alan came along right when I needed him, and I pray that if someone picks up this book twenty years from now, that person will read this, smile and say, "Aha, so that's how their story started."

The same can be said of my non-classical management. Evan Newman of Outside Music, Steve Zsirai of Zed Music Inc., and Tom Kemp of The Feldman Agency handle all my intangibles:

the "dream projects" that I try to keep off the radar of the super-judgy subsection of the classical world—lest I muddy the waters for the purists. Well, the cat's out of the bag, because these guys are too good at their job! All the folks in my camp, classical or otherwise, are ready and enthusiastic about working together. They understand that the unclassifiability of my output IS my brand. That the career I want isn't one that exists yet. Meaning, I'm hoping to break the mould and empower other artists to do the same. I can't be the only opera singer who wants to do chamber music on tour in non-traditional venues at different times of day in order to attract a new audience or just shake things up. I can't be the only soprano who is influenced and inspired by non-classical music and is willing to work just as hard to be as stylistically correct in other genres as I am in French *mélodie* or German Lieder or Spanish *canción*. For all my touting of nonconformist liberalism, it really all comes down to using the appropriate voice at the appropriate time in the appropriate place with the appropriate instrumentalists and singers. I am deeply grateful that the management I have now understands and celebrates that.

Beyond having a team who understand me well enough to facilitate my professional designs, I have to give them something to work with. The quality of my singing works in tandem with the strength of my appearance, with the ultimate goal of creating a complete package. Thankfully, I was raised to be a bit of a clothes horse. I come by it honestly, because my parents have always taken pride in their appearance. To this day I've never seen my father anything but clean-shaven. He is always immaculately dressed and presents himself to the world with self-respect, dignity and good posture. Additionally, my mother is my sole icon of beauty. She has a closet full of clothes that she presses, hems and tailor-fits to her petite frame. She also has flawless skin ("the best accessory," as makeup artist Jackie Shawn once told me) and knows to never throw anything out because it will always come back in style. She made all my gowns in my early career. The truth may have been that we didn't have the money to buy new, but the consequence was I looked better and stood taller than anyone next to me, because I was the pride of my parents.

As a result, part of my professional armour has become my wardrobe. It could be that I believe it is entirely possible to "fake it to make it." As in, if you look good, you will be good. If you smile, you'll be happy. If you keep your legs moving, your lips talking, your eyes focused and your hands steady, you're half-way there. Good posture communicates so much to the world around you because, as I often tell singers who lack confidence, the audience sees you before they hear you! Your posture can project confidence and make people think that you know what time it is. Sometimes that's all you need to get in the door . . . or the club. An appropriate, self-reflecting wardrobe—and the confidence with which you wear it—is essential to your under-cover mission of Total World Domination (TWD)!

My foundational style is dictated by comfort and convenience. About seven years ago, during a concert with Maestro Robert Spano at Symphony Hall in Atlanta, I realized I couldn't feel my feet. My tight shoes had cut off all the blood circulation to my tootsies. Throughout my final measures, I shifted back and forth from foot to foot, trying to create more blood flow. It didn't work. I knew that once the music ended and the applause started I would have to bow, extend my hand to the conductor and hold his hand while we bowed together. Next, I would have to shake the hand of the concert-master and—somehow—manage to walk off the stage. I remember thinking, *I'll have to exit doing that weird hot-potato dance—hoo hah! hoo hah!* And that's exactly what ended up happening.

That experience taught me one thing: no more shoes; it's not worth it. Why should I suffer for the occasional peek of footwear from under my floor-length gown? Far better to lengthen my skirts so that the hems pool on the floor, hiding blissfully comfortable bare feet, than to subject my fans to more hot-potato dances.

The way I see it, in this life there is enough discomfort to endure. You don't have to invite it on yourself.

Once I started travelling more and doing higher-profile gigs, I saw my relationship to Canadian designers as my own mini Canadian ambassadorship. Early on when I was still heavy, I usually wore a basic black velvet gown, splashed with colourful shawls that I would switch at intermission. This style developed because in Germany I was no longer available for fittings with my mother, my original gown maker (though to this day she would still only claim that she "does a little sewing"). The black dress provided a neutral canvas for the versatile shawls—made perhaps of chartreuse satin or a fuchsia silk blend—which I draped in ever more ingenious ways, pinning the shawls precisely in place to avoid a wardrobe malfunction or any fussing with them. They also taught me discipline, since I needed to train myself to never touch them while performing. I'd learned early on how distracting fidgeting can be, and it became one of my biggest pet peeves to see classical performers mess with their clothing onstage. Hello? We can see you. And that shawl or scarf or tie or jacket or bead of sweat or fallen hair curl is not who I bought tickets to see, so for the love of all things right and just, please stop making it the star of your show!

On the last birthday of this decade, when I was going through a particularly rough time, I decided to dye my hair platinum blond. I think I'd always wanted blond hair, but for a black girl from the dark side of Fredericton, it seemed a little ridiculous. I had originally planned to shave my head clean but thought better of it once I did a little reminiscing about the Britney Spears green umbrella incident, where she spiralled into more than a few well-documented cries for help. So

I backed away from the head-shaving option. I kept the length and changed the colour, instead.

If I'm being honest, I think I needed to hang on to the femininity that is traditionally associated with long hair. I'm not saying Jada and Halle aren't droppin' it like it's hot. I just mean that I wanted to feel like I could stand shoulder to shoulder with them before I did the chop. Things were kinda raw then in the Brueggergosman camp, and I didn't want to cut my hair out of desperation. I wanted my choice to be completely rooted in style and not because I was trying to make my life simpler. At that point in my life, given everything that was not working, I clung to everything that was workin', honey.

And thank God I did! I had no idea the year that I was in for. Despite the success in my career, my personal life was on fire. My marriage had broken down (for the second and, what looks like, final time) and I was shocked to discover that I was broke. I had never had anything to do with our finances, and the realities of getting a divorce and taking over my house given my dire money situation was beginning to take its toll. I didn't even know what a heat pump was or how to pay a cell phone bill—let alone where the money was going to come from to pay it. Then there were the implications of starting to parent my boys on my own—one of whom is gifted, with anger-management issues— while also maintaining my career (because it was sure not the time to get sick or stop making money). Putting out fire after fire after fire was overwhelming me.

All this to say that during the hard days of my thirty-ninth year, a simple compliment about my hair was sometimes all the encouragement I got. Something that might seem so superficial, from a stranger or a colleague, could douse the flames of self-doubt and panic that were threatening to consume me. Please consider that the next time you want to compliment someone but think better of it for whatever reason. There is never a bad time to give a compliment. You never know. It could be the one thing that keeps the recipient from giving up. Your compliment could be the perfectly timed push he or she needs to make it through that day. For me, there were some days when I was so close to not getting out of bed. Yet I knew I would because there was no way forward but through. And the compliments on my hair made me feel fierce for the fight!

I refused to lose hope. And circumstances that I could not have foreseen (or afforded) entered in. As I type on my seven-year-old MacBook Pro in a poolside room in the mountains at Tree of Life Cabinas in southern Costa Rica, I am humbled by the expanse and variety of my life up to this point. There is no way I can afford to be here on my own, but somehow, I am listening to the jungle sounds while I try to keep from sweating to death. How can I not think everything's going to be as it's meant to be? When the receipts are read, the "it's complicated" wife of Markus Bruegger and Mama to Shepherd Peter and Sterling Markus stayed juicy, adventurous and imperfect the whole of her life. And she wrote this book that let her lay herself bare and hopefully helped other people do the same.

Yes, my husband has moved out of our home, my finances have blown up (in a bad way), but my artistry is redefining itself (in a good way). On balance, my heart has expanded several times, my heart has broken several times, but it has also been strengthened every time in the healing. Rinse and repeat. That has essentially been this banner year for me. How I experience and react to all "the stuff" is at the fore of my mind. "Stuff" like touring what I consider to be my most personal album to date, *Songs of Freedom*; singing for Her Majesty the Queen of England (again); defending Madeline Ashby's *Company Town* all the way to the finals of a national book show called *Canada Reads*; and ending it all by making sure my babies were well taken care of so that I could take my newly blond half-shaven head to Costa Rica for two weeks and put the cherry on the sundae of this period in my life. Being here at my friends Ben and Nate's slice of heaven on earth ties a big red bow on a year that has been a verifiable shit-storm of all that could possibly burn up and take me with it in the process. But I remain standing and so will you. Whether the storms are here or their arrival is pending—some hurricane, tornado or firestorm hits us all eventually.

The most extreme emotional, financial and spiritual battles I've had to face to date have helped me to see how my mother's example of not throwing any quality article of clothing away would lead to an accumulation of clothing (and cosmetics) that has sustained me in my job and my life, since I have no money to buy anything new. I believe what we choose to wear, in addition to being a reflection of who we are, can also tell the story we want people to believe. I have known true discomfort, and at least where my wardrobe is concerned, I don't see the need to experience it while doing the job I love.

I'm confident that the unpredictability and instability of my thirty-ninth year will leave me standing in a truer version of my Self than I've ever known. The process of getting there won't be graceful or neat. At least, it hasn't been so far. One of the things I love about the teachings of the incredible Christian scholar and orator Bishop T. D. Jakes is that he states there is no way to be both effective and pretty. In his words: "The only way to become a wise woman is through the stupid things you've done." And if you're thinking, *If that's true, then I should be Solomon by now,* then you're my people. Everything in my life right now is an open wound, and I'm not going to keep stitching it up, because I'm coming to believe that I'm the most effective when I'm the most broken. I have to believe God can use someone who isn't a perfect parent, or who has survived divorce, or who is under a crushing debt load. What keeps me from total despair is that I can't be disqualified from grace because I cheated on my husband or have back taxes to pay. I refuse to lie down and curse myself for the sins of my past. Besides, I'm too busy building an empire to feel ashamed and guilty all the time. I am not defined by my mistakes, and instead, I will use them to encourage as many people as will listen, because the presence of dirt in my life is also the presence of Truth and Beauty.

Date: Sunday, May 23, 2010, 9:03 am
From: Measha Brueggergosman
To: Nearests and Dearests
Subject: Out of the Frying Pan . . .

What a difference this time has made. I'm praying for all of your support. I've realized that while there's tremendous joy in parts of my life (because God is faithful), if I'm being honest, I haven't been truly content for a long time, and that dissatisfaction has seeped into all my relationships and my work. I've managed to cope and, in some cases, thrive up to this point, but I knew if I didn't take this time for myself, things would only get worse.

Thank you for following me on this journey. It has been gruelling and exhausting and humbling. I know some of you out there like to envision what I'm doing so that you can think of me, pray for me or just feel like you're with me in some way. That, along with my bulldog, steel-clad determination, will sustain and edify me. Believe that.

Humbled and grateful,

Measha

Once you come to a place where you acknowledge your worthiness and create (or even elbow into existence) the space you need to move forward, ready and hungry for your purpose, how do you go about reaching your goals? Accomplishing your desires? Hitting your mark? Fulfilling your destiny?

How do you get what you want?

However you phrase it, I hope you'll forgive me for simplifying, but . . . well . . . you ask. The act of asking is in itself its own first step. It requires precision, succinctness and articulation.

Who do you ask?

Whoever's got the power to give you what you want.

This may require some courage. This may require a good look in the mirror. This may also be where opinions might diverge, because this could also be a chance to get all existential, which might result in you doing nothing since what would be the point in fighting the inevitable? What I hope is that it results in the realization that no one has control over anything. Including who you think might have the power to control your own fate.

But then, who is in control? I mean for sure, for sure. I know what I believe, but I can't say for sure. No one can. So then, perhaps it's best to deal with the here and now. Oprah (can you hear the angels sing at the sound of her name?) once said that one way to accomplish your goals was to map them and retrace the steps from your destination to your current starting point. And then perform them in reverse, starting with the one closest to you. This simplifies the situation to a series of locks and doors. Locks that need to be opened and doors that need to be walked through. Questions that need to be asked and answered. A road map. If you want to be a mechanic, you don't show up at a garage, point at something and say, "I'm here to repair that." You would likely be escorted out rather quickly once they realized you were serious. Several steps were skipped before walking into that garage, all of them necessary. Licence, diploma, school, money for school, interest and someone's car are just a few.

Don't nitpick with me. I may not know the exact trajectory of the career mechanic, but I do know it doesn't just happen. Just like anything you want. The sandwich doesn't magically appear in your hand while you binge-watch *Scandal*. You have to make it. The point I'm trying to illustrate is that the goals we set for ourselves, no matter their motivation, can be mathematical in their execution. The steps, no matter how tiny, all have an order. To skip any would lead to a different result. You'll have choices and distractions. I'm not saying there won't be variations to the plan, or even that the plan won't completely implode and need a reboot. Sometimes it will feel like you have no options but to go in a direction that feels backward. I would challenge that it is still forward; it's just the second or third or fourth time you've been there. But you're not the same. That would be impossible, since change is constant, no matter how minute. The destination can change, depending on the path you take. There will be surprises.

Hell, sometimes the bottom will fall out completely. What will ultimately steer your course and ensure its inevitability is how you react. There are several paths to the ocean, and you have to have faith that they will all eventually end in water.

To be clear, I haven't come close to achieving what I believe my deepest contribution will be. My children are young, my voice and body are constantly changing, and no one knows what the future will bring. I could use the illusion of early success as my most concrete evidence and my most alluring deception. It could be perceived that I was getting everything I wanted, and in some areas of my life that was true. But I have to be sure I'm giving value to the right things or, in the end, I'll come up empty.

For where your treasure is, there your heart will be also. (Luke 12:34) Your heart and your treasure are always found in the same place. Without fail. They mutually define each other. If you find the statement confusing, maybe you've been forcing yourself to believe something that isn't true about your job, your relationship, your finances, your kids. For my part, every new day is an exercise in prioritizing the sustainable and irreplaceable. I fail regularly, but I keep trying because I will have nothing to show for all my efforts if I don't enjoy the bumpy journey to wherever it is I'm meant to be going.

This is why I say to you that when you ask what it is you want, don't forget to listen to the answer. And if you don't get the answer you want, ask again. And maybe again. And then check your ears. Because maybe you're only hearing what you want to hear. The answers may sound the same, but I assure you, they're not. Get all the information you can possibly gather and then change. Small variation, big variation. It doesn't matter. Change something. Because the definition of insanity is repeating the same thing and expecting a different result.

There may be a fine line between persistence and perseverance, but it all ends inelegantly. Messiness and inelegance are important distinctions. Witty repartee versus a shouting match. Fries or frites. Scolding a child or shaming him.

Be fair to yourself. Recognize when things have gone well for you and take your bow. Acknowledge your sacrifice and bask in how it paid off. Toil, struggle, fight and bleed. But take a beat to raise a glass and *hip hip hooray* yourself. Take up the space you're going to take up on this earth. There is enough room for everyone. Strut your stuff. Give yourself a high-five because you bet on you and won. When it's earned, be blessed enough to say, This is mine. I own this. I deserve this. I worked hard to get here and this is my moment. No one can take it away from me. I will not be robbed. I will be who I deserve to be and people will gravitate toward the generosity and empathy that seep from my pores. The meekest among us shall be protected by the strongest above us. All are safe. All are worthy. I am special because I know this and I serve this. I am a frequent loser but a good and generous winner.

The wisdom in any moment is that the difference between

the winning and the losing is of no consequence if your mind is right. For me, that means my mind is fixed on Jesus. That doesn't make me anywhere near perfect. But it does make me highly favoured.

I believe there are circumstances in which you can feel enough contentment from having the weapon that you don't even need to preoccupy yourself with winning the war. Because if God is the weapon, then the war is irrelevant. It ceases to exist. The struggle is useless against an opponent who isn't even fighting because He has already won. We don't need to fight or struggle or tie ourselves into knots. We've already got the prize. If God is for us, who can be against us? Our job is to persevere. Our job is to work. Our job is to pray without ceasing. To build the bridge to the other side, even if the other side is ablaze. Throw the lifeline anyway. Because if you're on the winning side, you have the answer to a question that, in its asking, always leads to the same answer. So, go ahead. Ask a question with the expectation of an eternal answer. I dare you.

And even if you don't believe what I believe. If you've cultivated the knowledge, the resources, the discipline and the mental wherewithal to articulate what it is you really want out of life, or even just what you want out of the day, then for heaven sakes, don't give up now! Go do it.

Don't overthink it. Go do it.

B ecause something is always on fire, I had a series of career highs starting in 2010 while also suffering devastating tragedy in my personal life. On the one hand, I sang the "Olympic Hymn" at the Opening Ceremonies of the 2010 Vancouver Winter Olympics and released my second Deutsche Grammophon album, *Night and Dreams*, with Justus Zeyen on piano and compositions by Brahms, Liszt, Duparc, Debussy, Strauss, Schubert and Mozart, among others. My Wagner's *Wesendonck Lieder* and Beethoven's *Symphony No. 9*, with Franz Welser-Möst and the Cleveland Orchestra, would also be released over the next couple of years on the yellow label. On the other (much heavier) hand, Markus and I had reconciled our marriage after a rocky year or two. Shortly after getting back together, we got pregnant and then lost both our twins, one at ten weeks and one at twenty-one-and-a-half weeks. To this day, the grief of that loss chokes me, but at the time, I honestly had no sense of where my life was going or if I was even going to get there.

Still on the mend, and two years after I sang in the opening ceremonies of the Olympics, I flew back to Vancouver and made my way to Merritt, British Columbia, in search of healing at a ten-day silent Vipassana meditation course. By then, through displacement, heartache and busyness, I had accumulated so much calcification in my emotional joints that I was ready to try something radical. I was also in my first trimester with our first son, but Markus and I were not ready to go public.

Vipassana is a silent practice of meditation. The first course—the sole method with which you can initiate yourself into the practice—is a full ten days. Ten days of total silence. From the minute I'd heard it described to me, it sounded like paradise. My Bikram yoga practice had been leading me toward this type of meditation—justifiably described as extreme. But . . . nothing ventured nothing gained. I had done a cross-Canada audition tour as a judge on *Canada's Got Talent* from the fall of 2011 into 2012, and we finished taping right before I took the Vipassana plunge. The show was exciting and glossy and cacophonous and relentless, in a good way. It was a huge, ridiculous party and I loved every minute of it.

My husband and I had started trying to get pregnant straight away after we lost our second twin, August David, in August 2011. By December 2011 we were expecting, but after our double loss, I was pretty gun-shy about letting the cat out of the bag. I also wasn't sure I'd have the willpower to go my whole pregnancy without drinking. My wine-loving, alcohol-appreciating pregnant ladies and mothers out there know what I'm talking about. (You're just pregnant. You're not suddenly a different person.) So, when we finished the audition tour for *CGT*, to illustrate the disparate personalities of the judges, Martin Short went to record voice-overs for a Doritos ad campaign, Stephan Moccio went to Turks and Caicos with his family and I went to be completely silent for ten straight days. Just me and the baby in my belly.

Something was definitely on fire and it was me. The entire ten-day journey felt like I was being dipped repeatedly in a detoxifying inferno: painful and beneficial, uncomfortable and empowering. Some targets for detox were old lovers, my emergency open-heart surgery, the remorse of my marriage almost ending (the first time), losing babies. All of it had to be revisited, seen for the power it was having over my life and future, then put in its rightful place: either in the past for good, or tucked into a place where it could rest, remain a part of me but not do any damage. I had to mine deeply because I'd been pushing all that stuff down for a long time, pretending it wasn't there or underestimating how sad and powerless it was gradually making me. This was my time of being good to myself while also facing my darkest moments again. I had to find my way back to who I was and what I wanted.

Vipassana is a difficult process even when you don't have all that stuff to exorcise. It was the first trimester of my second pregnancy, so I spent pretty much every waking minute of the first few days trying not to fall asleep. Unsuccessfully. When I would come up for air, my energies were spent pushing distractions out of my own mind, and bringing the guidelines for the practice in, and trying to ultimately create space for everything—but never being able to be truly still. Try meditating when you're gassy and hungry all the time. It's pretty difficult to achieve a state of Zen if all your concentration is being used to stifle a fart.

Though I knew that Vipassana, like hot yoga, was an extreme Eastern discipline, I didn't really understand what I was embarking on when I boarded the bus for the three-hour journey from Vancouver into Merritt to the Vipassana centre. Located on fifty-six acres in a pine forest, it consisted of a four-winged, two-storey building with sexually segregated accommodations for about sixty people, a meditation hall, a dining hall, and bathing and administration facilities.

Vipassana means "to see things as they really are." Based on techniques taught by the Buddha 2,500 years ago, it defines suffering as the result of craving, aversion and ignorance. Theoretically, eliminating these *sankaras* through mental purification leads to balanced living and, ultimately, Enlightenment.

Because Buddha himself taught orally, his meditative techniques were thought to have been lost. However, an upsurge of twentieth-century interest led to the discovery that they had been preserved by the monks of Burma. In 1955, S. N. Goenka, a Burma-born industrialist, may he rest in peace, used these techniques for mind purification, incidentally curing himself of severe migraines. In gratitude, he founded the Vipassana International Academy, outside Bombay. That was in 1971. Now Vipassana is taught and practised all over the world.

As a new student, I was committed to completing the course by complying exactly with my teachers' instructions without addition or subtraction. Specifically, I was to refrain from the killing of any being, from stealing, from sexual activity, from lying, from indulging in intoxicants. This extended to all drugs, cigarettes, tranquillizers, sleeping pills and other sedatives. Even my blood pressure medications had to be reported to my teachers.

Because Vipassana claims to be non-religious, all forms of prayer, worship or ceremony were banned for the duration, including fasting, burning incense, counting beads, reciting mantras, singing, dancing and yoga. Any student who had brought any religious items, including rosaries, crystals, talismans, crosses, was to deposit them with management. Musical instruments, radios, recording devices, cameras, reading and writing materials were also banned.

From the first day of Vipassana until the morning of the last full day, I was to observe Noble Silence, which meant refraining from all forms of communication with other students: speech, touching, eye contact, gestures, sign language, notes. I was allowed no outside communication except in an emergency, which meant no letters, phone calls or visitors. Cell phones, pagers and all other electronic devices had to be deposited with management.

The only sanctioned exercise was walking during designated times in designated areas. Clothing should be modest and comfortable. Simple vegetarian food would be served.

The strictness of the environment reflected the discipline of the practice.

The cost of Vipassana, including all meals and accommodation, was zero, with a voluntary donation, according to one's means, only after completing the course. To preserve Vipassana's purity, the global program receives no institutional or government grants, and the teachers and organizers are unpaid. As it was explained to me, this is so that we "householders" (essentially, anyone who owns anything) can temporarily take the Buddhist vow of poverty and temporarily live off the generosity of others.

According to the schedule, I was to rise at 4:30 each morning and retire, with lights out, at 9:30 p.m. I would receive a breakfast break, a lunch break and a tea break (in place of dinner). I would meditate for a total of nine hours and forty-five minutes every day, sometimes in my room, sometimes in the group hall. The cardinal rule was to meditate as if alone—with mind turned inward—while taking care not to disturb anyone else and ignoring any distractions caused by others. I could ask questions of our teachers during designated periods—which was the only time I could speak. Each evening I would hear a forty-five-minute teacher's discourse.

Because of the timing of *Canada's Got Talent*, I arrived at the centre the day the silence began. I was relieved that I didn't have to make pleasantries with strangers and could just merge into the process undetected.

Once in the meditation hall, I was assigned a permanent place where I was to sit on cushions in a comfortable upright position. Though crossed legs were preferred, stretching them out was also allowed, and because I was pregnant, I could lean against a wall for support.

We received our instructions for meditation via video and audio recordings by S. N. Goenka. We were told to concentrate our minds by observing our breath, which is the link between our conscious and our unconscious. Specifically, we were to focus on the tiny space between the tip of the nose and the top of the upper lip. I thought, *Okay, I can do that.* Oh sure. Though seemingly a simple task, it's nearly impossible for prolonged periods, given the uncontrolled mind's desire to wander. How could I fill ten days with silence? I struggled to stay awake. Silence is so unusual in our noisy lives that it cued my mind to sleep. Conversely, the snoring and restlessness of the students with whom I was sharing a room caused me strong nightly annoyance, even though I knew overcoming these distractions was part of the process. I was grateful when, after three days, I was offered a single room. Being pregnant has its privileges.

I discovered that I liked the regimented schedule and the comfort of always knowing where I had to be. The meals were adequate for survival, but the absence of my beloved coffee seemed harsh.

As the days passed, Goenka gave us further video instructions for perfecting our meditations, allowing me to gain deeper insight into my behaviour. In the language of the practice: I typically suffered from the *sankara* of boredom, which meant that I was always looking to the promise of the future instead of being satisfied with what the present offered. To increase emotion, I created drama, leading to unnecessary hardship.

The first six days I wanted to crawl out of my own skin . . . when I wasn't dozing off. But, somehow, these occasional five-second stretches (usually less) emerge, and you find yourself suspended in a golden stillness. In this space, no matter how small, you renew yourself. Something rebuilds from the inside out. You get a glimpse at what a clean house might look like. It's a satisfied exhale, a glass of wine on a comfy couch after a long day; it's a date with yourself where everyone gets lucky. And then it's gone. It's fleeting, but it's everything and nothing simultaneously. I don't mean to make it sound like magic, because it's the presence of nothing that gave my mind and brain the relief it was so desperately seeking. Eventually—and with the requisite frustration and sense of failure that comes with it—you string those few seconds together into a longer succession. And then it's time to get thrust back into the noisy outside world. Where, praise God, there's meat.

Buddhism teaches that the suffering of the world and those who inhabit it is created by a desire to make the good last forever and to end suffering as soon as possible. Since everything always changes, equanimity is attained by freeing the Self from both an aversion to the negative (suffering) and an attachment to the positive (pleasure). The understanding that both are temporary allows you to enjoy the good and to accept the bad. This does not mean detaching the Self from life in an apathetic way, but freeing the Self from false desires and projections in order to engage more deeply.

Because my singing career is built on the breath, Vipassana's emphasis on breathing was very helpful. My yogic practice had already taught me that strong emotion, either good or bad, changed my breath. With fear, we typically hold on to it, stopping its free flow. When singing, how I take a breath is directly related to the phrase that will follow and its length—how full of tension or devoid of tension my musical choices will be—because of the quality of the breath I have to work with. Vipassana also taught that the further I was from consciousness of my breath, the further I was from awareness of myself and the acknowledgment of how I felt. This was one of the big lessons that I took from the course, and that I still carry with me.

During my interviews with one of our two mentors, I found it difficult to articulate the confusion caused by everything swirling in my head. When I did formulate a request, it was along the lines of, What should my process be when I leave here? Where is all this leading?

Typically, I was wanting to know the future rather than being content with the present. Once again, this was my *sankara* of boredom, manifesting itself in goal-oriented ambition. At times during Vipassana I did experience the true breadth of stillness, which gave me insight into its antithesis, which is my norm: the desire to always be moving. This helped me to understand that my feelings of breathlessness were not related to my blood pressure but to a spiritual condition requiring me to take a deeper spiritual beat and relax already. I needed to expand my spiritual lungs, which would also strengthen my physiological lungs, creating the oxygen for a full breath. The cleansing path to stillness is narrow, allowing room for only one person, and I found it hard to get to that solitude with its prescribed singularity. At least I now knew that the channel existed and that to be a fully formed human I must make that effort.

I hit a bump on day six. I could not believe I had four more days to go, locked inside my head, talking to myself. It helped to walk outside, doing the meditative shuffle, though what I really wanted was to throw myself into a snowbank and roll around—so I did that a few times. This was motivated not by joy but by my desire for a release through contrast. At the same time, I knew I had to let this impatience wash over me and trust in the process to do its work in me.

Vipassana was challenging in so many ways but ultimately highly powerful. Its ripple effects have changed the way I warm up for singing, as well as how I live my life. It has instilled in me a sense of control, so that now I experience both joy and adversity more objectively, as if viewing them from a greater distance. Since my volatile schedule doesn't allow me to practise every day, I have brushed up with a few one-day Vipassana courses.

Half a decade later, I understand the unfolding layers of that experience more and more. My triggers, my pitfalls, my deficiencies are held in a context of me never wanting to be bored—the illness of restlessness. If I'm not careful, my need to be entertained will force me to jump from sparkly thing to sparkly thing.

Which is a problem for me, since now I have kids. Falling prey to an inability to live in the moment means I could miss a lot of moments if I'm not careful. To be motivated by an aversion to boredom means that I have avoided being still for any reason and by any means necessary. By not allowing the natural cycle and rhythm of life to deepen my experience, wisdom and humanity, I risk banishing myself from the engagement of being a parent.

To be fair and balanced with myself, I also see this *sankara* as a hunger for life. It's the insatiable nature of my ambition that gets me home on fumes of sleep so that I can see my sons for as long as possible. But sinking deeper into the consistencies and commitments of the day in, day out realities of my children's needs is a challenge for me. I'm not naturally wired for it. And I'm supposed to feel guilty about it because my ambitions were meant to suddenly morph and align with those of my children's as soon as I gave birth? Screw that. Yes, the stakes are higher because I now have two sons I plan to raise into men. But, Shepherd and Sterling, if you're old enough to be reading this, Mama was a card-carrying member of society before you got here, and now you'll fall into step behind her until you can light your own torch (when you're old enough to play with fire). At that point, you'll light your way and mine. Because eventually, my offspring, our relationship will be reciprocal. You'll be raising your own babies by then, but yeah, eventually we'll be friends. If I like you.

(At this point in their lives, my sons are fully entitled to the entire scope of all the love I have to give. No questions asked.)

Being a full-time opera singer, performer, artist, narcissist and mom means strengthening the important connection between my restless desire to be everywhere at the same time and my deeply rooted dissatisfaction, because as strong as my hunger is for success, I'd like to think my hunger for healthy spiritual growth is much deeper. The older I get (the thirty-nine-year-old stifles a chuckle), the less apologizing I do for my attraction to sparkly things. Do I still feel guilty and ashamed and like I've missed important moments? Absolutely. But if I don't live long enough for cloning to become a reality, I have to make my peace with (and find the joy in) being where I am and who I am.

My Vipassana experience solidified the value I place in isolation: carving out your own place in the world and taking up the space you need in order to recharge. The goal of meditation is to accomplish this within the Self, but practically, my fix for satisfying my inner isolationist was to move to the country as soon as I could after the birth of my first son. Beyond the logistics of being close to my parents, my primary goal in life was to not have neighbours or be able to see any public road from my house. I wanted an oasis of space in the hope that my busy mind might take the cue and relax.

My environment has so much influence over my state of mind. I have incredibly thin skin for someone who makes her living being looked at and listened to. And, as I'd established, the teensiest sparkly thing could veer me off course. There are already enough cooks in the kitchen of my head that I really needed a place for them to all spread out. Without this expanse, I become tense and insecure. My breathing becomes shallow and I don't laugh as easily. It's not that my problems don't follow me home (because they do), but there's something about having more than one room to walk into, or a kitchen to cook in, or a fireplace to build a fire in, or a proper place for everything, or my own wine to drink, that gives me at least the illusion of control. It's not even about sleeping in my own bed or wearing my own clothes. I rarely unpack, actually. It's more about the buffer that exists between me, my sons and the rest of the world.

I also like being able to get my bearings from my space, from the heat pump turning on, to the creaks of the structure, to the weather against the windows, to positioning myself in the day based on the comforting constant of CBC Radio. There are no errant car horns or voices or sirens or machinery. I find it very calming to be able to identify every noise in my environs. I'm that much of a control freak. But it makes room for the sounds I should be taking in: my boys laughing or crying, the eagles on my lake, the voice telling me to stop procrastinating or the voice asking me, *How could it be procrastinating if what you're cooking will feed your family?*

Like the clothes you wear, the food you eat and the voices that get inside your head, where you choose to live can determine the ease with which you radiate from the inside out. Obviously, for some the opposite is true. These peeps are turned on by action and options and a consistent blanket of sound. I have friends who can't sleep without traffic blaring all night long. They recharge to the subway thundering outside their window. My point is, even superheroes need a place to regenerate and quiet the voices vying for supremacy over their motivations. You can only be expected to maintain the illusion of invincibility for so long.

This raises a question: Where does strength come from? When I'm singing and am expected to make you "believe," or am inviting you to the well of music for a deep, long drink, what am I telling myself to get myself to go beyond the notes on the page and into your memory forever? I'm so glad you asked.

In the fall of 2014, I gave a Walrus Talk on "The Art of Conversation," at Mount Allison University in Sackville, New Brunswick. In the talk, I maintained that the ongoing conversation or dialogue we have with ourselves is arguably the most important exchange we'll ever have. It is the well from which all motivation springs. For instance, if before a performance I was to think, *I am going to crash and burn, this is going to be awful, there's no way this is going to go well,* then I would spend the entirety of my time onstage trying to prove myself wrong. Whereas what I choose to believe is, *This is going to be amazing, your lives will all be forever changed, and you will leave from here, cure cancer and instigate world peace.*

I have a lot of conversations with the dead. Barely any of the composers I sing are still alive. In fact, they're likely to have been dead for close to a hundred years or much, much more. They can offer no audible advice save for what's left behind in the written score. Consequently, my stylistic decisions are informed by context and experience, and in the arena of technique, my mind has much to tell my body before I even make a sound. Backstage before a performance, I'm usually talking myself off the ledge, trying to convince myself to move forward, swallow the fear. I check to make sure there's no lipstick on my teeth, that my hair isn't going to fall in my face, that my dress is on properly, that a bra strap isn't showing, a boob isn't hanging out, my Spanx are hiked and doing their job. Any number of things that could go wrong I expect will go wrong. And then, I come out, I see all of you, and I am immediately calmed and assured (and reassured) of my responsibility to you. Reassured, because I know I'm fulfilling a purpose. I choose to believe it is the purpose of God's will over my life, and that takes off a tremendous amount of pressure, because I know I am called to do my part and anything after that is up to Him. I come to my spot. Sometimes my pianist is about to start playing; sometimes the conductor is about to indicate the downbeat for the orchestra.

For my part, I am focused on looking pristine, like I am in total control . . . I'm also wondering what the first words are. And then, there is breath, but before the breath there is posture, and within the posture there is alignment, and with alignment comes a good breath, and when you take a good breath, it has to be well timed. It has to be perfectly in time. It has to be devoid of tension but purposeful. It can't engage the jaw. It can't involve the tongue. It has to raise the soft palate. And then, you have to think about the consonant. If there is even a consonant. Sometimes there's a consonant. Sometimes there's not. Sometimes everything begins with an open vowel; sometimes the vowel is closed. Sometimes it's a mixed vowel involving the tongue and the lips; sometimes it's an open *ah*, which for me is the worst thing ever.

All of that is running through my mind as you watch my pristine, immaculately put-together, beautiful dress, and you know from the expression on my face exactly what it is I'm trying to tell you, and you are sucked into me. And that's my responsibility as the artist whose name is on the ticket you bought. The conversation that I'm now making you privy to would otherwise be none of your business, because I'm meant to make you feel like I'm in total control . . . which I am. As your singer, the things I command myself to do are relax, have fun, give nothing away—you, in concert with the music, are enough. Breathe. Repeat.

I would encourage you to examine the nature of the conversation you are having with yourself. How do you talk to yourself? Are you constructive? Are you discouraging? Are you realistic?

Would you say the same things to yourself you would to your best friend, a child or someone you love?

Answering these questions goes a long way to steering the most important conversation you'll ever have in the right direction and will reveal what you want and how to get it.

Part 3

WHAT'S HOLDING
ME BACK?

DATE: SUNDAY, MAY 30, 2010, 8:57 PM
FROM: MEASHA BRUEGGERGOSMAN
TO: NEARESTS AND DEARESTS
SUBJECT: SOMETHING CLEVER

Hello Nearests and Dearests,

Well, I'm afraid I'm gonna keep this update pretty short. I'm not in the best of places at the moment and I'm pretty exhausted. I've spent the majority of my weekend doing various household things and memorizing dialogue. Plus, when I opened up my inbox, there wasn't much news from any of you, so I'll just assume everything's fine on your end and that I'll hear from you eventually. But it's always nice to be able to read something in addition to writing something . . .

It's getting hotter in the desert, which means it's getting hotter in the yoga tent. We're getting to the point (55 classes in, with 45 left to go) where hydration and food intake are NOT optional and some people are struggling to keep their energy and electrolytes up. I basically alternate between litres of water, coconut water, Pedialyte and several packets of Emergen-C (electrolyte vitamin packets) and can usually put in about 11 litres a day if I monitor it correctly. And a TON of protein. The problem is we don't have a lot of time to eat and one is never hungry right after class, so you have to just have food on you all the time. But my blood pressure's good and I've had no cramping, vomiting, digestion "issues," headaches or the shakes, so I think I'm doing okay.

I don't know what this week has in store, but apparently, we're a pretty good bunch of trainees and are ahead in the dialogue, so maybe they'll find a whole new level of torture with which to afflict us. Or maybe they'll take it easy on us. Who knows? I'm trying not to have any expectations, so I'm not disappointed either way. In general, I'm trying to stay open and relinquish control, but I kinda feel like I'm not getting any better at it. Thanks very much to those of you who sent me mail this week. That was really great and I hope you know I truly appreciate it. And to those of you who promised to send mail but haven't yet? Well, I guess I understand that, too. But to that person who sent a letter and had it returned, jumbled up and wet? I'm really thankful you tried, and, if you have it in you to try again, I'm here until June 19, and hopefully we'll have victory over the US Postal Service.

I think I'd best sign off now. Sorry to be such a downer. Hopefully next week will be better ... or tomorrow ... or an hour from now.

Namaste,

Measha

It can feel downright impossible to figure out what's holding us back, because some of us are only willing to face forward, desperate to outrun our past. The fact is, I'll likely be divorced by the time this book comes out. You're right to feel a sense of déjà vu, because this past year was actually the second time that my husband and I separated. I'm quite sure this time it's going to stick. While I was at the Semperoper in Dresden with my boys, he moved out of the house and closer to his work. My first instinct on hearing the news was to feel betrayed and abandoned. Like he'd waited for us to leave and then made his escape. But my husband had said repeatedly that he wanted a divorce and had it not been for our boys, he would have been gone already. And I would defend his choice with my dying breath, because I've broken his heart so many times and I can see now how bitter it has made him. He should get out while he can still laugh and find the good in life with someone else. In a way, I can see how I've been spared the bedfellow emotions of confusion and resentment that come from seeing the boxes packed and piled in the front entryway—the drawn-out regret and push-pull of agonizing that there must be some way we could make this work. But he's left the only home we shared together with both our sons.

I was so stupid when I got married in May of 1999. I didn't know how to do anything or be anything for anyone else. Markus, by contrast, seemed perfectly suited to marriage. The sun rose and set on his partner and he had no reservation whatsoever about putting all his proverbial eggs in one basket. We were incredibly in love, but I don't think either one of us actually thought there'd be work involved. So, when you see marriage as a utopic destination instead of an ongoing series of fires you have to put out, your bubble gets burst really quick. Especially when your wife cheats on you and your world comes crashing down twelve years, and then again at fifteen years, into your marriage. And he has forgiven me probably too many times. And yes, I do feel like a disgrace and failure some of the time. And the rest of the time? I need all my energy to try and not feel like a disgrace and failure.

My husband is justified in divorcing me, because throughout our entire marriage, I have not been faithful to him. With my heart, yes. With my body, no. I've never loved anyone as much as I love him and he is the absolute best human I have ever met, but if I'm being honest, I never really thought marriage was for me. The religion I prescribe to essentially says to not have sex before marriage and to stay married forever. Well, there was no way I was going to go through life without sex. And once that bell was rung (on my wedding night), I couldn't un-ring it.

I met Markus when I knew what I was going to be doing for the rest of my life. Anyone meeting me at that time would have had no choice but to board the Measha Train. I don't know that much has changed, actually. I still tend to think my direction is strongest, my ideas are best, and you may find yourself justifiably feeling a few steps behind or wondering if you can do anything right, because I prefer to take control of everything and then complain that I have to do everything. What has changed is that I know that thinking of something first or having a plan doesn't make me right . . . but I do have a will that is likely to outlast yours. Sigh. It's not always a good thing and I'm working on it.

Markus seemed to be willing to make my desires his own. We never really found any common interests, although we did do some things at the same time. But there's a difference between being on the couch and watching the same movie, and being at the same dinner table and sharing things that excite you. What we do seem to share is a general aversion to people. He's a man content with himself and I'm a woman who has very few confidants. My spaces and environments change all the time, so the consistency I seek comes down to someone to whom I do not need to recount the entire backstory. That's what I'll miss the most: the witness we have been to each other's lives. You don't get many people like that in your lifetime, and the steel fortress of Markus's intimacy and trust is, by far, my greatest and most tragic loss. For the months before I left for Dresden, he was sleeping in the basement of our house, while I was upstairs with our boys. I'd come home to a space where the parents were civil to each other but no love was exchanged. We were clear on the fact that this was the moment to pull the trigger on our relationship because it would do the least damage to our boys, since they're so young. By no means does this leave the adults unscathed, but I think it's the price you pay to keep your kids out of harm's way emotionally. In our more clear-headed moments, we hypothesized that it would be best that their earliest memories be of us not together, as opposed to putting them through the volatile process of married parents, fighting parents, unhappy parents, divorced parents.

But we continued to coexist under the same roof for all those months because we were in the limbo of being each other's child care and not having the money to make any kind of move. I'm the first to admit that we lived our financial lives in the moment and probably beyond our means. I was paying little attention, so after Markus left I was shocked to find there was a ton of debt I knew nothing about. I tell myself, *It's just money*. But that doesn't keep me from the recurring dream I've been having of my house being on fire with me and my babies inside and me having to choose between getting us all out or just letting the blaze engulf us together because there isn't enough time to unblock the door and get out. It's literally a nightmare I keep having over and over.

I will always remember the final year of my thirties as being the most disastrous I'd ever experienced to date. I can't remember a time when I was so poor, sad, busy and heartbroken. I honestly don't know how I got here. I have a house, two cars, two boys, two cats and no money. I have every kind of tax bill pending—property tax, federal tax, general tax, personal tax, provincial tax, income tax, pleasure tax, liar tax, cocktail tax. You name it, I owe it. I've taken baby clothes and equipment to a consignment shop and tried to sell my shoes online. It has been a humbling, humiliating and exhausting year. And as I write this, it's not even over. In fact, it will likely get worse!

I know I can't be the only person on earth to look at her children and think, *You're the only good thing I've ever done.* Dear God, let me keep them healthy and out of prison. I can't be the only Christian woman to have cheated on her husband. I can't be the only person to believe that I have no one but myself to blame for where I am. I can't be the only woman who has no idea how money works, where it goes or how I've managed to end up with so little of it. Dear God, do not let me be the only human to have ever overspent, miscalculated and lived in denial. It brings me no small amount of comfort to believe that I can't be the only person to say to herself, *I know I'm no prize on so many levels, but I won't roll over and die, either.* I simply can't because I have things to do. I may feel like I'm alone and I brought all this on myself, but there is a still, small voice inside me that says I'm not and I didn't.

So I never thought I'd get married, and when I did, I sucked at it. So now what? I did get married, and over a decade later, I gave birth to the two perfectest boys in the history of the birthing of males. I am where I am and I've made my choices—some good, some incrrredibly bad. I have to believe that if I move forward, forgiven and undefined by the mistakes of my past, then I'll be able to empower others to do the same. I have to believe I'm not the only person who feels this way and that I'll come out on the other side, wiser and stronger. I don't know when that will be or how much longer I'll be juggling, holding my breath and faking it to make it, but that day is coming.

In the spring of 2009, my husband and I celebrated our tenth anniversary shortly after purchasing our first house in Toronto's Parkdale neighbourhood. Though I was travelling a lot, it was a haven I loved to decorate with the things we'd collected over the years, including the only plant we ever knew how to take care of: the Chinese money tree bought from Ikea. There were big antique letters hung above the patio door that told me where I was: H O M E.

I was enjoying a full schedule of recitals and concerts throughout Europe and Asia. I was also having fun as a host and guest on several European and Canadian TV shows: *Arte Lounge, Toronto Variety, MTV Canada Cribs, The Surreal Gourmet, Bravo Arts & Minds.* The first full-length feature documentary about me, *Spirit in Her Voice,* was released (the second one, *Songs of Freedom,* would be released in February 2015) and I had starred in a handful of music videos featuring classical repertoire like Aaron Copland's "Heart We Will Forget Him," William Bolcom's "Amor" and Jules Massenet's "Rêve infini."

I really enjoy the intangibles, as I like to call them. Anything that doesn't involve me actually having to sing: interviews, appearances, acting, writing. When journalists were looking for snappy sound bites or an upbeat interview, I was a go-to celebrity:

Your favourite colour?

Turquoise.

Your idea of happiness?

The sound of my husband laughing.

The quality you like most in others?

Consistency.

Your favourite drink?

The Caesar.

Your present state of mind?

Equanimous.

On what occasion do you lie?

In the morning.

What is the greatest love of your life?

My Saviour Jesus Christ.

Where would you most like to live?

In the Maritimes.

What is your favourite journey?

This one.

What word or phrase do you overuse?

"Whuddup?"

Which talent would you most like to have?

To speak more languages.

Your favourite aroma?

Black truffle.

The person you'd call in an emergency?

My husband or my parents.

The person you'd call if you wanted to laugh?
My husband.
What do you consider your greatest achievement?
My relationship with my mom.
If you could choose what to come back as, what would it be?
A predatory animal.
Who are your favourite writers?
Alice Munro, Jonathan Coe.
What is your motto?
It's a horrible idea. Let's do it.

Could my life have been any sweeter? I felt like I was swimming with the current. Everything was falling into place.

And then, on June 8, 2009, my aorta exploded.

And then, in the summer of 2009, I failed my marriage . . .

In the fall of 2009, my husband moved out of our Parkdale home and I took off around the world with a guy I thought I loved, but barely knew.

Two thousand nine was not the first time I stepped out on my marriage. I was less than a year into being a wife when I had my first affair. I had gotten married to the love of my life, but I didn't really know what came after that. I had unlocked the floodgates of my sexuality, and it never occurred to me not to take it for a test drive, because for my whole life I'd been on a solitary journey of discipline and reward. I had waited until my wedding night to have sex, and now that I'd given my virginity to the most worthwhile candidate I had ever met, I was free to explore. I know how twisted it sounds, but let me try to explain: I am a soloist in a niche profession; I enjoy a certain level of fame, a broad level of access; and when it comes right down to it, the end of my work day ends in thunderous applause. I believed the rules didn't apply to me. Fidelity in my marriage felt optional because no one was watching and I usually got what I wanted if I worked hard enough for it.

Do you know how much lying, cheating and compromising need to be done to sustain an extramarital affair? It's a lot, and I don't have any excuses because I excelled at it for more than a decade. What I wasn't prepared for was how un-conflicted I would feel about it at the time. I honestly didn't feel any sense of moral accountability. That's not to say I trumpeted my infidelity from the rooftops and told everyone I knew. No. I knew enough to keep it a secret. But I framed my life in such a way that I could always allow my lies to somehow weave into my everyday life, experiences, travel and work. And it's not like I didn't have a moral compass! I was raised in a Christian home, lived my life as a Christian and had waited until I was married to have sex. Some Christians will judge me. They'll say I was never really a Christian at all. I mean, how could I be living my life for Christ and act that way? The non-Christians will claim that I married too early (twenty-one) and that waiting to have sex so late led to an opening of the floodgates, to which the only logical conclusion could be infidelity. I'd argue that it's like a mixture of both. But also neither.

Though no Believer has ever walked up to me and pro-
claimed, "Hey! I have never been faithful to my husband, either,"
again I can't believe I'm the only one. I'm not saying that makes
it okay. I'm just saying that it has taken me my entire adult life
to even voice the words "I cheated on my husband" without the
weight of shame bearing down on my chest and crushing my
heart from the inside out. I can only hope that a brother or a
sister out there will read this and know that with time and trans-
parency, you can move forward, be forgiven and, perhaps the
hardest part, forgive yourself. And encourage others to do the
same. Marriage isn't for all of us. But I took a vow and I broke it.

I always felt like it was someone else engaging in those relationships. Not in a schizophrenic or bipolar way—I would never
trivialize people with mental illness by using it as my excuse. I
will say, however, that I'd appointed for myself a sort of "movable
do" of morality. Movable do is a term in solfège (the do-re-mi
system of identifying music notes) where the tonic—*do*—
moves around the scale, and in response, all the other notes con-
textually organize themselves around this tonic, or this root. As
opposed to the "fixed *do*" system, where, as you can likely guess,
the tonic stays the same, regardless of the musical context or key
signature. I told myself that because I lived in a different context—child prodigy, opera singer, artist, traveller, whatever—
morality could organize itself around me. Whatever I wanted
was relative to myself as *do*. Everything—my faith, my marriage,
my finances—could morph to my needs and not the other way

around. If I was reading this about someone else, I'd be all, *Tsk, tsk, Delusional One. This will only end in total destruction.* And it has. I'm talking to a book.

For all of you out there whose lives are also rooted in and guided by religion—Christian, Jewish, Hindu, Muslim—one of the decisions most influenced by your faith, followed by the influence of your family, is when and with whom you will spend the rest of your earthly life. I can only speak for myself as a young Christian woman from a small town. Despite having never seen anything close to dreams of "marital bliss," I didn't see a reason not to marry young. I still don't. And marrying a Christian had been programmed into my DNA. Plus, I loved him deeply. He was supportive, kind, gentle and fair. He didn't hold me prisoner or yell at me. He didn't insult me or wake me up in the middle of the night to fight with me. I felt no contempt for him. He didn't try my patience and I didn't tolerate him or feel like I had to compromise any part of myself to be with him. He didn't hold me back or pressure me to do things I didn't want to do. He didn't like the taste of alcohol and I didn't drink (at the time). Neither of us wanted to have children (at the time). We chose each other not as some act of rebellion but because we had found our truest match. Essentially, he was my unicorn and we were madly in love. The only thing left for us to do after dating for four years was get married so that we could have sex.

Given my schedule, there was no time for premarital counselling (huge mistake), so I went into my marriage placing one logical foot in front of the other, without really knowing what marriage was supposed to actually be. What I did know was that my relationship wasn't like my parents' and that was good enough for me.

To this day, I'm not entirely sure how I was supposed to feel. The wedding day itself went off without a hitch. A joyous occasion that could not have gone any better. But, as I've said, I don't like crowds or strangers (ironic, I know) and by that point I was used to people assembling in my honour for my job. As a result, my wedding day felt a bit like going to work. But I know God was there and I know He blessed us and our families and friends that day. We were pretty much set for life until I effed it up.

And to those of you not guided by religion, spirituality or any labelled belief system, I would offer that my active interior life, cultivated through early soloistic musical development and success, was very isolating. I have always talked to myself in full sentences. Not just the odd thought here and there. Full-on conversations, with debate and the weighing of options and, inevitably, conclusions that I believe to be quite insightful (she pats herself on the back). These conversations, thankfully, are not held in a vacuum. They are informed and guided by outside sources like my family, mentors, friends and my own history. But I've spent a lot of time inside my head, and any artist out there will know exactly how intimate a space that is. There is barely room for your own desires and goals, let alone anyone else's. And the same self-centred voice that leads me to incredible professional success is the same voice that guides me in my personal choices. Why wouldn't I trust it?

All the evidence presented led me to believe that marriage was the only logical conclusion to a long courtship that had nothing wrong with it. There was no better choice for me. But should I have gotten married? Maybe not. Except, the point is moot. I *did* get married, and it's only recently that I started calling my actions "infidelity," because I had so greatly distanced myself from any of its personal implications.

Beyond that, we are all of us the sums of our histories. No, I didn't attend a cathedral with an abusive priest, and I wasn't a victim of a residential school or a violent sexual assault. But I was molested by my cousin. Honestly, I don't think he knew what he was doing. That doesn't excuse him, but it helps me put into context what happened to me and why I feel how I feel about my body. I was exposed to these tingly sensations at an early age. I didn't know the feelings were sexual until later. And I wasn't afraid when it happened. But I was undeniably coerced and what happened to me was wrong. Period.

So, what do I do with that? It wasn't my fault. I bear no responsibility in what happened to me. But I know I have to do something with the experiences that form who I am. Acknowledge and use them, instead of them enslaving and shaming me. In the subjective context of "self-discovery," my molestation fell right in step with my musical discovery, because there IS a reason for everything. I say that only because I have to believe God can turn around and use anything for His glory. And I do mean anything. He has shown me over and over that I don't have to mourn whatever innocence I lost, because He will never use what I don't have.

Singing is a full-bodied experience and I choose to believe that the early awareness cultivated in me through a depraved act has led to an awareness of my physical self. To go beyond that, I also know how I can be made weak or my judgment can be clouded by sexual desire. And I understand the power I possess to incite that in other people. I recognize that this may not be how I'm supposed to feel or how society tells me I'm supposed to feel about being molested. But after therapy and journaling and counting the abundance of my blessings, it's the conclusion to which I've come.

I'm truly grateful that, as an adult, I love sex. I don't see it as immoral or indecent or tainted by premature exposure. I think it is a beautiful union between two people who have consented to make each other the focus of their pleasure. I'll also qualify that by saying it's not necessarily the act that interests me. It's always such a letdown when some hot guy you've been sussing out and investing in comes at you with monster tongue. Or busy hands. Like, zero game. I'm sorry, but no woman likes it when she can't tell whether she's making out with someone or being frisked. Nah, it's the prospect of the journey of attraction leading to the destination of coupling that interests me. Some would call it "the chase," but it's also a kind of exploration, because if I take the time to truly understand someone, falling in love with him isn't far behind.

I've never been successful at curbing my curiosity. I don't think I've ever really tried. But I've had to work to identify it to keep myself from jumping off a cliff in total despair over my inability to conform.

None of these explanations, clarifications or elaborations are meant to serve as anything remotely resembling an excuse for any of the choices I've made. The only reason I would ever contemplate suicide is to rid my partner of all the pain that I caused him with my constant selfishness and infidelity. I would often think of how I had won the lottery by meeting this guy so young, before "everything," and if he had just ended up somewhere else, on another day, in another year, under different circumstances, or the butterfly had just flapped its wings one more time, he wouldn't have been made to suffer as much as I've made him suffer. Wouldn't it ultimately be the best thing if I just died and spared him any more misery? He could move on, the stoic widower, and, after a respectful period of grieving for his lecherous, cheating whore of a wife, he could remarry and get the relationship he had deserved from the beginning . . .

After much of that therapy I mentioned, plus meditation, yoga, alcohol, weed, self-destruction, self-reconstruction and analysis, I now have a clear idea of how massive a betrayal I repeatedly committed in my marriage. I may not deserve to have my marriage saved, but I certainly won't be destroying myself as some martyr-like self-sacrifice on the altar of morality while I define and deepen my own sense of accountability.

I have to believe that there are souls who will read this and know that whatever their system of belief or the voice in their ear, they, too, are worth saving and celebrating. This can't be the end. I hope someday to be able to fully forgive myself, because I know there is such joy in the redemption of forgiveness. And if I allowed my indiscretions and flaws to hold me back indefinitely, my flame would be extinguished forever. I don't want to live in the shadows, ashamed and afraid, because that's not life. And if being the one who writes down all my inequities—and how I've made the choice to not have them rule me—brings you closer to living your life with pride and conviction, then I may have several more books in me!

Everyone has a type, and over the years I've come to notice a pattern in the type of man I'm attracted to, and, depending on the season of life in which I find myself, the type of man who is attracted to me. I've decided, in the interest of protecting the innocent, to create a composite of all my lovers. (And yes, I hate the term lover. Yick.) Conjuring this composite was an exercise in accountability, as well as a platform to vent. Throughout the journey of this book, there has been an undercurrent of unease for me about how best to broach this touchy subject with some level of insight and humour. I felt ready to ruminate

March 2017. Westminster Abbey. Queen Elizabeth II is in the front row. Prince William's in the second row. Annie Lennox gives me the nod when I come offstage. Colossal mic drop.

Just givin'r! I wouldn't suggest this as a default jaw position. But technique-schmechnique. Sometimes the Spirit just moves you. Both gowns above by Call and Response Clothing (Toronto).

I've still never seen the video of my performance during the opening ceremonies of the Vancouver 2010 Winter Olympics. Why? Because, as breathtaking as it is, this is the image everyone saw. But only I saw what I saw from the perspective I saw it. I don't want to ruin that. Gown by Dsquared2 (Milan). Hair by Maria Bertrand. Jewellery by Myles Mindham.

San Francisco photo shoot with fellow Maritimer Mat Dunlap at the start of my non-classical rebranding.

In rehearsal and performance with the New Brunswick Youth Orchestra. Antonio Delgado is conducting and Aaron Davis is on the piano. Antonio, like Gustavo Dudamel, is another star pupil of El Sistema in Venezuela. In the spring of 2017, in celebration of Canada's 150th anniversary, we toured spirituals from my album *Songs of Freedom* and premiered a new piece commissioned from Oscar-winning film composer Howard Shore.

After the very last class of my Bikram yoga teacher training course. Nine weeks of practising twice a day.

Advanced camel pose. I have no idea who this is or why she would contort her body this way. (Heh. It was 2010 and I was drinking lots of the yoga Kool-Aid.)

There are some photos that you just have to get if you can. Leonard Nimoy didn't even hesitate to give me the Vulcan nerve pinch when I asked him after a performance I gave of Beethoven's *Symphony No. 9*, with the Cleveland Orchestra, in Miami in 2007.

My homeboy, MTT (a.k.a. Michael Tilson Thomas, conductor and composer). He and his husband, Joshua, have an array of curiosities throughout their home, including a gong given to them by the Grateful Dead (to show their gratitude) and some of James Brown's performance jackets. I'm wearing some kind of crown unearthed from their exotic travels.

I'm always looking for new ways to innovate, and I'm constantly searching for people willing to break the mould. I had to include a photo of the string quartet that checks both those boxes: the delian::quartett. This is us after we debuted a mixed program of Mendelssohn and Weill on the final day of the Kissinger Sommer festival in Bad Kissingen, Germany, in July 2017. I'm excited by the space the classical music industry is going to make for us and those like us.

The Banff Centre and Project Trio: I have been a massive fan of both these entities for as long as I can remember. I wrote most of this book at the Banff Centre. Beyond that, Banff afforded me the opportunity to begin a collaboration with the Brooklyn–based maverick ensemble Project Trio AND bring my babies with me! L to R: Sterling Brueggergosman, Eric Stephenson (cello), Shepherd Brueggergosman, Greg Pattillo (flute) and Peter Seymour (bass).

On the 28th of June, 2017, I began my next decade on this earth. My fortieth birthday was a two-day fiesta extravaganza, but it started at the beach in the Annapolis Valley, Nova Scotia. My best friend, Jeff, carved this into the sand for me because he's awesome.

Me and Jeff. Our journey started in kindergarten. He knows where all the bodies are buried.

Sharing the stage with my youngest at my birthday celebration, surrounded by family and friends.

LISA MACINTOSH.

In addition to the five bands that came and played for my birthday, graffiti artist Kim Taggart tagged the initials of everyone who has made my house a home: MB/SB. To complete my fortieth birthday guestbook, my friends and family took turns spray-painting their names onto the foyer wall that greets me every time I come home.

LISA MACINTOSH.

June 28, 2017: The Original Five in my living room on my fortieth birthday. As the years spent themselves, we've had fewer and fewer of these moments. But my family has always been there for me. Always.

The last child I'll ever give birth to: Sterling Markus. He is the namesake of my father and his daddy and every bit his mama. My youngest comes by the habit of putting his index finger in his mouth honestly. I've done it my whole life while I'm thinking, when I'm nervous or just to pass the time.

One of the only times my boys will peacefully sit together is when we read. Here, we're genuinely perplexed as to why an old lady would swallow a dog to catch a cat to catch a bird to catch a spider to catch a fly.

You don't have to be a parent to understand why my whole life has led to these boys. No matter what they become or who they choose to love, may the Holy Spirit keep their hearts and minds fixed on Him.

without griping, because I sensed myself opening up as I teeter on the brink of taking a vow of celibacy; I knew I'd likely never be this objective again.

So I have named my composite *Jacob*.

Jacob is a loner, even though he has friends. He is seemingly social, but it takes time to get beneath the surface, and although he is well-liked and respected, most people do not know him the way I do. He is very opinionated but happy to sit back and allow others to speak. However, he will very rarely acquiesce in an argument. Despite making you feel like he sees your point of view, he will very rarely change his mind, because he truly believes that he is right.

He has a strong character and a well-defined aesthetic. I am a breath of fresh air to him, and the only person to have really challenged him consistently, intelligently and with a sassiness he truly enjoys. Until I came along, his circle of friends believed him to be an infallible, impenetrable force. It makes perfect sense that he is with me because they knew Jacob would eventually find a woman worthy of his calibre. Jacob enjoys a close, if qualified, relationship with his mother. (Yep. I went there.) He is accountable to her in the sense that he is loyal to her and her opinion matters to him, but there is something about her that keeps him from truly trusting that she has his best interests at heart. She also occupies a large stake in his "livelihood," if you will. Whether it's her say over his life choices or her influence on or oversight of his finances, she is referenced and considered. Jacob's father is present in his scope of influence, but, as is the case with most man-boys, Jacob's father does not take up as much space in Jacob's world as his mother. I am like his mother insofar as I am a strong personality who has persevered in forging my way into his life, but Jacob doesn't know that by being with me he's mirroring the relationship of his parents. He is proud to bring me home, happy to show me off. Chances are his parents have been to one of my concerts— or will go eventually.

I am a good listener and allow Jacob to express his truest self, eat what he wants, enjoy his vices, whisper in my ear what he truly thinks in any given situation. I go so far as to facilitate Jacob living out his dreams, no matter how out-of-reach or un-lucrative they prove to be. Travelling together, meeting a mentor, turning a hobby into a career: chances are, I know someone or some way to make it happen, and I am happy to do it because Jacob is very gifted . . . but in a very specific way. He has one or two niche "callings" (as might be his moniker for his aversion to the nine-to-five grind) and he makes money in an unconventional way. I am deeply fascinated by Jacob's chosen profession and seek to find out as much as I possibly can, because to me information is intimacy. My consumption of him and his life forms the substance of our relationship.

The sex is good . . . but Jacob doesn't necessarily need sex, in the traditional sense. That's not to say he isn't a sexual being. Sex doesn't exist as a hunger, more a happy consequence rife with conflicting intangibles I can't quite put my finger on. He isn't entirely free, but I wouldn't describe him as inhibited, either. At times reactionary, at times intuitive. Open to the hint of suggestion, but sensitive like a ripe peach. For me, sex is more of an intimacy barometer to see how into me he is (pun intended). His reactions couldn't be confused with those associated with "simpler" men. Jacob's brain never turns off. My satisfaction is rooted in inviting him to be more present with me than he has ever been with anyone else.

I don't want to be indelicate, so I'll say that Jacob can have a hard time reaching his destination and doing the same for me—though he would never know it . . . Our relationship between the sheets gets progressively better as I delve deeper into his life. There is a crucial connection for Jacob between my acceptance of him—my seeing him as a dominant male—and how ready he is to abandon himself to the moment. That isn't to say he can't get there . . . because (and yes, I'm tooting my own horn here) I don't leave any job half done.

He finds me beguiling, exotic. It is my absolute pleasure to expose him to things, because he has less money, fewer professional prospects, less life experience (which is not to say he's younger, necessarily); he's just not established yet.

Sometimes, I get the impression that Jacob feels like he's owed something—like, maybe, while he was growing up, his mother praised him for, well, nothing. So, as a result, Jacob is expecting that the fates will eventually smile on him and manna will fall from heaven. I mean, he has landed me, hasn't he? While the relationship is working, I am like a shiny, lucky penny. And I will absolutely bestow on Jacob characteristics and talents whether he deserves them or not.

Jacob's memory is miraculous, and though he says he forgives, he holds a grudge. He can be vindictive—though he'd be the last to admit it. At first you consider this a sign of uncompromising strength, but in the end—like most things—it is used against you.

As our relationship spirals deeper, I stop the emotional hemorrhaging by showering him with newness and dinners and personalities to fawn over and learn from. He meets his heroes and his favourite drink is always within reach. His universe and scope of experience expands and Jacob gives me the credit, while secretly growing more and more resentful that his woman is doing everything for him. He feeds a mounting fear that he's getting man-candy side-eye from the very people from whom he wants respect (or a job). When we fight about it later, I'm dismissive and frigidly ask him how any of this is my problem—I mean, maybe he *should* be doing more with his life.

I say none of this during our relationship, but Jacob, insightful man that he is, eventually grows wise to my thinly veiled (albeit well-intentioned) contempt. To spare his ego, I am content to sacrifice my own standing, since it will still be intact after he inevitably leaves me.

In the beginning Jacob is not emasculated. He is simply made to feel like he is being given access to experiences in which he always knew he could thrive. And he does . . . at first. Until he realizes the implications of none of it having been built by or belonging to him. He has no ownership. My life is like a kingdom behind glass, and in response, he either takes on a sense of entitlement or he's overly grateful. But I do not want him to feel indebted to me. A man indebted to a woman is the height of un-sexiness. Jacob will soon come to that conclusion on his own, but for now he is sucked into what I offer as my "life."

At his core Jacob is kind-hearted. An old soul who is perhaps a bit naive. I tell him repeatedly that none of this—the fame, the attention—is real. What we have is real. But, I'm also thinking that I'm not sure if that's entirely true, either. But I want him to believe it. Jacob is not maliciously manipulative, but he likes to have the upper hand (and I don't mind giving it to him when the stakes are immaterial). He sees me as having chosen him, even though I make him feel like he chose me himself. It's a win-win. Until it's not.

Beyond his desire to have his own balls back—to make his own money, to keep his own schedule, to make his own choices, to have his own success—my relationship with Jacob ultimately ends because I'm constantly dangling a life in front of him that I know he will never be able to belong to. (I remain openly married during these relationships, after all.) It is equally plausible that Jacob eventually decides I'm crazy and wants to get as far away from me as possible.

As someone who can invoke a sense of intimacy from the jump, I know that the best part of any relationship with any Jacob is when I repeatedly create scenarios that allow him to believe I could be his. And the best parts of my relationship with him are when I can fantasize about somehow fitting into whatever exotic world Jacob has revealed to me: a niche culture; a language I don't speak (or wish I spoke more fluently); a lifestyle; an exotic profession, philosophy, sport or cuisine. You name it, I consume it and it endears Jacob to me because I wholeheartedly embrace him.

Jacob introduces me to his whole family, his circle of friends, his world. I assimilate myself into everything that is him because I love him and want to be a part of whatever matters to him. The reverse cannot be said. That doesn't make Jacob selfish. Quite the opposite. He gets rejected at the border of the life I've sworn to protect, and eventually he starts to feel that inequity between us. He feels exposed in the gap between all that he has given and all that I have taken. It dawns on him (slowly) that he will never truly have me. He concludes that it will never be enough.

If that's not ruthless enough, Jacob doesn't know that I dug my heels even deeper into my own sovereignty when I had my sons. There is a force field around my offspring that no one can penetrate. At least, that's how I have felt up to this point, and I've met no one who possesses whatever it would take to change that. Including their father. Don't get me wrong. He is an amazing father. But my boys grew in my stomach, and although the father-son relationship is life defining, it's not the same as the bond between mother and son. My boys came from my soul and are my greatest accomplishment. My sons and I are not a quid pro quo. I'm not going to go introducing them to some random Jacob, no matter how much access he's given me to his life.

The tender morsels of myself that I do offer him would never, ever fully satisfy or sustain him, or our relationship. They are also possibly not what he was looking for in the long term. Exciting and novel, yes. But when I'm reading the receipts, I clearly needed to be someone else, somewhere else, doing something else, with less going on and more time or commitment or understanding or whatever. Jacob realizes that I am in truth very selfish and uncompromising. Maybe that's what first attracted him to me, but now? It's really stickin' in his craw. I like to think I became an exceptional part of his process of elimination.

The heartache I experience when he (inevitably) leaves me is real, prolonged and deep. Despite all the dissecting, I do know that I loved Jacob with my whole heart. I went to great lengths to bring him joy, and my investment was real. It was impossible to reconcile this great loss with the love and commitment I felt for my husband, whom I also loved with my whole heart. They simply did not exist in the same space. In my mind, they were compartmentalized, separate and unconnected.

As the veil lifted for my dear Jacob, and he realized how narrow his access to me actually was, his disillusionment would send him into fits of mystified not-quite-anger and then, eventually, radio silence. I could always see the end coming, even though I fought hard and did my best to suck out every juicy tidbit and stave off the inevitable. At the outset with a Jacob, I seemed so generous, but in actual truth I was a chemist throwing him in a petri dish to see how he'd react under different forms of duress and newness. I pushed and prodded and pressured and pleaded until he broke.

I am not friends with the early Jacobs, the ones to whom I was truly open and innocent. We don't check in or hang out. After you've seen someone's Oh God! face, it's hard to un-see it in polite company. I don't know how I didn't connect the dots at the time, but I was simultaneously engaged in the traditional process of elimination—also known as dating—while also being someone's wife. I killed two birds with one stone, and a little bit of me died at the hands of my deception and infidelity, as well. Now, through a process of trial, error and elimination, I am happily independent. The only ex I'm interested in being friends with—one of two men I've ever truly loved—is the one I gave myself to first. The one who gave me the two beautiful boys who put my world on its axis.

P art of truly being inside someone is also knowing when you've hit the unyielding wall. I knew my husband had reached his breaking point with me because he couldn't look me in the eye. It's like he had moved on and I was an afterthought that he had folded up and neatly tucked in the glove compartment in order to get back to driving his own life. He gave me the worst case of freezer burn in the history of the Arctic. He looks at me now like he knows exactly what I'm incapable of, how I've betrayed him, and like he has to get me out of the way so he can clear his head and make room for his next family. I feel like he won't listen to a word I say because he assumes it's a lie. And it's true, I've lied to him more than enough. Yet I can absorb all that because he is completely devoted to our boys. I can tell he has more he wants to do with his life and he is resolved to me not being involved. This is the wall I walked into every time I came home from a gig during the months we were living together but apart. It's an agony I do not wish on my worst enemy but one that I earned. I do my best to describe it, because I again refuse to believe that I'm the only person to have ever gone through this. And as long as he shoots that venom at me and not at my boys, I will pay my penance, swallow my medicine and take my lashes.

Before I had children, if I loved someone, I would give the person access to all the material things that, ultimately, make people comfortable but not happy—the house, the money, the dinners, the hype. I like those things, but I'm not attached to them, because they're an illusion. The real motivation behind my work is the process to which no one is privy and for which I get no glory (save for knowing I've done my due diligence): highlighting a new score, coming to terms with how much music I have to learn and how much work it's going to be not only to learn it but to sing it until it feels comfortable, second nature. I get excited just thinking about it! Because then, in the same order every time, there's the translation or deciding what the text is about. I decide on the big emotions in the music: Is this happy or sad and why? If there's time, I'll do some light harmonic analysis to see where I fit in the compositional scheme of things. I do an inner happy dance as I write in my international phonetic alphabet (IPA) symbols over every syllable; fill in every accidental; colour-code the time signatures, the dynamic markings, the key changes, the composer's notes; and then (finally) I start to learn the actual music by playing my melody over and over and over with the bass line and the instrumental cue that precedes it so that I can understand my harmonic context and get my pitch from them.

Let's say I start with twenty-four bars of singing. I will isolate the section and sing it on every vowel down the octave, lip-trill (or motorboat) it in the actual register, re-sing it on every vowel (still no words), and then I'll speak the words to the twenty-four bars in rhythm—with the metronome that has been beating this whole time anyway. I'll say the section over and over and over until my mouth has conditioned itself around the words and I know what consonant is coming, and plant the muscle memory of the shape of the vowel that comes after it. I do this with every intersection where vowel meets consonant meets vowel again. I train my jaw to relax and hinge freely instead of tightening itself to the consonant I'm about to shape, I flatten my tongue (in vain, because I have a tongue that sometimes moves in rhythm to my vibrato when I sing in my higher register), and then I proceed to sing the line, in tempo, but only on vowels so that I can make sure I'm not wasting any air when I finally do add the consonants. I do not add said consonants until the vowels are clear and pure and distinguishable from one another—not some gobbled, mushy mess of imprecision. Pure. I might go back and repeat this process again to make sure I can hear the melody I've just learned in my head before I have to create pitch. That's the only way I can be sure it's totally internalized. Only then will I add the consonants, bar by methodical bar, making sure my *t*'s and *d*'s are released properly, that my *l*'s are placed forward enough that I don't swallow the vowel (which would disturb the flow of the legato by changing the vowel's place of resonance) and my upper lip springs upward whenever there is a *p*, *b* or *m*, for the same reason. It won't be perfect. I won't be happy with it. But it will be time to move on to the next twenty-four bars.

To any young, inexperienced, lazy or unemployed singers out there, I would humbly advise that you make your peace with (good) singing and musicianship being this much work. I'm sure there are singers better than me who do much more!

Who are more thorough, more disciplined; who speak more languages; whose lives are wholly dedicated to their voice, its health and what it sounds like. For me, the balance and variety of my life are what make me a good artist. But, my dear young singer, you need to learn *who* you are and *how* you work. But it is a lot of work. If you enjoy the solitude and the repetition of the uncompromised, then this job is for you. But it doesn't just happen. All those singers we look up to—the Jessyes and Kiris and Pavarottis and Montserrats and Renées and Cecilias and Placidos and Leontynes—they didn't just stumble into excellence. It wasn't luck that made them fabulous. It was a willingness to put in the extra hours, beat the pavement, and a refusal to believe they were put on this earth to do anything else.

Truthfully? You are onstage maaaybe 5 percent of your whole career. The rest of the time is spent, at least in my case, creating a life that makes it easier and more fulfilling to do that. I understand, from the outside looking in (at least before you picked up this book—ha!), that my life appears very generous and ample and varied. And I enjoy sharing this luxury with people I love, especially with someone seeing it for the first time. But my real reward is in executing the lessons that I learned from Mary and Edith, as well as the coaches who made me better than I was. My real reward is troubleshooting my vocal technique and rendering things easier or more efficient. The closer I get to any subject, the less willing I am to see what would've been clearer had I kept my distance. And when your friends see things that you can't, don't blame your friends. Take what they say into consideration because they love you. But if you're bullheaded like me, you'll need to come to your own conclusions, in your own time.

I n the fall of 2009, when I arrived back in Toronto from a trip to Korea, they were standing in the arrivals terminal at the airport in a trio, waiting to save me from myself: my husband (who had moved out of our house two months before during our first separation), my father and my brother. My husband had staged an intervention. While his concern was undoubtedly well-meaning, I could never respond positively to that kind of pressure. I'm not sure if I've fully forgiven that group that gathered, but even now I'm not sure what else they could have done that would have gotten my attention. I'd had my blinders on for quite some time and had convinced myself I needed to stay focused in order to keep working. The reality was that I didn't want to deal with any of the trouble—financial, health, marital—I'd gotten myself into and Jacob was the most accessible escape. But I wasn't about to tell them that.

I went with the Interventionists to the Toronto home that, according to a separation agreement, I now owned, along with the mortgage and all our debt. The best neighbour in the world, who'd been staying in my house, was waiting in the living room. He was accompanied by a collection of my closest friends. I don't want to name names because who was there wasn't important. There were people I trusted, and they were there to right a ship they were convinced was on course to run aground.

Each person spoke to me in turn and I listened to everyone, but I heard nothing. When I wasn't dumbfounded by the shock of it all, I was seething mad and concentrating on not giving them the satisfaction of seeing me cry. Their words were drowned out by the rage throbbing in my head. I think I could've sung the actual pitch that rang in my ears I was so angry. I could taste blood in my mouth, and at times I was so overwhelmed by the intrusion that I was on the verge of blacking out. I kept silent. It was me against them, and although I could understand what they'd hoped to accomplish, I was not going to give them anything. Not. One. Millimetre. It was all so humiliating. I like to think it would eventually dawn on some of them that there was no way this was going to work on me, but by then it was too late. I'd already shut down. First I was publicly mortified at the airport, and now I was being privately shamed by the only people I had trusted. I felt ganged up on and betrayed, because they had clearly been talking about me and devising a plan behind my back. How little did my family and friends know me? Why would they approach me by committee? I felt completely alone.

Mary was there on the phone. As always, she was the best. Strong and upbeat, but slightly bewildered, she said, "I'm not really sure what I'm doing here, but what I do know is that these people clearly love you." How horrifying! I could hear in her voice that this all felt a bit too personal for her to be involved in but that she cared enough for me to be part of something she had likely been told would help.

No one knew what was going on with me, apparently. I was unreachable. I wasn't present. I was running from my fear about my mortality and I had disappeared into my gallivanting, disappeared into my work schedule, disappeared into my guilt and, according to them, I was nowhere to be found. And they were worried where it would all end if they didn't voice their concerns.

Of course they were right! I was completely lost, I had no idea what I wanted, I didn't know where my priorities had gone and nothing seemed to have any meaning. I felt dead inside and was jumping from high to high—professional and recreational—in the hunger to feel something. One thing with all the Jacobs is that they tended to insist they were *always* right. Which made me? You guessed it. Always wrong. But still I was willing to bear it because I thought it was all I deserved, considering how badly I'd treated my husband and how I'd blown up the only relationship in which I truly flourished as a Christian, a woman and a partner. I believed I deserved all the hardship that could rain down on me, because I was a cheater and a liar and I didn't deserve to be loved properly, so why not be with some guy? Why not allow myself to go into crippling debt? I didn't deserve to have anything anyway. And I certainly didn't deserve to be happy.

After my husband moved out (the first time) and I had confessed my infidelities to my family, my brother was the first to reach out. The eldest, my brother, who is quite possibly the wisest human I know, told me that no matter how much I felt I had screwed up, I was not to live my life motivated by guilt. I had a family who loved me (all of me!) and I was not to keep punishing myself over and over for the wrongs for which God—and this family—could forgive me. He repeated that accepting forgiveness was just as important as asking for it. He told me that the process of forgiving yourself was ongoing and would require several attempts, and that if we were not careful, we could fall prey to satan wanting to keep us down and sink us lower than we ever thought possible because *satan prowls about like a roaring lion looking for someone to devour* (1 Peter 5:8).

Seven years later I'm in the same position for the same reasons, but this time I will not allow my guilt to shame me into abusing myself like it did during that difficult period. I can see the parallels between my life then and my reality now, and I have chosen to strive for a different outcome. I already feel blessed this time around, because instead of a dissected aorta, I have two beautiful sons; instead of trying to keep a house in Toronto, I am trying to keep a house in Nova Scotia, close to my parents. I am older and the stakes are higher. Though my marriage would reconcile in 2010, it will likely end permanently in 2017. And the end of my marriage will force me to become what I should already be by now: financially responsible and independent. It might take me a decade, but I'll get there. I have already said that God won't use what you don't have, so I refuse to obsess about what I've lost. And now that I have tiny eyes watching my every bob and weave, I need them be confident Mama is a fighter they can bet on.

Looking back on that fall of 2009, in the living room of the house I could no longer afford, I now recognize the downward spiral from which those half-dozen people were attempting to save me. At that time, I took a deep breath, kept my eyes bone-dry and said, "Thank you all for taking the time to voice your concerns to me. I've just come from a very long trip and I need to rest." I went upstairs and didn't come back down. In retrospect, I do forgive the husband who left me for caring enough about me to set this in motion, but I still regard it as horribly invasive. Why didn't he intervene when he saw the first signs of my self-destruction? Why did he assemble an arsenal of embarrassment that would only serve to humiliate me? I know I'm not the easiest person to confront, but the situation had become so polarized that an intervention could only make it worse.

I know there won't be any interventions this time around. He has flicked the switch to off, and the only way he can get out the door is if he leaves and justifiably doesn't look back.

~~~

The moments where reality snuck in and burst my fantasy bubble were the moments my Jacobs revealed what they were truly made of. It could be an airport confrontation, an unwelcome phone call from my spouse, or a stranger asking how my husband was. My commitments outside of the world I'd created for him in our relationship chafed against the reality of what I was willing to offer, and ultimately he was forced to recognize that my loyalties—unlike my body—did not lie with him.

Such a crossroads came when I had to tell Jacob I was pregnant. With my husband's baby. After Markus and I had reconciled in 2010 and had our first son in 2012, we were trying for our second because I wasn't about to raise a serial killer by having an only child. Jacob already knew I was committed to having another baby by the same man, but I lied to him and told him I'd been artificially inseminated, so that he wouldn't think I was still with my BabyDaddy. I also wanted to give him plausible deniability with his own tight-knit, conservative family. My husband and I had gotten pregnant faster than either one of us had expected, and part of me was so excited to share this with Jacob, because, after all, we were modern adults and we understood each other. We'd met each other at a time in our lives where these things were happening. Sure, I thought, our "life rhythm" might be slightly off, but we were in sync where it counted. Plus, he was in no position to be fathering a child, and I wanted the same father for both my boys. I was nowhere near famous enough to have multiple BabyDaddies. I grew up in a small town (and currently live in one) and I know that having multiple babies with multiple men out of wedlock is something only real celebrities (with real money for nannies and several houses) can do and get away with.

If I'm being completely honest, I also wanted to see whether Jacob would stay the course with me. I was having another man's baby, but I still wanted Jacob to be happy for me. It was crazy, not to mention the height of selfishness. Of course he wasn't happy for me! Not at first, anyway. I was not looking to hurt him, but I was pragmatic: I did not have a lot of baby-making years left and I wasn't willing to risk my son not having a blood ally in life. I was not willing to put Jacob's needs, expectations or feelings ahead of the designs I had created for my actual family. I knew I was throwing a carpet bomb on our love, but I did it anyway. I was open to being pleasantly surprised, should he decide he loved me enough to stay.

Jacob did stay. He had an incredibly open, empathetic and selfless heart to see me through my second pregnancy. He would sing and talk to the baby growing in my belly and kept my secret before I was sure I wanted to go public with the news. That made him the second great love of my life. When my youngest was born, Jacob sent me a note wishing me all good things and gave me space to enjoy this blessed event with my family.

But that's just it. I didn't enjoy it. I'd shot myself in the foot. By deceiving and undermining and, frankly, shattering the boundaries of decency, I almost ruined arguably the best thing to ever happen to me since the birth of my first child. Granted, in response to the losses we'd already suffered, I was equally gun-shy about telling anyone about my third pregnancy, but what was supposed to be a triumphant pregnancy for the woman the doctors said shouldn't have children because of her enlarged aorta got downplayed because I didn't feel I could truly be happy or demonstrative about being pregnant, lest I risk hurting Jacob's feelings even more than I already had.

Sure, he came around. But his initial reaction to the news involved yelling, screaming, slamming doors, and eventually total silence. He tied himself up in knots trying to wrap his head around what I was putting him through. When he finally did make his peace with it, the damage was already done. I know how ridiculous it might sound now, but I didn't want to do anything to jeopardize "the peace," so I downplayed my joy and accepted my penance. Meanwhile, with my husband our relationship was just there. Sort of content, sort of secure, sort of happy. It's not actually fair to compare the two, because Markus and I were the pregnant parents of a beautiful only child. I loved our life and what we had built.

I recount this as an illustration of how, even when God chooses to bless me, even the most delicious of happenings can turn to dust in my mouth if I'm living a life of deceit and compromise. I knew, even as the months of my pregnancy progressed, that I needed to turn this prognosis around, because I feared it would affect my unborn son. That somehow Mama would send him these in-vitro signals that he was not wanted or that his arrival was anything short of miraculous. I agonized between my external pressure to please and my interior passion to nurture. I would wake up in the middle of the night and sob and sob and beg God to please let my baby be born healthy— mentally and physically—despite my inability to get it together. I desperately prayed that by the time my Sterling Markus came into the world, his pride of place would come from the God of all things, because Mama did not have the strength of character to be unreservedly happy about her pregnancy. I wept ceaselessly and begged God to make sure my youngest knew he was wanted.

I wish I could go back and love every single minute of Sterling's pregnancy. It's truly a testament to God's grace that He has entered into that space I couldn't fill, because in the beginning every cuddle I gave that boy was tinged by the guilt I harboured about not keeping his time in my womb devoid of personal turmoil. God's unmerited favour has made that almost a distant memory now, as the waves of love I have for both my boys wondrously continue to grow in intensity. I hate that I felt one ounce of conflict about Sterling growing in my belly; that I let some man come between me and my miracle. I unreasonably resent Jacob for not immediately understanding how much of a miracle this pregnancy was for me and that the tension of his reaction tainted everything that came after.

Please keep in mind that I'm saying all this for the first time:

the composite Jacob, the pattern, the implications on the life I wish I could have made work. You might be asking yourself where Markus was through all this. She might not be "considering" him, but he hasn't disappeared, has he? All of this was locked inside and gangrenous. I got to where I needed to be, I sang my concerts, I chose to live in blissful ignorance about the state of my finances and had affairs. The infidelity I brought into my marriage, combined with how much I was away working, rotted everything from the inside out. And before that happened, it felt like I had two hearts but one life. I suffered under the illusion that my life with Markus was unrelated. Invisible. As in, visible only to me. I liked what Markus reflected to me when it was just us. That is to say, it was a sacred space. I was grateful that he understood and respected my job (you'll remember he had been my manager), but after we separated the first time, he left the family business and pursued other interests and income streams, which further disconnected us.

Markus and I have always been private, and that goes double for our children. My marriage, as I see it, slowly died over time, but my respect and admiration for Markus is as bright and shiny as the day we met. I would even say we were happy. For a while after our post-separation reconciliation I was even satisfied and fulfilled. We were new parents who had been bonded by the grief of losing our twins, rejuvenated by the arrival of Shepherd and excited to expand our family. Once Markus had successfully completed his paramedic studies and we travelled together as a family for my work, my confidence as a mom grew. Consequently, the part of me that was hungry for new experiences resurfaced and I went back to my old habits.

The last and final time Markus confronted me, I wasn't going to insult him by denying it the way I had done in the past. This is how a strobe light got pointed at my relationship with Jacob. I was doing the very thing my brother had cautioned me against. I was living my life motivated by guilt. Nevertheless, it took me several attempts to leave Jacob. Because I don't give up.

The first time I left I convinced myself it was the right thing to do for my self-worth and mental health. What was wrong with me that I couldn't just be happy and satisfied in my marriage and with my two beautiful boys? If I could just get my head right and keep my blinders on, this life could really work for me.

My first gig after my second baby was in São Paulo, Brazil, three weeks after Sterling was born. I was the soprano soloist in Tippett's *A Child of Our Time*, with Mark Wigglesworth conducting. For Sterling's arrival the month prior, Markus and I had invited my saintly Swiss parents-in-law to Nova Scotia to ease the transition to Big Brother for my eldest while I got on a consistent nursing and pumping schedule, got my voice back in shape and Markus ran around getting Sterling's travel documents for Brazil in order. At one point Markus drove twelve hours to the Brazilian consulate in Montreal to apply in person for Sterling's visa to be sure it got processed in time. (Why a five-minute-old baby would need a visa is beyond me, but he did!)

Meanwhile, I was in Halifax trying to get Sterling's passport processed in time. I still can't believe it all worked out.

I thrived after Sterling's birth. His older brother had the undivided attention of his paternal grandparents; I was travelling with my family and singing like I was in my twenties. I told myself I was keeping Jacob on ice, but the fact is, he hadn't written to me for weeks and in my mind it was over.

I wanted more. I also believed in my heart that I deserved more. It's not about money or position or prestige. It's about dependability, reciprocity, discipline and loyalty. Plus, by being with Jacob, I was not living the way God wanted me to live but instead was deceitful, secretive, prideful, guilty. *No wonder I'm so unhappy*, I told myself. *It's so cold and lonely when I create such distance between me and the Divine.*

One thing I like to do is write emails and not send them. I get to say whatever I want to say and exorcise myself of all the conflict that is raging on the inside. *Better out than in!* as my mother would say. I've written countless unsent emails over the years to all the Jacobs. They're unsent because once I've written them I feel better and don't see any reasonable justification for sending them. Plus, I never have to be vulnerable—glued to my phone, desperate for a response. That doesn't mean I obsess any less, mind you. The text message time stamp is the stalker's worst enemy. (*The fact that I can see that you were just online not writing to me is frankly ALL the abuse I can take.*)

When it came time to end things with the Jacobs, I told

them in unsent emails that they were nothing but fuel for cheesy poems and heartsick love songs and that I had to get out or I wouldn't have a leg to stand on when it came time to teach my sons how to treat their partners and build lives independent of me that they could be proud of. I told them that their so-called sacrifices were purely self-serving because in the end I set things up so that they didn't have to actually risk anything. Meanwhile, all that I am has been called into question as I repeatedly second-guess myself trying to figure out how much I'm entitled to and whether I should be more understanding.

I always left the recipient line empty, lest the email be sent by mistake. I knew who I was writing to, and I knew any response I'd get wouldn't satisfy, or it would be filled with excuses that would just make me feel worse or leave me with more questions. I knew that the only reason I wanted to even send the email was to elicit a response, and I didn't want to *want* a response. By not sending anything, I never gave him the satisfaction of seeing me truly laid bare. It seemed to me that I maintained some semblance of dignity by articulating how I felt without needing his reaction to it. (Instead, I saved it for a book. Ha!)

Still, I lost several years of my life and a few chunks of my heart contorting myself into knots for the Jacobs. But as I've noted before, T. D. Jakes teaches that there is no way to become wise without doing a TON of stupid stuff. And God, in His infinite wisdom, turned a crime into a blessing when my phone got stolen this past summer, along with all the photos and videos

I had of him. I'd already saved all the photos of my babies into the Cloud, so I didn't lose anything of true value . . .

If I could go back (which I can't), the first thing I would tell my younger self is that I wasn't fat. At all. But I would also warn her that she would have to work really hard to be solely attracted to one man for her entire life. Nobody told me you had to work to stay completely devoted, mentally and physically, to the same person. I thought it just happened. Nobody could have convinced a twenty-one-year-old me that I wouldn't love my husband anymore or that I would live long enough to suffer the anguish of him not loving me anymore. I realize how naive it sounds for a thirty-nine-year-old to be saying this, but in my marriage I was still very young because we never really grew out of the roles we'd established for each other in our teens. He was good at math; I was bad at finances. I was a master intuitive cook and decorator; he tossed unseasoned chicken into a frying pan and threw it over a salad, while also thinking that an inflatable Darth Maul chair was a viable piece of furniture for a formal living room. He paid all our bills; I made most of our money. I cooked all our meals; he sorted and took out the garbage. He was a person born to be married; it never occurred to me to be faithful.

Nobody tells you when your marriage is over, but you're still living under the same roof, that the absence of love is just as painful as waterboarding. That the silent killer of any hope of reconciliation is contempt, and that coming home to what once felt like the perfect haven now feels like a punch in the stomach when your partner looks at you with dead eyes. And you convince yourself that he must have a point when he questions your parenting, your priorities, your ability to make it on your own, because you're the one who cheated, so all the instincts you trusted before must be fruit from the poisonous tree, including the instinct to love and provide for your children when he leaves you. You don't even think you have the right to be angry or question him, because he just seems so sure and because he's your husband! You never thought he could be wrong about anything. And he is such a good dad that you're willing to swallow the misery of feeling so painfully misunderstood. Oh, and you're the one who cheated. Just in case you forgot. But the worst of it is, he says he has forgiven you. He's just done with you.

So what I want now is to feel like I can get it all under control. The finances, the shame, the regret, the remorse, the sadness. What I want *now* is to trust God to bring me through the fire and know that what doesn't kill me makes me mad, and what makes me mad keeps me moving, and if I'm moving, I'm going to do so with purpose and effectiveness, because, oh by the way, I still have to get my babies to kindergarten on time. And they're watching. They see everything. But they don't see Mama, the skank who cheated on Daddy. They see Mama who helps them into their PJs, says their prayers and sings with them, makes everything better when things break, blows on their food even when it's good and cold, gives them cuddles when they go to bed and gives them kisses and tickles when they wake up.

I write this memoir knowing that my sons will inevitably read it and gain a deeper understanding of who their mother is or was. ALL moms have some idea (vague or precise) of how they want their children to perceive or remember them. But I know that I have no control over that. I can only control how much I love them and how hard I fight for them. With my dying breath, I will savour their names in my mouth. I know I am not unique in this. I am a mother.

When I say that I believe you can have it "all," I mean that planting the seeds and nurturing the growth of things that will bear fruit in the long term is essential to creating a life of substance—which is "all" I need. It might not sound sexy to write in my rhythms or wash the dishes or go to bed early or say no to that invitation to dinner, but those kinds of sacrifices keep me focused on the good stuff. I would argue that counting the poops and pees, and Febreze-ing the gowns IS the good stuff, because it monitors the health of my baby and ensures my colleagues will want to stand next to me—seeds planted that nurture the growth of excellence and efficiency. There are steps that can't be skipped; not if you expect to see maturity in your investment or you plan to proudly stand shoulder to shoulder with giants.

Ideally, your professional and personal desires should align and support each other. I'm at my most content when my personal desires bleed into the professional, meaning my innermost source of purpose is gainfully employed by what I choose to do for money. This is what would happen in a perfect world, the caveat being that all bets are off when it comes to parenthood because those little dependants require you to make the ultimate sacrifice: to not put your own needs first. In fact, the law isn't even on your side! Don't feed them? Jail. Don't clothe them? Jail. Leave them alone? Jail. You're pretty much legally obligated to put their needs before your own. Childhood is the height of leisure. (I'm speaking strictly from a southeastern Canadian perspective.)

We in the Western world have the luxury of viewing our children as a choice. Some of us women view having children as a personal goal, forgetting that motherhood is forced on girls less than a third my age. When I drag my sleep-deprived bones out of bed after my child wakes me up at 5:00 a.m. wanting milk, I forget about the parent who reaches for milk and finds none there and no means to replace it. When I'm watching the clock wondering how I'm ever going to plan the hours between the end of nap time and strapping them in at suppertime, I forget about the mother who has a plan to throw her body over those of her children when the bullets inevitably come. And when I'm impatient with their questions, screeching the car to the side of the road because they won't settle, or wondering how many hugs it's gonna take to get me out of the daycare and back in the (empty) car? I have to think of the single woman raising her granddaughter, the father bailing his son out of prison and the parents desperate for the phone to ring.

Can you indulge my gooey parent long enough for me to say my babies are so beautiful? At the time I write this, Shepherd Peter is four and Sterling Markus is almost two. Seeing one picture of them while I'm away (or even when they're sleeping in the next room!) can reduce me to tears of joy, longing, guilt, tenderness and fear. I think of what makes them smile, how they are untainted by pressure or weariness. My heart aches to realize the crushing blows yet to come their way. Having babies could turn me into a glass-half-empty person because it almost feels like their lives can only go downhill from this clueless state of bliss and innocence.

I had my children during incredibly optimistic periods of my life. My spiritual life was what could be called "stable," my marriage still had love in it, my financial outlook was much rosier and I was disenchanted enough with my singing career to believe I'd be happy to change my focus to motherhood. I feel that bringing children into the world is a kind of investment in what you believe could be good about life and the future. But the yang to that yin is the crippling fear that anything will harm them. The inevitability that some idiot will infringe on their childish state of elation and they'll come home with questions you won't be able to answer. Tears roll down my face when I speculate on my reaction to things that haven't even happened. The good parts of my childhood were good, but bad parts of my childhood were baaad. When people say that struggle and strife breed character, those same people should be asked if they'd subject their children to the same struggles that made them who they are today without the guarantee that the outcome would be the same. Because my boys, Shepherd and Sterling, are going to be who God intends them to be. I will have no say in the matter, except to keep them from lighting each other on fire or going to prison.

No one tells you how conflicted you will feel about being a parent. Yes, it's hard, and yes, it's rewarding, yada yada, cliché, cliché. All that stuff is true. But the GUILT. The crushing guilt that comes with even querying: If you had it to do all over again, would you choose to become a parent all over again? Even allowing the question to enter your mind is grounds for crucifixion in our society. The fact is, I can't go back. So the question is moot. But do I have real doubts about my effectiveness as a parent? Or even my calling to parenthood? You better believe I do! It's hard to be motivated by love when you just need to get to the bloody bathroom before he pees himself, because you don't have an extra set of pants. It's hard to get down on the carpet and play Lego when you know that piece of music isn't going to learn itself. And staying calm when he just keeps calling "Mama" over and over and over and over and over from the back seat and you're on the phone with yet another person who needs something really important from you right this very minute. How do children not know everything isn't about them? I mean, there are other people in the room and they are talking to people other than you. What makes kids think they can just barrel in with a request or a completely unrelated topic with the unshakable belief that the entire environment revolves around them? It makes me want to tear my hair out. And then I watch them try to eat spaghetti and forget what I was complaining about.

Because you also know that children are an investment, so if you don't put anything in, you won't get anything out. And it's useless to complain, because you are their world. For my children, the only thing that stands between them and the big world (and the scary sound the coffee grinder makes) is Mama. There will never be another point in their lives where I fulfill their needs so wholly and completely. Markus is as committed as a daddy can be to his sons . . . but he's not Mama.

Granted, you need money to raise them, and beyond money, you need a contentment with yourself that can only be cultivated by living your best life. And then they become an inextricable part of that Best Life. Heck, sometimes they are quite literally the best part of your life. I never thought I'd be that much of a cliché, but with the inferno blazing in most areas of my life right now, seeing my children is the best part of my day. My son sometimes asks to hold my hand. I never say no. Sometimes I need to hold his hand, too. It's a love language between us, and in the precious evenings when I get to put him to bed and he doesn't want cuddle time to end, I tell him to close his eyes and focus on the feel of Mama's hand in his. I tell him to commit how it feels to memory—the grip, its tightness, the warmth—and know that even when our hands aren't physically linked, we can still remember how it feels. And even as my heart is bruising from the guilt of desperately wanting to be left alone to drink the glass of red wine on the counter downstairs, he gives over to the assurance of things unseen and lets go of Mama's hand with his eyes still closed.

My Shepherd is already teaching me the consequences of time well spent. Both he and Sterling can read me like a book. They're not children. They're tiny Buddhas. And they're always watching and they forgive me so easily when I invariably screw up. I tell them that giving and getting forgiveness is equally important, because if you can't give forgiveness, you can't get it, either.

I've heard it said so many times that having children can make you a better person. I don't know if I agree with that, but I do know that being observed by eyes that are seeing things for the very first time has a way of making you examine yourself and your actions. The first time Shepherd came home with a note saying he'd used a bad word at kindergarten, I told him that coming home with bad words was the same as bringing the flu into our house. I said that Mama understood that he's intelligent enough to understand the power that words have; otherwise he wouldn't be acting like someone who knew he was about to be punished. I told my beautiful boy—who is clearly sorry—that using bad words is the same as kicking or spitting on someone, because our words have the power to do much more damage than our fists or feet. God should be in everything we say or do because He made us to love Him and others.

I don't speak to my four-year-old like he hasn't got a brain. He may still believe that vegetables can talk or think his birthday can be every day, but he also understands that there is more power in him than he has yet to acknowledge, and it's my job to help him self-actualize so that he can contribute to this world in his unique, positive way.

Mama's still working on, well, everything (aren't we all?), but it doesn't make trying to teach self-worth (to my sons—and to myself, while I'm at it) any less of a worthwhile pursuit.

When you think of the things that are holding you back, sometimes the answers aren't what you'd expect. It's not that my children hold me back necessarily, but having them sleep in the same room with me while I'm working definitely impedes my ability to get a good night's rest while they sleep, well, like babies. I don't begrudge them their time with Mama. I just need to know that if I can't afford a four-bedroom apartment in downtown Madrid for the six weeks of my contract at the opera house, I'm going to have to wear earplugs and be prepared to be slapped in the face by my four-year-old a few times during the night.

By the same token, it's a good thing I'm an opera singer, because if I wasn't, I'm quite sure I'd be a stressed-out chain-smoker. What's holding me back from my career in smoking is my career as an opera singer. I know it is the height of stupidity to smoke cigarettes given what we know about the death sentence that comes with inhaling carcinogenic toxins into your lungs, but it just looks sooo cool. And I have a very strong oral fixation, so smoking would really work for me if I wasn't an opera singer. The one thing I won't do is sacrifice my livelihood for the sake of looking cool. Plus, cancer sucks.

I signed up for a life of humidifiers, lozenges and herbal tea. I know the benefits of vocal rest outweigh the stress of singing with a voice that is less than fresh. I'm not saying I can't tie one on with the best of 'em. It's just that the sacrifices I make for my profession are worth it, because I want to be good at my job since it also happens to be my calling.

Can I say the same about motherhood? There is such a steep learning curve to becoming Mama. I know there are instinctual things that do come naturally—I could recognize my babies' cries, could sense what they needed, understand their first seemingly unintelligible words. I know that for them, there is no substitute for Mama. But I'm not a roly-poly mom. I'm not the least bit interested in building blocks or toys. I see those as distractions that allow me some freedom or a few moments of peace. I'm not going to spend an entire afternoon doing fingerpainting. What my boys understand is that if they need something cooked, or a book read, or a piece of art praised, I'm the mother for that. I am their biggest fan. If they've got a scratch and need a bandage—or if they just like bandages and want to wear one—then I'll hand out the superhero bandage. Why should you have to get hurt to wear a bloody bandage? But the playground? I'll keep you from cracking your head open, but we're not playing tag.

With my twenty-three-month old, he's just happy to have me in the same spot so that he knows where I am and can bring me things or sit on me. We have full-on conversations despite all his sentences not being filled with actual words. I believe I know what he's saying. And what does it matter if I'm right or not? He's my son. I had to make my peace with the strengths and weaknesses I bring to their upbringing, resisting the pressure of allowing the type of mom I am to be influenced by factors not privy to the intimacy that exists between my sons and me. So, that would mean everyone. I'm blessed to have a job where, for the most part—if I'm not learning or singing music—my time belongs to my sons when I'm at home. That's a real gift. But it was an adjustment. All you parents, take a minute to remember what your life was like before you had kids and then fill in the blank: "Before I had kids, I could . . . "

Parents who say they can't remember what their life was like before they had kids are lying. Or they want to wilfully forget because it depresses them too much. Leaving the house whenever you wanted, getting enough sleep, day drinkin'. I swear half my life is spent fastening and unfastening those blasted car-seat safety straps. And when the boys have winter coats on? The Seventh Circle of Hell will be nothing but fastening screaming children wearing winter coats into their car seats.

Whenever I get frustrated, or need a reboot, I always take a deep breath followed by a swift exhale: in and out through my nose. Hot yoga, Vipassana, you name it. It's just something I've conditioned my body to do. My four-year-old has started asking me about it. Because it happens a lot. I explained to him that it sometimes means that Mama is frustrated. I see it as an opportunity to teach him about the power of taking a deep breath to calm yourself and see a situation more clearly. But yeah. Most of the time it means I'm pissed.

My days as a mom require far more energy and endurance than my days as an opera singer. If anything, by comparison, becoming a parent has made being an opera singer easier. There's a longer detrimental consequence to screwing up your kids than there is to screwing up an entrance in *Tales of Hoffman*. I'm much easier on myself as Singer since becoming Mama, because I know that at the end of the day, my performances are not seeds that bear sustainable fruit in the spiritual sense. They are a snapshot. A gorgeous, profoundly moving and complex snapshot for which I am paid a livable wage. They end, and after I give myself to you, I get to come home to myself, in a sense.

To unpack that a little, I don't mean to imply that art doesn't matter—or that classical music doesn't matter. I just don't think I can take playing dress-up and screaming for a living as being as consequential as changing my absolutely dependent baby enough times a day that he doesn't get diaper rash. Some might think it's not fair to compare the two, but why wouldn't I? It's all the same life and I'm one of a large demographic living the same work-life matrix. I'm also not going to dismiss what I've accomplished by saying, *I'm hardly curing cancer*, because I do believe that music is balm to the soul and the human voice reaches people in a very special way. Only that being responsible for two tiny humans is hardly the same as deciding if I go with the sequins or the satin. I knew I was fully Mama when I was standing in the drugstore with only enough money for false eyelashes or diapers and it was a no-brainer.

Yes, I am both Mama and Singer. But not to my boys I'm not. By the same token, the entertainment industry doesn't care that I'm a mom. But within myself, the two must work in tandem and reconcile themselves to each other. I just know my job and my other job make each other better. If Mama and Singer don't find a way to work together, then the conflict between the two will make both suffer. If I've not organized myself to be fully present when playing my roles, then why bother doing either one?

I chose to become a mom in a much more conscious way than I chose to become an opera singer. Singing was my calling so early in life that it hardly felt like a choice. I wasn't forced or coerced, and I'm grateful it found me, but there is no question that singing is something I'm meant to be doing full-time—for as long as it works out. As I get older in this job, I realize that time away from it is essential. The aging opera singer can be a beautiful thing, but it can also be a bastion of bitterness and regret. Like any job that can take everything from you but give very little in return, being a classical musician isn't generally something you just fall into. It demands that you work and sacrifice and eat a lot of crap in order to pursue your dreams. And the higher up you are in the food chain, the bigger the stakes. Slap a coat of conservativism onto the old-guard mentality, the gay mafia, the politics of voice classification, sizeism, ageism and people not even in the game having something to say about "your last *Antonia*," and you've uncovered some of the downsides of my job.

I don't want to live that way. I don't want to think that I'm only as good as my last gig. I don't want to beg to be liked by people whose opinions—and the inherent exclusionism they're couched in—don't scratch the surface of what my *actual* goals are. I want my memories to be more than short-term and my relationships to be lifelong instead of the length of a contract. I don't want to equate not being in my own bed for months out of the year as some badge of honour and my lack of dependants as true freedom.

My mother and I once watched a movie called *Quartet* together about a retirement home for aging opera singers. It starred Maggie Smith and Michael Gambon. There is no potential outcome more depressing to me than spending my final days with a group of people who did the exact same thing as me for their whole lives. That the sum of my life could amount to reliving my glory days—gossiping about dead conductors, listening to old recordings—would be a fate worse than death. Tears streaming down my face, I sat and watched, horrified, unable to breathe from the panic, slowly shaking my head. I honestly bawled my eyes out from start to finish at the very premise that if I didn't cultivate more things of value in my life, that could very well be me one day: perishing in the ashes of recordings no one listens to anymore from programs and productions I can't sing anymore. What gets me up in the morning is the prospect of cultivating a life where, in the end, I will be surrounded by people who loved me for the person I was and the adventures we conquered together, not the repertoire I sang or the voice type I was. The movie *Quartet* is my *Scream*.

I grew up, as I've said, the youngest of three—the singular achiever—with my husband as my manager, handler and baby maker. And despite not being the most natural fit, the role of Mama grows more and more fulfilling to me, because it is played to a tiny, exclusive club of two (pint-sized) superhumans who happen to have lived inside my body before they ever saw the light of day. It tickles me to think that the same people I'll want beside me when the career is over and the crowds are gone were made in my own belly. It is a very elite club and I don't take lightly the fact that, at this point, that is how my young sons see it, as well. I belong to them. Their worlds literally collapse if I'm in the room and they can't get to me.

As they grow older, I know that bond will evolve and develop into whatever they need. It will become increasingly creepier for me to put their feet in my mouth or watch them while they sleep . . . not that that will stop me.

PART 4

WHY AM I HERE?

~~~~~

DATE: SUNDAY, JUNE 6, 2010, 9:17 AM

FROM: MEASHA BRUEGGERGOSMAN

TO: NEARESTS AND DEARESTS

SUBJECT: PRESSING ON

Hey Gang,

Another Sunday has arrived and I'm still here. It may sound like I'm counting them down because I can't wait for it to be over, but I'm also ;-) amazed at how quickly the time is going. This week was the most emotional I've had so far. But the funny thing is, I feel absolutely fine now. There was a bit of panic, of feeling raw and overwhelmed. I melted down and then poof! Over. It kinda felt like the sweat that comes out of my pores (in massive amounts) every day. All these emotions and unexpressed "whatevers" are there percolating in the bones. They have to come out somehow in order for the body and mind to balance and regulate itself, and after they do, they dry up like sweat. Mind you, it's painful. Lord, is it ever painful. Nothing worthwhile is ever easy. For a lot of the students here, this past week has been Meltdown Week: yogis in tears in the elevator, on their mats before/after/

during class, in the Porta Potties, you name it. You can't predict where or when the meltdown's gonna strike. It's an intense process. You all know that I prefer not to cry in public, so my release happened in private, in my room, and I had some pretty wonderful support.

But there have been a lot of tears. This process is a lot like a refining fire, and I'm still trying to find my rhythm. There's 90 minutes of dialogue to memorize. We're also expected to learn their 26 Sanskrit titles. Try to make "Dandayamana-Bibhaktapada-Paschimotthanasana" roll off the tongue and you'll have some sense of what we're going through. The first posture, Half Moon Pose (Ardha Chandrasana), is the only posture in the series done in front of Bikram himself (and all 350+ of us). I completely crashed and burned on my first attempt. I'm not exaggerating. I thought I knew it (famous last words), but I completely fell apart. Bikram eventually had someone pass me the written dialogue and had me read from it. Yes, I was pleasant and cracked a few jokes that absolutely killed, but I'm really fighting to let it go by telling myself all the usual clichés and mantras. I just wish it had gone better.

Pressing on,

Measha

The greater the hurdle, the sweeter the victory. With each stumble, with each fall, I get back up stronger than I was before. I don't focus on how many times it happens—I focus on how quickly I can see what I'm meant to be learning. To say it another way, what I think is important about the discomfort of burning off the things I don't need to move forward is my reaction to the fire.

I know that's not how we're supposed to think. I know the pervasive belief and overwhelming trend is to run at the very whiff of discomfort. Why force it? It shouldn't be that hard, we say. It just wasn't meant to be. If it doesn't bring immediate pleasure—or reap fast rewards—then it must be the wrong path. We misinterpret hardship as a signpost directing us to a wider, more populated path instead of this rocky, narrow one. I believe that there are plenty of times where walking away or not staying the course (especially when it gets hard) is a sign you didn't really want it—or that you weren't willing to sacrifice the sweat, hours, tears, money, pride, research, endurance and sacrifice to get it.

There are Christians who believe your hardships are brought on by your sin, and therefore you deserve everything you get. Well, I'm not that kind of Christian and I would argue that that isn't actually how God works. He tells us to *consider it pure joy whenever you face trials of many kinds, because you know that the testing of your faith produces perseverance.* (James 1:2–3) Meaning, Hold on! I'm using whatever and whoever to show you something about yourself that you need to fix so that you can properly handle the blessing I have for you. Don't give up!

There are things we need to know about how to get through this deluge of manure so that when things do work out (and they will), we'll know how to move forward. Your capacity to deal with pain and pressure determines your level of responsibility. When God says, *Be strong and courageous! I will never leave you, nor forsake you* (Deuteronomy 31:6), He's saying to trust Him— there are blessings He can't give you unless He tests you first. Nothing happens to you without His knowledge (He's omniscient!), but there are some things you can't see unless you're at the bottom. We can be destined to run out of everything just so that He can give it to us better than before and we'll know where it came from. Nothing we do can separate us from Him, and in the same way you wouldn't leave a baby naked outside in a snowstorm, God won't leave us to fend for ourselves.

What I find hugely comforting is that He isn't telling me that if I'm good in this life, He'll reveal himself to me in the next. (If that were the case, we'd never get to spend any time together!) God is with me now, engaging with me in the morning, noon and night. At the helm, steering the ship.

I've said repeatedly that my life can be incredibly isolating. My work and study can only be accomplished alone and no one can do it for me. I've come to realize that that creates a sense of loneliness that, if not balanced with community, can lead to some pretty self-destructive mischief.

The wonderful thing about the Christian God is that He wants me more than I want Him. Warts and all. I mean, He's literally waiting. For me! Revelation 3:20 says, *Here I am! I stand at the door and knock. If anyone hears My voice and opens the door, I will come in, and we will share a meal together as friends.* As friends. What a comforting sentiment. When life inevitably runs me aground—and it has more times than I can count—there has to be somewhere for me to look to and know the answers will come. And if I don't have the wherewithal—or the will—to find them, I choose to look up.

The first time I got pregnant was in the spring of 2011 while my husband and I were "practising to try." I had become a Bikram yoga teacher in June 2010, so my body was still humming from all the yoga it had been doing. I had expected to be fertile, but we hadn't expected to get pregnant so quickly, and there hadn't been time to seek out any medical advice. I was thrilled—and terrified because I wasn't mentally prepared.

Our terror was echoed by the medical profession, but not our joy:

With your dissected aorta and hypertension, we wouldn't advise this.

Are you sure you want to continue?

Maybe we should consider all our options here.

Do you know what you're doing?

Remembering this still makes my blood boil. First of all, the medical profession had never seen a dissected aorta present itself in a patient so young, so they had no idea what my follow-up care should be or what "options" were available to me. (I was even turned into a case study based on the rarity of my condition and survival.) I wasn't going to live my life under a microscope, tiptoeing around stress or denying myself the things I wanted out of my life, no matter how truncated that life might end up being.

I informed my obstetrician that the train had already left the station and she was to get on board or find someone who would, because this pregnancy was happening. So, despite my medical history and all the red flags it waved, a team of physicians was called in to oversee my care, because mine was such a high-risk pregnancy. I felt like I was having these babies in spite of my support team, instead of with them. They didn't even consider the glass to be half full. And yes, I mean babies, because, you'll remember, I was pregnant with twins.

I was also in the middle of rehearsals for Opera Atelier's new production of Mozart's *La clemenza di Tito* in Toronto. I would be singing the lead of Vitellia, daughter of deposed Emperor Vitellio. I worried that my corsets might hurt my babies and that my costumes wouldn't fit by the end of the production.

Because of my high-risk medical status, ultrasound tests were initiated well before the usual ten to fourteen weeks—that was how I had learned the wonderful news that I was carrying twins. Then at the next ultrasound, at ten weeks, we learned we had lost our first baby. As soon as I saw the technician's sombre expression and heard her silence, I knew something was off. She had the worst poker face. She told us, "There's only one heartbeat. The other has stopped. I'm really sorry."

As I've said, I hate to cry in public. I don't care how shocking the news or emotional the situation. I do not like to cry with strangers around. I wanted to shout, *Okay, now leave! You've done your job. We're not your friends. This intimate moment doesn't involve you.*

I wasn't going to cry in front of a stranger, despite how broken open I felt. I know I was focused on the wrong thing. But if I thought about what was actually happening, I wouldn't have been able to keep it together. My pride helped me retain my dignity, in some small way. When she finally did disappear, I pulled the sheet up over my face, then buried my head in my husband's chest and wept. The kind of weeping with no sound. Where you hold your breath and squeeze out the tears until you have no choice but to take a breath and start over again. I cried and I cried, while stealing glances at that blank ultrasound screen, hoping to see that second heartbeat, praying for a miracle.

This is the process that would teach me that I am consoled by information. The more you can tell me about my dead baby and her journey (because I've always thought of her as a girl), the more I can join myself to her. I learned that the body of our dead baby would be absorbed into the wall of my uterus. I was told, "You won't feel a thing." Which was ridiculous, because of course I felt everything. Perhaps the pain couldn't be seen or measured physically, but I was so devastated I didn't know if I'd even be able to walk out of the room.

We remained thankful that we still had the other baby, and he seemed to be doing well, but before I was to leave to sing in Norway later that summer, my checkup at the hospital revealed that the left chamber of our second baby's heart was thickening. That meant it was working too hard to support the other side, which wasn't developing properly, but that it might self-correct. I learned this was a side effect of my blood pressure medication, taken prior to my pregnancy. While in Norway, halfway through my second trimester, I went for another ultrasound. The test revealed that though our baby's medical situation hadn't improved, it hadn't deteriorated, either. I was hoping for the best, trying to prepare for any possibility, yet not wanting negative thoughts to affect the outcome. I wanted to believe that through the power of positivity, I would will my baby's heart to grow and function properly.

When I got back to Toronto at twenty-one weeks, my first desire was to have another ultrasound. As Markus and I anxiously watched the monitor at Toronto SickKids Hospital, we could see that our baby's heart was slowing down. By now we knew he was a boy. We watched his tiny heart as it struggled to beat.

The word sad doesn't begin to describe how we felt, but I can tell you, sad as it was, it was also helpful for us to be a part of this fleeting moment. Since a mother can't possibly feel the heartbeat of a baby at this stage, not even slightly, we were booked, as well, for a fetal cardiac ultrasound the next day. When I relive the memory of that time, I think I knew what we would see.

My husband and I were staying at the home of our dear friends Joan and Jerry Lozinski. As I was lying in bed, I knew our baby was gone. I told my husband, "His heart isn't beating anymore." The fetal ultrasound the next day confirmed what I already instinctively knew: On August 22, 2011, we lost our August David at twenty-one-and-a-half weeks.

The nurse at SickKids told me I was to head over to a different hospital. When I asked why, I was told it was to induce labour and give birth to my baby.

I was stunned and horrified. I'm not ready. You can't make me give birth until I've processed what's happening. I won't let the death and birth of my child just happen to me. You can't dictate that! He's not going anywhere. I'll call when I'm ready and schedule the delivery. It might be later today. It might be tomorrow or the next day. You can't prematurely force me into this.

If there are any couples out there who find themselves in the same, unenviable position, I would encourage you to insist on following your own instincts and emotional needs by shutting out as many voices as possible. There's no right way to grieve.

You have to take in the information, decide what it means to you, then come to your own decision.

We went back to the Lozinskis' and called our parents. My parents had attended all the major events in my life, including the medical ones. In 2006, my mother had stayed by my side for a week during my gastric bypass. In 2009, both my parents were at my bedside when I came out of emergency heart surgery. Now I wanted them present for the birth of August David.

They arrived in Toronto the next day and we went to the hospital together. Because of the stent in my aorta and my chronically high blood pressure, a cardiac nurse was present. She told me that I would be kept pain-free so as not to raise my blood pressure. This would be achieved through an epidural, which would deliver continuous pain relief to my lower body while I remained fully conscious.

That didn't happen. I was a critical patient, in a state of deep grief about giving birth to a dead baby, and yet it was some resident sent to administer the epidural. Apparently it was hard to find the place of insertion between my vertebrae while I sat hugging my knees. He tried twice, which felt like being slapped in the back with a mace—twice. I told him, "You have one more chance, and if you fail, go find your teacher, because I can't take this anymore."

On the third try, the needle went in. I wouldn't know until much later that the epidural didn't work and I would end up feeling everything.

My labour was long. The contractions and the physical pain were excruciating, while the emotional pain clenching my heart was immeasurable. I was pranayama deep breathing to save my life, and I was confused about why I was in so much pain. When I look back, I see the sad irony in the whole process: This was the only time I would give birth naturally, without surgical intervention, and my baby would be dead.

My mother and my husband were with me in the room when August David arrived at 2:40 a.m. on August 23. I was able to hold him, and he was the most beautiful thing I'd ever seen. He had super tiny eyes with membrane-thin lids that would never open. He fit into the palm of my hand. His little fingers weren't quite separated yet and his skin was purplish and translucent, but he already had a brush of hair. His head was proportionately big the way babies' heads are supposed to be at that stage. I could already see his Gosman nose and his Bruegger lips, and where his eyebrows would have been. He was my son.

I was still in physical pain and my blood pressure was so high. Thankfully, I was already in the intensive care cardiac unit and they ushered August David away while they brought my blood pressure down. The memory of the nurse leaving with my stillborn baby in her arms, still warm from my womb, is one that is burned into my mind forever.

Then the fatigue of the prior seventy-two hours set in and I slept. Hard. The next day, my husband, my parents and I met in a counselling room, where August David was brought to us, dressed up in a white outfit knit by angel volunteers. We took turns holding him, and we were given literature—"So You've Lost a Child"— to help us move forward in our grief.

We named August David after the founder of the Roman Empire and constitutional democracy and the biblical figure who also lost his first-born son, respectively. That our August David had been twenty-one-and-a-half weeks at birth was essential to our grieving process. At twenty-one weeks, a baby is entitled to a birth certificate and a record of having existed. I knew my baby long before twenty-one weeks, but I was grateful my pregnancy progressed far enough for us to fall under these customs that helped my entire family to grieve.

With a stillborn birth, the reality of seeing and holding that little body takes on a powerful place in memory and recovery. Until August was born, I was the only one who could feel him. But the loss wasn't just mine alone. Daddy, Nanny and Papa, Oma and Opa in Switzerland, with whom we'd kept in touch by Skype, also had their own loss to grieve, along with August David's cousins, aunts, uncles and our family friends. By having the privilege of giving birth to him, he became more than a blurry image on an ultrasound screen. He was Markus's and my first-born, and a grandson and a nephew and a cousin.

I sanctioned an autopsy because we wanted to know if there were any genetic reasons that had caused August David's death, some congenital heart problem that might afflict another child of ours. For this, we had to submit his body for three days of tests. A chromosome count would also be done to confirm what we already knew about his gender.

This meant three days of waiting until we could bury August David. My parents joined my husband and me in Chatham, Ontario, where we were living at the time while he completed his paramedics course.

This is where my grieving began in earnest. It was unfamiliar territory, and I wasn't sure how it was going to unfold or how long it would last. I wanted it to be exhaustive. I knew there were stages I had to go through, and that if I missed any or tried to rush, I'd have to go back and repeat them. I knew I would be doing a lot of crying. I knew I would be doing a lot of staring off into space, wishing things had turned out differently or wondering if there was anything I could have done.

All four of us busied ourselves, and since we had recently moved into the top-floor apartment of a big old Victorian home and I hadn't quite unpacked, we had plenty of projects to tackle. I was raised by a doer, so my mother and I mobilized. We organized shelves. We went to the Salvation Army, found a bunch of old chairs, stripped them and repainted them. We unpacked boxes and purged doubles of things we'd brought out of storage. When I wasn't doing, I was suffocating from grief, crying in the bathtub, crying in the bedroom, clinging to the banister while I climbed the stairs, collapsing on the occasional step to let my sadness pour out. When the cloud would lift, I would get back to work.

This would prove to be some of the most meaningful time that I would get to spend with my mother. We had always been close, but we had almost skipped the maternal relationship because from very early on, we'd rallied ourselves around my career. There is no occasion more intimate than sharing the loss of a child. For her, it would have been the birth of her youngest baby's first baby. To watch her child grieve and to try to find a way to be supportive must have agonized her, but she and my dad were exactly what I needed. In the middle of painting a chair, I would burst into tears, paintbrush in hand, and she would put the brush back in the can and then sit and cry with me.

My father, as a pastor of visitation, was used to visiting shut-ins, the sick and the grieving. He was so strong in his silent presence while undergoing his own loss. Sometimes you can have people around you who are mystified and grief-stricken by the event and you end up spending your time and energy bringing *them* to terms with *your* loss. My father's not like that. I was blessed by his invested stoicism. My husband and my father share that characteristic. They were both present to share and to help. My husband grieved in his way and I grieved in mine. Though he was also so sad, I was happy to have him around. We were all trying to move forward while not wanting to rush it. Grief will not be coaxed or tricked into leaving. It has to go on its own, and never all at once.

After our three days together in Chatham, we returned to Toronto for August David's body. The autopsy had confirmed that his problem had not been congenital. Losing my twins did not confirm my doctors' prognosis that I should not give birth. My blood pressure medication was not intended for pregnant women. Even switching after I was pregnant wouldn't have helped, because the medication would have remained in my system long enough to affect my babies' development. I tried not to blame myself or anyone else. The doctors didn't know I was trying to get pregnant and I didn't know about the possible side effects. The twins had taken everyone by surprise.

My parents flew home to Kentville, Nova Scotia, while my husband and I drove August David's body from Toronto to the Maritimes for burial. At first, we had wanted to fly with him, but that would have meant a lot of red tape to get his body on the plane. The journey turned out to be a blessing. It was the pilgrimage we needed to bring the body of our child home. As much as we would have enjoyed guiding him through this life as his parents, we believed he had skipped the challenges of the temporary and moved straight to Glory, where we would all meet one day.

When passing through Quebec, we stopped among rolling hills devoid of people, sounds or cars and felt the peace and promise of creation. I liked the idea of wandering into the forest and sitting somewhere—to cry, to pray, to meditate or just stare into space. And that's what we did. I'd never experienced the rejuvenating powers of being in nature before I lost my babies. But it is very real: wind rustling the trees; the smell of grass or rain or fresh air; an organic colourscape; the ocean eternally turning over on itself; deep root systems as elders, confessors, witness. All my relations. Nature only requires me to be still while it does all the work by just being itself.

We stopped again in Nackawic, New Brunswick, which boasts the world's largest axe, weighing over fifty tons and standing almost fifty feet high, with a head twenty-two feet high. My home province of New Brunswick is famous for having a lot of "the biggest"—the biggest blueberry, the biggest spud, the biggest coal, the biggest frog, the biggest peanut and the biggest axe. We took crazy trompe l'oeil pictures of the axe sticking in our heads, and of one of us wielding the axe while the other pretended to run away.

We understood that grieving was a process with no discernible end, because even while we laughed together, we carried the place in our hearts that the loss of our first-born had created. The time we had together on our drive to the Maritimes was a practice run for lives that incorporated our grief into our emotional DNA. Losing a child is never not a part of you, but as my Vipassana ten-day silent meditation course would teach me about five months later, the mind filters out the toxicity of the pain so that the heart can find a healthy spot for the memory to peacefully rest.

We took August to Kentville, where we gave the brown box holding our child to a funeral director. My father, having led his share of funerals as a pastor at New Minas Baptist Church, had arranged it. He knew this funeral home was a symbol of compassion in the community, but the hardest part for me was giving them August David's remains, because they would prepare his body for burial, and this would be the one part of the process that I couldn't oversee. I wanted to know where his remains would be and what would happen to them. Just handing over that box, after we'd carried it for twenty-one hours, after I'd carried him for twenty-one weeks, almost broke me.

We still had to pick out a cemetery plot and order his marker. I never thought I would ever live to see "Brueggergosman" on a tombstone with a single date, but there we were, placing the order. On August David's grave marker, we chose to carve his name, his date of birth and Psalm 139, acknowledging that he had existed, that he had been loved and that he would remain a significant part of our family and our marriage moving forward.

Should he be in the shade? Will his plot get enough sun? We would discuss these options with the cemetery groundskeeper, as if any of this mattered to a child who had never seen trees or the sun. Despite the grief that chokes me, I know my child is not actually there. Even as we were picking the location where the box containing his remains would be buried, I wasn't making the decision based on whether my baby would like it. He was in heaven having the time of his life! What we were in truth deciding was where we would like to visit to appease our own grief and to remember this chapter in our family's life.

My husband wanted to dig the grave himself, which I completely understood, but we were told this wasn't permitted for insurance purposes. However, we were allowed to watch the grave being dug, so we arrived at 6:00 a.m. on September 1, 2011, the day of the memorial service, and silently watched the gravedigger carve away the square of grass where our tiny brown box would fit, shovel out the dirt of our child's grave and carefully pile the earth to one side.

I have such beautiful memories of that day. The gravedigger was a warm, soft-spoken, middle-aged family man with a dog, a man who seemed to have been tailor-made for this kind of ministry. He told us that most people wanted the loose earth covered with AstroTurf, which I guess creates the illusion that your loved one isn't being covered in dirt. We wanted to see the pile of dirt and we wanted to refill the grave ourselves.

To someone who has not experienced a child's death, bearing witness in this way might seem unnecessarily morbid, but I wanted to know the full process of burying my child. As his parents, it would serve as the only journey on this earth that we would get to oversee. I believe all these steps braided us into the condensed life of August David. I had prayed that my grieving process would be unqualified and complete, and bearing witness to every detail was how that manifested for us.

When the rest of my family arrived for the memorial, we put our brown box in the prepared place and had a short but beautiful service, opened in prayer by my father. My brother spoke encouraging words and my sister read Psalm 139:

1 *You have searched me, Lord,*
     and you know me.
2 *You know when I sit and when I rise;*
     you perceive my thoughts from afar.
3 *You discern my going out and my lying down;*
     you are familiar with all my ways.
4 *Before a word is on my tongue*
     you, Lord, know it completely.
5 *You hem me in behind and before,*
     and you lay your hand upon me.
6 *Such knowledge is too wonderful for me,*
     too lofty for me to attain.
7 *Where can I go from your Spirit?*
     Where can I flee from your presence?
8 *If I go up to the heavens, you are there;*
     if I make my bed in the depths, you are there.
9 *If I rise on the wings of the dawn,*
     if I settle on the far side of the sea,
10 *even there your hand will guide me,*
     your right hand will hold me fast.
11 *If I say, "Surely the darkness will hide me*
     and the light become night around me,"
12 *even the darkness will not be dark to you;*
     the night will shine like the day,
     for darkness is as light to you.

13 *For you created my inmost being;*

    you knit me together in my mother's womb.

14 *I praise you because I am fearfully and wonderfully made;*

    your works are wonderful,

    I know that full well.

15 *My frame was not hidden from you*

    when I was made in the secret place,

    when I was woven together in the depths of the earth.

16 *Your eyes saw my unformed body;*

    all the days ordained for me were written in your book

    before one of them came to be.

17 *How precious to me are your thoughts, oh God!*

    How vast is the sum of them!

18 *Were I to count them,*

    they would outnumber the grains of sand—

    when I awake, I am still with you.

19 *If only you, God, would slay the wicked!*

    Away from me, you who are bloodthirsty!

20 *They speak of you with evil intent;*

    your adversaries misuse your name.

21 *Do I not hate those who hate you, Lord,*

    and abhor those who are in rebellion against you?

22 *I have nothing but hatred for them;*

    I count them my enemies.

23 *Search me, God, and know my heart;*

    test me and know my anxious thoughts.

24 See if there is any offensive way in me,
and lead me in the way everlasting.

This Psalm would also be the very first thing my sons Shepherd and Sterling would hear as they entered this world. What initially attracted me to the passage was how David talks about the Almighty's omnipotence being made manifest even as God knit me together in my mother's womb. But, in the years my grief has had to morph and change in the light of my life with my sons, I find myself drawn to David's humility to God's sovereignty when he says the night will shine like the day, for darkness is as light to you. The power to transcend darkness and see night as day is the super power I am cultivating now. The spiritual ability to "see in the dark"—or see the night as day—takes away all power to enslave; a spotlight is shone on the deceptions and fears that would continue to enslave. By the blazing, revelatory light of Truth, the prison door is flung open and we are set free.

Markus and I brought the memorial for August David to a close by describing the whole trajectory of his brief time with us, and how it was okay to be sad and okay to acknowledge this as a tragedy, even though we had faith that August David was in Heaven. We said that we knew we lived in a broken world, with illness and injustice, but the brokenness is meant to point us toward Christ. That when we search for answers or want to give in to bitterness, we must remember that God isn't responsible for the brokenness. That He is the healer of our brokenness and that there are heavenly benefits to skipping this earthly existence and going straight to Glory, as August David had done.

We filled in August David's grave, exchanged condolences and took our turns holding each other.

Blessed are they who mourn for they shall be comforted. (Matthew 5:4)

To turn its corners, the grieving process transforms and rediscovers itself: It changes its position in the middle of the night; it jostles for supremacy and finds a comfortable place to lie dormant. It doesn't leave you, because it's the latest in a collection of experiences added to who you now are.

In the fall of 2011, I had cleared my entire concert schedule because I was supposed to be having my first baby and then caring for that baby. Now I was staring down a six-month, dark and empty tunnel with no place I was supposed to be and nothing I was supposed to be doing. I hadn't had that much time off since I'd done Bikram teacher training, and that was only nine weeks. This was a phenomenon I'd never experienced before. I consciously tried not to panic.

I trusted that whatever time was free was whatever time I was meant to use to grieve, and then, in whatever state I was in, I would be in whatever state of readiness I needed to be in in order to accomplish whatever was to come next. About five minutes after coming to this conclusion, I was thrown a lifeline: the invitation from the Canadian broadcaster CityTV to become a judge on their newly launched reality variety show, *Canada's Got Talent*. As a spinoff of the British series, it would feature singers, dancers, magicians, comedians and other performers of all ages, competing for a prize of $100,000. Auditions in Winnipeg, Calgary, Vancouver, Montreal, Toronto and Halifax would begin in mid-October for the show's debut in March. The winner would be chosen by audience vote from contestants preselected by the judges.

Well, if you had told me when my career started that I would be a judge on a reality talent program, I would have never believed it. I love reality television!

Let me quickly qualify that statement by clarifying that I am a fan of *talent*-based reality TV: *Dancing with the Stars, Project Runway, The Amazing Race, So You Think You Can Dance, RuPaul's Drag Race*. I gravitate toward the campy, to be sure, but I like the presence of a distinct qualifier: a passion to train, or launch your business, or hone your craft through competition. I can also go in for a good *Survivor* marathon, though you won't catch me auditioning to starve myself and lie to strangers. But I'll watch it.

The producers of *Canada's Got Talent*—John Brunton's Insight Productions—had already hired comedic genius Martin Short as the panel's supernova. I was added, along with the pianist and composer Stephan Moccio. Through *Canada's Got Talent*, I was handed an opportunity to fill in some crucial gaps—financial, professional—at a time when I needed it most. God knew that I wanted to be working . . . but not really working. That is to say, I was thrilled to be having so much fun with a production company I loved, with two co-hosts who were so incredibly kind and generous to me. The show ran for only one season, 2011 to 2012, the only time in my calendar that allowed me to do it. I'm not saying I wouldn't have done more seasons if we had gotten more seasons. But it served the purpose it was meant to serve: fitting neatly into a narrow, calendrical pocket. I could have thought greedily about how I could have used the money or the fame, but that's not the role this experience was meant to play in my story.

Our chemistry as panellists was wonderful. I never expressed to Marty or Stephan how essential they were in healing my heart and soul. They, along with the team at Insight—though they may not know it—played a major role in easing my profound grief. You never know what will trigger the construction of more supportive scaffolding under your grieving heart, but for me it was a national parade of star-searching misfits and undiscovered geniuses—and the "support staff" that came with them.

We finished the auditions for *Canada's Got Talent*, which finally wrapped at the end of January in Vancouver, and I went to the ten-day Vipassana course to press the reset button on my inner life. I had the best of all possible reasons: I had become pregnant over Christmas in Switzerland.

After August David's death and birth, my husband and I

waited for a month, then began researching ovulation tests and timing and began trying for a baby. Another month went by, then two, with no result. Maybe we were trying too hard? As a healthy, fertile couple, why not just have a lot of sex because it was fun, not because I was ovulating? So that's what we did, and that's how we got pregnant.

We didn't tell anyone. The last thing I wanted was this big announcement on TV, coupled with the pressure of staying calm while the professionals around me stifled their nervous empathy over the two babies I'd already lost. I'd originally shared the loss publicly because I had also been public about being pregnant, and wanted to share my story in the hope that it would bring hope. I knew our story was shared by countless families, and when the newspaper article ran nation-wide, people across the country were incredibly respectful and supportive of our grief and loss. But this time around, I would not be telling anyone who did not need to know.

My blood pressure medication had been changed, so we were in the clear on that potential complication, but I was still afraid of compromising my pregnancy, especially during the critical first trimester. That's why I made the choice to do the ten-day silent Vipassana course. I wanted to get my head right. I needed to do whatever I could to cleanse myself and emotionally reboot. I've described how crucial that experience was for me. The baby train had left the station and I wanted to joyfully climb aboard.

I know that there are couples out there who justifiably wait to get pregnant after the loss of a child, and those who justifiably jump right back in the saddle, like my husband and I did. For my part, I knew I wasn't getting any younger and I saw getting pregnant again as closing the circle of my grief. It was just an image I had in my head of August David (and his sister) morphing into the ongoing cycle of life.

My heart also goes out to those couples who do not get pregnant as quickly as I did, or who have to make their peace with not having children at all for whatever reason. I can't imagine a dream that hurts more to have unrealized than wanting children but not being able to have them. I don't know what God's plan is in those circumstances. But I honestly believe there is one. I would not have been strong enough to keep trying and trying and trying without success. So that wasn't my fight. We are each of us handed losses and struggles that to someone else would seem unfathomable and unbearable in their depth. These losses redirect us into experiences we would never have dreamed possible; like having my grief appeased by being a judge on a reality show. But God sent the unexpected to me, and I do know that God hears you in your grief. You are not alone.

You will press on toward the goal to win the prize for which God has called you heavenward in Jesus Christ. (Philippians 3:14)

People often assume that I am a high-energy person. That I have boundless, bottomless, truckloads and football fields of energy. How else would I be able to accomplish all that I do?

Makes sense, right? Well, let me dispel that myth. This could not be further from the truth. Honestly. I don't wake up and yell, "Hellooo, WORLD!" I'm not bright-eyed and bushy-tailed and practically climaxing at the day's potential. The fact is, I am tired. All. The. Time. There isn't a millisecond in the day when I don't wonder if my time could perhaps be better spent lying in bed. I'm barely awake most of the time. Yes, I may create the illusion that the energy is there, but that's the fallacy of the highly "energied." We fake it till we make it. That's the only thing that separates us from those who seem to be low "energied" or even average "energied." We're just better actors. But trust me, we're exhausted.

When I'm working, I know my day is coming to a welcomed end when I finally get off the frickin' elevator of some hotel and put one sluggish, heavy leg in front of the other sluggish, heavy leg. Then my injured left hip—for about five years now—starts to scream at me that it needs to be replaced, already! I start to get cold and achy, because the powerful balance of pressure and expectation that I use to distinguish myself from the crowd all day is also releasing itself. I take one last look around me to make sure I'm alone, and then I draw in the deepest breath of my life so far and exhale one long, audible "Aaaaaahhhhhhhhh . . . " I might even release a few tears. Because it looks like this day is finally going to end.

Because what's the benefit of coming to the end of your day with energy to spare? A life half lived? Opportunities lost? Problems ignored? Why run from your problems? Success is attached to problems. And yes. Matching the tough question with the right answer may require taming the beast and killing the dragon. You'll likely come home bruised and bloody from battle. But it's that kind of courage, resolve and innovation that earns you a seat with the elders—surrounded by people who know more than you and are more accomplished than you. (If you look around you and realize you're the most accomplished person in the room, you need to find a new room.) To again quote Bishop T. D. Jakes: "Seize every opportunity to look forward." Your reward isn't behind you. Everything that matters is ahead of you, so don't let the pain of your past obscure the brilliance of your future. Use every scrap of strength and resolve you have to fill in the blank cheque of your destiny.

I can sleep when I'm dead. I've had people watching me my whole life and I choose to be grateful for how preoccupied I've been able to be with the creative process. On the mornings when I can actually hear my bones telling me not to move, I think not only of the people who sacrificed for me to be where I am but also those who would hungrily take my place. Sometimes my strength comes from a place of faith, and other times all I have is the belief of a few and the envy of a few more to spur me forward. Whatever my motivation, I always somehow manage to get my young bones moving.

If it's not already abundantly clear, I'm a Christian. In this day and age, I feel like it's almost something I have to apologize for, since the persecution of Christians has become the accepted position for the "intellectual" or the "scientifically minded." Like the belief in God is synonymous with abandoning all reason.

Don't get me wrong—Christians can give as good as they get it. (And they have for centuries.) But I'm talking about my own right to exercise my personal faith and then being made to feel naive or stupid for wanting to live my life for Jesus. You have your business and I have mine. As a Christian, I am taught to not judge, but that doesn't mean I don't feel the urge to punch you in the esophagus if you roll your eyes at me when I confess to constructing my home and career according to biblical principles. I'm also human and I want to be liked. Thankfully, I have Jesus to get me out of that kinda trouble more often than I'm willing to admit. And He is the source of wisdom and energy that I tap into daily. Do I always get it right? If there were a word stronger than NO, I would use it here. But do I know I can always go back and be enveloped in boundless grace and perfect love? Unquestionably.

I have made so many mistakes and endured so much self-inflicted hardship I'm wondering how I'm still even here. But if the attacks and demands on my life weren't personal, they wouldn't mean nearly as much. I'm not here to be comfortable; I'm here to be effective. If I'm not hit where it hurts, how will I claim victory when I get back to running my race?

This is the memoir of an incredibly flawed individual. But I'm not going to cut off my nose to spite my ear. I'm not going to render myself ineffective because there are parts of my life

I'm not proud of. Sure, sometimes I "fake it to make it." There's nothing wrong with that, so long as I make it. What I'm saying is that the end doesn't have to be pretty. It rarely is. I stumble and fart and drool and stutter myself to victory every single day. The granola bars I find in the bottom of my purse might be in pieces, but my kids still get fed. I may not have had the time to shower or brush my teeth, but I'm on time for rehearsal, with my music learned. It's not pretty, but it is what it is.

We are sometimes faced with impossible decisions. Compromises take new shapes and we tell ourselves we have failed our friends, our family, our colleagues and whoever else will listen. But take heart. They're thinking the Exact. Same. Thing. So fail forward. Because failing forward is still forward! He truly is a great theologian and preacher, so I'll quote him again. T. D. Jakes talks about "stumbling into place." He also says that there's no way to be effective and pretty. The flies are swarming; I'm swearing and cursing the world, thinking horrible thoughts; I haven't showered for days; and still I find a way to steal a chuckle or put things into perspective, because really, I know how crucial it is to have this time away from my kids to do my job or to concentrate on writing this book in order to share the life I've lived so far, along with the lessons I'm still learning and un-learning.

My life can sometimes feel like an open wound, but I'm not called to be pretty—I'm called to be effective. God, in His perfect time, is the one who does the stitching, and when, bruised and bloody from the war of life, you stumble into place, you still end up where you're supposed to be. God directs the traffic; you sit back and enjoy whatever ride you're on, knowing that you're loved, blessed and worthy of good things.

~~~~~~~~

DATE: SUNDAY, JUNE 13, 2010, 2:37 PM
FROM: MEASHA BRUEGGERGOSMAN
TO: NEARESTS AND DEARESTS
SUBJECT: LAST POSTURE!

My faithful Beloveds,

End of week 8 and I delivered my last posture last night!! All I can say is that after my last update, which I have lovingly titled "Pressing On," I had to make a conscious effort to refocus my energies into positivity because although I never doubted I'd see this through, it was tough going there for a while . . .

This year, I've really committed to seeing and experiencing as much as I possibly can. Because let's face it, I've been so very many places and seen so very little. This brings me to my next reason to celebrate: June 10th marked the one-year anniversary of my dissected-aorta surgery. At exactly this time last year, I had come out of the post-surgery haze, after having had my chest torn open, and was recovering in Toronto General. Although I was mainly concentrating on staying alive, the thought did cross my mind that I wouldn't make it here, or that I wasn't meant to make it here. But it's poetic (and preordained) that I did, and I am truly grateful.

I can't believe the end is so quickly approaching. I have mixed feelings about it because this "yoga bubble" has been the exact right thing for me given what the past year has been for me. I know my life priorities and direction will undoubtedly change after this, but what I do need you to pray for is the music I'm preparing for the gigs I have this summer. I hit the ground running to Norway this Sunday for concerts in Risor, so I'm pretty focused on that rep. After that I have concert perfs of *Carmen* (Bizet) in Caracas with Sir Simon Rattle and the Simón Bolivar Orchestra. Should be fun. And after that I'm in Verbier for two concerts before hitting the Rheingau Festival for a recital with the incomparable Justus Zeyen. Then a bit of time off before playing Jenny in Weill's *Mahagonny* in Madrid at the Teatro Real for 2 months. A bit insane, but I agreed to it and I'll make it through somehow. But your prayers and support would be greatly appreciated. I can feel the pressure of the "real world" slowly closing in and I'm hopeful I'll be able to keep my head once I leave here.

In other news, I've so enjoyed the outpouring of support and mail and well-wishes that have come from you all over the past weeks. I GOT SO MUCH MAIL!!!! You have no idea how encouraging your kind words and prayers are to me. Proverbs 16:24 says, *Pleasant words are like a honeycomb, sweetness to the soul and health to the bones.* Well, my soul has been sweetened by your words this week. It really does do me a world of good to see your handwriting and feel you're with me. And yes, with all the encouraging Bible verses I've written down on Post-its, YOU surround me in my room: on the fridge, the bathroom mirror, the walls, on my bedside table. You're everywhere and I love it!

Big love to you all, and Namaste,

Yogeasha

Before my emergency heart surgery in June 2009—after I'd painstakingly freed up nine weeks for teacher training—my biggest worry was that my exploding aorta had ruined my chances of becoming a Bikram yoga teacher. Among other things, the surgery taught me how important achieving that goal actually was to me.

As evidenced by the excerpts from the emails I've included in this book, the course was the hardest, most rewarding journey I'd ever undertaken. I knew it would be a gruelling nine weeks, physically and mentally, and I was going to need help. When I arrived at teacher training, my husband and I were still separated (for the first time), I'd remortgaged my house to pay for teacher training, I couldn't really summon the energy to even have a desire to sing and I was convinced I was destined to retire from classical music and open a yoga studio in my hometown. I was grasping at straws and looking for strength wherever I could find it. Although I had a pretty good idea of "who" had gotten me to Las Vegas, I wasn't ready to be confronted by my Christian faith—which I had lapsed on. When I say I "prayed" for help, it was more of a blithely wishful conjuring that I sent vaguely upward into the ether. I was also taking the time I needed to actually question my own faith by looking at other systems of belief.

My three literary sources for strength during this harrowing process were *The Heart of the Buddha's Teaching* by Thich Nhat Hanh, *Autobiography of a Yogi* by Paramahansa Yogananda (whom some would call "the original yogi") and the Bible. Since I knew that some (non-confrontational) strength from the Bible could be helpful, I chose to read one chapter of the book of Proverbs (for the adages and subjective wisdom) and one chapter from Psalms (for the positivity and poetry) daily. Every night before I went to sleep, and every morning after I woke up, I would tap into all three resources to refill my tank.

We were strongly discouraged from having contact with the outside world. We were told repeatedly:

Don't let anyone or anything intrude into your yoga bubble.

Avoid emailing or going online.

Give yourself the benefit of total immersion in this nine-week journey of self-construction and betterment.

Trust the process.

As the weeks pressed on, I took to writing little passages on Post-its and taping them to the lampshade by my bed so I would see them first thing in the morning, on the bathroom mirror so I could meditate on them while I brushed my teeth, on the TV so I wouldn't be tempted to turn it on. I began to see a pattern in the succinct practicality of the Bible verses:

In the day when I cried out, you answered me, and made me bold with strength in my soul. (Psalm 138:3) This one was on the lampshade beside my bed.

Let the wise hear and increase in learning, and the one who understands obtain guidance. (Proverbs 1:5) On the mirror in the bathroom.

A little sleep, a little slumber, a little folding of the hands, and poverty will come upon you like a robber, and want like an armed man. (Proverbs 6:10–11) Bedside lampshade.

The Lord is my light and my shadow; whom shall I fear? The Lord is my strength and my life; of whom shall I be afraid? (Psalm 27:1) On the inside flap of my yoga dialogue book.

Blessed is the one who finds wisdom, and the one who gets understanding, for the gain from her is better than gain from silver and her profit better than gold. (Proverbs 3:13–14) On the TV.

A heart at peace gives life to the body, but envy rots the bones. (Proverbs 14:30) Bathroom mirror.

For the Lord gives wisdom; from His mouth come knowledge and understanding. (Proverbs 2:6) Bathroom mirror.

Ponder the path of your feet; then all your ways will be sure. Do not swerve to the right or to the left; turn your foot away from evil. (Proverbs 4:26–27) This I'd taped to the door so it was the last thing I saw before I left my room to start the day.

By the end of the course I had quotations on Post-its everywhere and, for the most part, they were Bible verses. The ones that actually helped me, anyway. These little notes to myself reminded me who I was, how I was loved and what my purpose was. I grew to be stable in accordance with God's plan, not to be blown around by emotional storms, and I felt that my hot-yoga practice was a part of God's plan for my life.

When I completed the course, it was a relief and an accomplishment to have survived, but I wanted to get back to my real job. I wanted to pack and get to my recital in Norway. I knew that being a certified Bikram yoga teacher was a huge achievement, and that everywhere I went in the world, I would seek out a Bikram studio, like finding a church. I also knew that after nine weeks of sweating it out together, my fellow teachers had become my cohorts for life. I could call anyone in my class anytime in the future and find a friend, because that was the nature of our teacher training experience. We had forged an unbreakable bond, like ex-cons who'd been in the joint together.

I was in the best physical shape of my life, but better yet, the process, gruelling though it was, had given me back my faith and my sanity, along with a clarity I'd never known before. I was definitely awake and I wanted to get back to singing.

It's difficult to describe the circuitous route back to my career as a classical singer. From the outside looking in, it probably didn't seem like I'd taken any time off or veered off course at all. But in my soul, I'd really lost faith in my pursuit of singing. I'd lost the fire in my belly. Somehow, through rigorously training myself in another profession, all indications pointed back to my birthright as Singer.

I was both stretched out and locked down, and definitely where I was meant to be. Like I said at the very beginning, I was born to this. In the way you can neither decide nor influence your own DNA, I was, more than ever, the animal possessing the compelling predisposition to be Singer.

As the cyclical nature of my life rounds the next seven-year corner from that moment after Bikram training to today, I find myself right where I was seven years ago. That's not to say I am back where I started. I know more and have the capacity for so much more. I have more faith in myself, I'm closer to my Creator and I don't spend my time trying to avoid hardship at all costs. The confessions I've made and the difficult conversations I've had with myself have resulted in understanding that I am worthy of contentment. I won't be kept shackled by my inequities, because shining a light on our sins and imperfections is the best way to rob them of their power.

Although it may be cute to say that I know less now than

I ever have, the fact of the matter is, I actually know even less about my finances and how to manage them than I did seven years ago. True, I became a mother in the interim, but the challenges of that job pale compared with all the other jobs I've had or will have—including being my own financial manager and disciplinarian.

I'm a big ol' cliché when it comes to being inspired by my babies to be more. More prepared, more aware, more honest, more present, more patient, more loving. The "Mama/Papa Bear" instinct is real (and it is strong with this one). I would rather starve and go naked than have my children experience one iota of anxiety. This attitude is parental and in no way unique to me, although I've always felt like my husband never really believed I was capable of being more than an artist. And I may have wanted to believe him because it meant I wouldn't have to work harder and sleep less to have it all. Finding the appropriate things to sacrifice to make my boys a priority was a big part of my learning curve. But the fire of ambition that burns in my belly got an extra source of heat when my boys came into this world. That's just what happens when you contribute to the creation of another human. That human is quite literally grown out of you, and you will do anything to keep that human safe and healthy. My sons are flesh of my flesh.

You don't have to have children, of course, to tap into a deeper sense of purpose. I know I'm where I am because of how I've reacted this time around to the same circumstances: I'm not lying to myself, and I'm willing to take responsibility for how I got here, because I understand the ripples and consequences that are cast into your life from action—and inaction. The nature of the work you put in reflects the desired result. But beyond that, I know that no one but me can execute the plan God has planted for me of forgiveness, money management, joy renewal and faithfulness.

I've said that the measure of ourselves is found in our response to hardship. When trouble comes, do you immediately go on the defensive? Do you hole up in the fetal position and wait for the trouble to blow over? Or do you assess the damage and rally? Do you identify the enemy and acknowledge his hold over you so you can break it? Are you willing to stop the bleeding at the source, or just be satisfied with a bandage?

M arkus and I might not be married anymore, but the years we spent healing our marriage prepared us to be parents. I would never speak for him, and I will always love him as the great love of my life and wonderful father to my sons that he is. Those years are some of the greatest years of my life. They defined and groomed me. I learned that I could be someone's wife and mother. It's no accident that that realization came in the same way that I learned I could be a Bikram yoga teacher, possessing the strengths required but not necessarily being what I am called to. It's empowering to have options, but there is a difference between your gifts and your calling. I believe that the two should support each other, but I also believe that we can have conflicting, though complementary, roles that underline our individuality and teach us to be better, more expansive and compassionate contributors to other people's lives. In my capacity as wife, I excelled as a provider and nurturer. Those are attributes I value and have learned are not meant to be consumed by the unappreciative—or the undeserving.

I've also learned that I'm a better mom if I'm good at my job, but my job means nothing to me if I'm not a good mom. And being a good mom to my sons is not going to look the same as you being a good parent to your sons. I have to be present to know what they need, but my being fully present means not bringing my work home with me.

Your definition of being present for the things you truly value will be unique to you. I've stopped trying to fit into the priorities that other people would like to impose on me. It's hard enough to deal with my own guilt without having to preoccupy myself with the pending disappointment of anyone who isn't inside my head, thinking my thoughts or living my life. Our races are our own to run. Knowing who you are, with all your warts, faults, triumphs and strengths, is sometimes the only thing you have to cling to when the shame of your past wants to impede the hope of your future.

When I lost my babies, I thought I was being punished for cheating on my husband. Satan was trying to convince me that I had to pay my penance before I could be properly rewarded. But the devil is a liar! (John 8:44)

As hard as it is to accept, sometimes God brings us hardships to draw us closer to Him. Knowing that we should lean on His everlasting arms while believing that He can bring us through the fire sometimes isn't enough when it comes to actually living it. As I look at my bank account and pray my five-year-old computer will survive the birth of this book, He whispers, *Do you trust me?* I am sometimes called to do just that. Trust.

In no way does that mean we are to give in to stoicism. God doesn't call us to grin and bear it. Or keep a stiff upper lip. What I'm talking about is humbling yourself to the process and allowing Him to finish the good work He promised He'd be faithful to complete in you. (Philippians 1:6) This is not the book that is going to tell you that all the power is within you, because that's just not what I believe. I do not lean on my own understanding, because it's limited and finite and flawed by motivations that are less than pure. I try in all my ways to acknowledge God so that He, and He alone, can direct my path. (Proverbs 3:5–6)

Instead of relying on a strength that has limits, I would encourage you to lean in to your tragedy and let God take it from there. It's in the darkest moments where God can reveal himself to be the master healer that He is. There is nothing He hasn't seen and nothing He can't conquer. Most important, He is empathetic to our pain. He doesn't sit in judgment, waiting for us to be perfect before we come into His presence. He wants us as the open wounds we all are. I'm so grateful for that, because I don't know about you, but if I had to wait to be perfect and pretty before I could spend time with God, I certainly wouldn't make it in this lifetime or the next!

When Shepherd Peter was into his seventh month of growing in my belly, my medical team told me not to do anything out of the ordinary. Good advice. My husband and I were living in Ottawa at the time, having moved there from Chatham, Ontario, while he finished his paramedic studies at Algonquin College. After he finished his school year, we flew to Cincinnati, where I would sing my first Bess in *Porgy and Bess*, with the Cincinnati Opera. I had been originally scheduled to make my debut in this iconic role at the Styriarte Festival in Austria in 2009 under Nikolaus Harnoncourt, but I'd had to cancel because of my emergency aortic-repair operation.

We opened on June 28, 2012, my thirty-fifth birthday. Porgy would be gorgeously sung by the amazing Kiwi bass-baritone Jonathan Lemalu, the same guy who had sung Porgy in Austria. My father had taught me from an early age that there is no such thing as a once-in-a-lifetime opportunity, and this proved it.

Porgy and Bess might just be the most magnificent-sounding example of racial appropriation, since it's an opera about poor black people written by two white Jewish boys. For my part, all I've ever cared about was the heartbreaking story and the original orchestration that gave the world such musical gems as "Summertime," "A Woman Is a Sometime Thing," "I Got Plenty o' Nuttin'" and "Bess, You Is My Woman Now," re-imagined by artists like Miles Davis, Ella Fitzgerald, Oscar Peterson, Louis Armstrong, Sarah Vaughan and Billie Holiday.

As an opera, *Porgy and Bess* offers three strong roles for black women—all soprano roles with wildly different personalities. Given a choice, I usually go for Bess because the opera is called *Porgy and Bess*—not *Porgy and Serena*, or *Porgy and Clara*. I had often been told that Bess was a role I was born to sing, but I didn't want to play it before I had established myself in the classical music industry. I knew the role would be there, but if I went to it too early, I feared being (stereo)typecast as "the black singer who sings that black opera with all the black people." But the music and orchestration of *Porgy and Bess* are singular in their richness and colour, so I was very keen to sing it. Beyond that, Bess is a complex and universal heroine. She is a survivor and a chameleon. George Gershwin manifests this compositionally in her duets with Crown and Porgy. He adapts and endears Bess to her male counterparts by having her take on their melodic language and rhythmic idiosyncrasies. I couldn't wait to dive in to the process, and under the sure-footed direction of the great Lemuel Wade (may he rest in peace) my highly anticipated debut as Bess was peppered with lots of laughter and great gatherings with my colleagues.

My real-life pregnancy presented a challenge to the wardrobe department, since they had to tailor my costumes to hide my burgeoning belly. Working my pregnancy into the script was briefly considered (I thought it could have been really interesting to have a pregnant Bess), but it was decided my wardrobe would just camouflage my belly. I let it all hang out, so to speak, while not showing my profile to the audience too much.

An opera singer's voice is a highly sensitive instrument. With my pregnancy, I discovered that the colour of my voice had grown richer, while my range had somewhat compressed itself at the edges—my highest highs came down a bit and my lowest lows went up a bit. I chose alternatives where I could.

This brings up an important debate that exists in the classical world: If you are the temperament, voice type, gender and timbre that a piece (or a role) calls for but said role contains one or two notes that could be "adjusted" to more accurately reflect your vocal strengths, do you opt to make those changes for the greater good? Or do you consider that role out of bounds? I'm talking notes above the staff and below. Because there seems to be a double standard in classical music about changing low notes versus changing high notes. In my experience high notes are regarded as sacred, and if you choose the lower note, you've essentially admitted to being a lesser singer than someone who could sing the high note. Forget that the person who sings the high note might not be able to act, is awkward onstage and has horrible rhythm. I'm going to go on the record as saying that I would choose the musicianship and the believability of a performance over the pyrotechnics of high notes. Granted, high notes are kind of why I got into this business, but connecting with my audience and unearthing profound musical moments and developing palpable dramatic experiences are why I've stayed.

I think it's important, young singers out there, to keep a score within your comfort zone (within reason) so that you can deliver every note with everything you've got. That means nuance and dynamics and drama. It means that you risk more of what's important, instead of making the experience all about you and what you can do. We know you can sing, but what are you willing to risk? How much of yourself are you willing to show us, the audience? How theatrically vulnerable are you willing to be? Because people respond to the inclusive spirit of authenticity with much more enthusiasm and loyalty than they do to someone who comes onstage and sings *at* them.

I am a staunch Keeper of the Grail, so to speak. when it comes to the appropriate reverence that must be shown for classical music, but that doesn't make the genre untouchable, and while classical music is also meant to be a living expression of thought and feeling, each individual singer must invest with his or her own sense of ownership. I've brought myself through the crisis of feeling compromised by the strict definition of "soprano" as determined by a span of notes on the staff. As I've grown older in my chosen profession, I know that all those constructs are arbitrary. While there are standards and sub-categories that exist under the umbrella of the major classical voice types of bass, tenor, mezzo and soprano, if you're willing to put in the work and back it up with flawless, believable, electrified execution, I don't care what voice type you say you are. Labels just make it easier for casting directors to slot you into a given production. But, my young singer, you should be sneaky enough to change your proverbial spots according to your own artistic desires and goals.

Case in point: one Sunday a few of us from the *Porgy and Bess* cast in Cincinnati went to a nearby church where Jacqueline Echols, the gorgeous singer who played Clara, was the worship-team leader. There she was, leading from the keyboard, singing, while the black choir responded, foot stomping and clapping as if Martin Luther Jr. himself might walk in at any moment. My only contact with American gospel culture had been through *The Preacher's Wife* and *Sister Act*, so to see it live and in the flesh changed me at the molecular level.

This kind of church service doesn't come with a printed program or a time limit, so maybe there would be an hour of musical praise and worship, all led by our Clara. Even before this latest feat of awesomeness, Jonathan Lemalu and I had heard her sing Puccini and Bellini and Bizet in an outdoor concert with the Cincinnati Pops Orchestra. Jacqueline moved seamlessly from gospel to classical music, and I know a lot of African-American opera singers do it. But the real coup was Jacqueline's playing and singing and leading and changing it up on the fly with improvised responses and repeats. I can barely chew and walk at the same time, so this was something new and special to behold. Jonathan and I kept looking at each other like, *What the?* We threw our hands up in the air and bemusedly watched and listened as our Clara rocked out in praise to Jesus, a beacon of hope to all us singers feeling we could only be good at one thing.

Fast-forward to 2017, when I released my album *Songs of Freedom.* It's a collection of songs chronicling the soundtrack of my ancestors who were among the handful of black Loyalists who escaped their slave masters during the War of Independence in what would become the United States of America. On penalty of death, they went to fight for the British. In exchange they were granted emancipation from their generational shackles of forced labour.

The album was the soundtrack to a documentary about me—also called *Songs of Freedom*—directed by Barbara Willis Sweete—which witnessed me on a journey through my genealogy. With Aaron Davis and L. Stu Young, I co-music-directed the soundtrack and produced the album. Prior to the film, through a DNA swab, we discovered that I was a descendant of the Bassa tribe in Cameroon. The film company travelled to Cameroon, where I would meet the Mbombogs, the elders of the Bassa tribe. The Mbombogs would cleanse me of impurities from the injustices of the past and welcome me back to my homeland. This ceremonial homecoming was so much bigger than I could have anticipated.

Bigger, because the film and album involved more than just Singer me. They were a gift to my parents, who throughout their lives had kept their nose to the grindstone to give my siblings and me a different reality than the one they'd grown up with. Additionally, I had always known that I was fiercely Canadian. I have never felt more connected to any other country and, more specifically, to the region from which I hail: the Maritime provinces. I like to think it has something to do with it being the first place my ancestors could live lives of freedom. They had been bought and sold against their will south of the border, but never in Canada: their Promised Land, where they were slaves to no one.

Now that I have children, I understand terms like heritage and birthright. And legacy. I feel a responsibility to either uncover it or contribute to it, and this album, my most personal release to date, was a legacy project. It is a collection of hymns, spirituals and folk songs, all connected to my history in some way. Purposefully, they reflect who I am, and consequently, they reflect my faith.

Touring this album in February and March of 2017 was no fun for me. I started the tour with no voice, and every concert of the eleven-city cross-Canada tour was a struggle. That's not to say it wasn't a huge success! Remember what I said about the bigger the payoff, the greater the resistance? There is always some kind of economic, social or political crisis affecting our ability to stay decent to one another. I wanted to do my small part to fight for decency in whatever way I could. I knew that bringing a message of hope and inclusivity into the social climate that emerged out of the end of President Barack Obama's time in office was going to be an essential contribution to the overall narrative. But I also knew the enemy would do anything to keep any light from shining into the darkness. My job wasn't to have fun. My job was to make sure we accomplished our mission of spreading grace to all who would receive it.

I had an amazing band that was a fascinating musical mix of whippersnappers and veterans. We collaborated with community choirs in almost every city. The only city where we didn't have a choir was Saskatoon, Saskatchewan. It ended up being a blessing in disguise because the band and I relished our chance to get even closer as a musical ensemble—to tighten our hive mind, if you will. Aaron Davis, Marty Melanson, Guillermo Subauste, Michael Eckert, Marko Simmonds and Dave Hillier all worked their butts off to be the master of their different contributions to the cause.

For my part, I felt plagued by a weight that without God's help I would not have been able to carry for the duration of the tour. I gave up alcohol, sugar and carbs in sacrifice to the success of the project. My prayer was that the band would stay healthy, God would make the path clear for our travels through Canada during February, and people with ears to hear or eyes to see would leave better than they came. I easily recognized the heavy weight—or dark cloud—that clung to me as satan's feeble attempt to rob me of my effectiveness for God's glory. I also knew that there were so many people praying for me—hoisting me, city after city, onto their shoulders and carrying me victoriously across the finish line.

~~~~~~~~

DATE: WEDNESDAY, JUNE 23, 2010, 8:47AM
FROM: MEASHA BRUEGGERGOSMAN
TO: NEARESTS AND DEARESTS
SUBJECT: RISOR, NORWAY: THE WRAP-UP

Well, my Nearests and Dearests,

I've made it safely to Norway, and sang my first concert since Bikram yoga teacher training last night. It was the Schoenberg transcription of Mahler's *Lieder eines fahrenden Gesellen* and I'm happy to say it went quite well. To be honest, the voice feels a bit awkward, because during teacher training, I'd only been singing in fits and starts on the weekends, but the voice is relaxed and rested, so that's good.

So I am now a certified Bikram Yoga Teacher! I wouldn't dare forget to write my final post so that you can relive the moment like you were there. And yes, I'm still there. I even created a Facebook profile so that I can stalk all the studio owners in the hope of getting some classes whenever I can. Me! But PRETTY PLEASE do not go on Facebook and request me to be your friend. If you're getting this email, you're already my friend.

So, I've left the "yoga bubble" but have landed in the tiny Norwegian seaside town of Risor and am collaborating with piano giants Leif Ove Andsnes and fellow Canuck Marc-André Hamelin. I couldn't have prayed for a better place to end up right after Las Vegas—or for better musical partners. I've gone from one unique experience to another unique experience, so I think how I really feel will come to the surface once I get back to Toronto this Friday.

The graduation ceremony was a wonderful event. We all got dressed up, sat in our assigned seats and waited for the moment of truth. Lots of hugging, picture taking, some tears and lots of laughter. NO surprise, Bikram made a grand entrance with two decked-out Vegas showgirls on each arm (VERY Yoga—eye roll) and that was after we'd been serenaded by an Elvis impersonator. The official ceremony opened with a playing of a recorded speech given in Japan in the '50s by Bikram's guru, Bishnu Ghosh, in which he expresses his passion for the benefits of yoga and lays out his mandate of bringing enlightenment through yoga to the West. Special awards were given, some senior teachers spoke, and then they started handing out the diplomas! I skipped like a schoolgirl onto the stage to get my diploma, I was so elated. I hugged everyone who would let me. I was almost out of my skin with glee!

And then. I remembered I still had to pack up my room. Although it didn't steal my joy, it was an ominous task that I'd pretty much avoided for as long as possible. I don't know if I ever described the sweet, elaborate set-up I had going on in my room. Essentially, I raided Walmart for any small appliance that would make it unnecessary for me to leave the yoga compound: kettle, smoothie blender, slow cooker, coffee grinder, coffee press, dishes and utensils from accumulated room service orders, a foldable knee-height picnic table and a microwave. And then there was all the food and Pedialyte and coconut water and organic instant noodles and cans of tuna and nuts and Emergen-C and produce and, and, AND ... There was just a TON of stuff.

This brings me to my major point: friends. Oh. My. Goodness. What would I do without friends? You ALL have supported me with your letters and emails and phone calls, but a few of you actually jumped on a plane and made your way down here. It got me through a couple of pretty tough weeks by getting out of the hotel and into some of the most gorgeous natural settings I've ever seen. But the unforeseen bonus of Jess and Jeff's visit to be here for my graduation (!!!) was that they wilfully helped me get packed AND they took the majority of my crap back to TO so I wouldn't be bogged down with all of it in Norway. Thanks to you for suspending your lives and coming to support me in person.

I've made a scrapbook of all your letters, cards, poems, comics and well-wishes. I'd written down different verses and encouraging words and taped them wherever there was space in my room, so those have also found their way to the scrapbook that will always be with me when I travel ...

So, now that I've done A to Z, I'm starting back at A again. And just like in my day job as an opera singer, you never reach Z. All the fun is in the journey and the process and how you get through it. From this point on, perhaps everything that comes at me will be measured against the hardest thing I've ever done: the 9-week Bikram Yoga Torture Chamber. I'll always be able to say, "This is nowhere near as hard as the time at teacher training when . . ."

Aha! The first, tasty morsel of perspective on the process they were constantly telling us to trust!

I love you all very much,

Measha

I know the woman who wrote those letters and I know the excitement and trepidation with which she embarked on the next phase of her journey, because seven years later I feel the same way. I know more and I am more. I've expanded my territory and strengthened my resolve to keep hustlin'. I've learned a lot of hard lessons and experienced profound joy.

On July 8, 2012, after my final performance of *Porgy and Bess* at the Cincinnati Opera, Markus and I drove back to Ottawa on what we called our Last-Chance Road Trip. We took our time meandering through West Virginia, Pennsylvania, up through Vermont, on to Maine, and crossed into Canada at the

St. Stephen border. From there we drove to the coast and caught the ferry to Grand Manan Island. We had wanted to take that beautiful drive from Cincinnati to the Maritimes as a kind of pilgrimage to parenthood. The last time we'd embarked on a road trip of this length was when we were carrying August David to his own memorial service, but this time, Shepherd Peter was a very active baby in my belly.

Because of my enlarged aorta and hypertension, I've known exactly when and where my babies would be born. With both my sons, I had what I coined a "scheduled, super-civilized Caesarean section." Both my boys had to come out at thirty-six weeks because in the last trimester the mother's blood pressure rises to create more blood for the baby. Going deeper into that third trimester would have been too dangerous for me after my dissected aorta.

In August of 2012, at Ottawa General Hospital, I gave birth to Shepherd Peter, named after a family descendant and his paternal grandfather. I was awake the whole time, though numb from my knees to my belly. You're conscious, but you can't feel anything. Pulling the baby out is a pretty athletic process because the surgeon creates as small an incision as possible. My surgeon knew I was a singer and that my diaphragmatic muscles were an essential part of my livelihood. Since Markus was now a paramedic, he was allowed to look over the sheet, acting as my eyes. His happy face was reassuring. Shepherd also did his part. Apparently, his last-minute swim in my womb had tied his umbilical cord into a perfect knot. Praise the Lord he hadn't wrapped it around his neck! Just like his brother Sterling Markus would do two and a half years later, he was screaming before he was even out, maybe because of all the screaming Mama had done while he was in there. When the surgeon turned him around so I could see him, he started yelling again: *Hello, World, this is Shepherd Peter! Let's get this umbilical cord cut so we can get this party started!*

The medical staff cut the cord, and counted his fingers and toes, and weighed him, and performed the necessary tests to make sure he was all there and healthy. Then they brought him back to me. I recorded the whole event on my phone so that later I could relive his birth.

As I've already described, Markus and I recited together Psalm 139, the citation carved on August David's gravestone—the very first thing Shepherd heard upon entering this world. I gratefully accepted the miracle that Shepherd Peter had arrived almost a year to the day that August David left us. Everything went smoothly and according to plan. During the whole process, my heart rate only went from ninety-one to ninety-four beats a minute, then went down again. Though there's no upside to losing a baby, at least my body had a better idea of what was expected of it this time around.

Shepherd was classified as premature because the C-section had interrupted his development process. Though he was fully cooked and apparently perfectly healthy, he was a compact five pounds two ounces.

The nurse tried to take him away: "We want to monitor him to make sure he stays warm. You'll have him for six or seven minutes every hour."

Wait. What? Oh, that is not happening. "Shepherd will receive his heat from Mama and Daddy," I said. "If there's nothing wrong with him, you can come every hour and remove him for six or seven minutes, then bring him back to me, instead of the other way around."

I fought for that contact, and I believe all mothers and fathers have a right to make that demand. All research says that the best thing for a newborn, particularly a premature one, is to keep him warm and get the colostrum into him to increase weight, and these nurses wanted to take him away? I'm sure they meant well, but I wasn't letting him away from my skin unless it was absolutely necessary.

A few years later, when Sterling Markus was born in April of 2015, I was so thankful that his birth also went off without a hitch. We recorded the birth on a voice memo, and like his brother, a reading of Psalm 139 started his life outside my tummy. I had moved my growing family to the Annapolis Valley in Nova Scotia to be closer to my parents and to raise our boys in the Maritimes. In contrast to our experience giving birth to Shepherd in Ottawa, the Halifax hospitals don't have their cardiac and obstetrics units under the same roof. It's absurd. This meant that Sterling had to be incubated and transported in an ambulance to what is now the IWK Health Centre down the street for his checkups, while I stayed at the Queen Elizabeth II general hospital. It was the worst. When he was with me, his stats would improve . . . he would gain weight; and then, after less than a day over at the children's hospital, Sterling's weight gain would slow down because he was away from his mama. They were having me pump colostrum at another hospital to transport to him at the children's hospital so that they could get him strong enough to send back to me. It seemed ludicrous and it was beyond frustrating.

I stayed in the hospital for two days—the standard length of a hospital stay for a C-section in Canada. Both my boys took to nursing really well, and I am grateful for the time we had to bond. I often heard breast milk described as "liquid gold," and to us low-yield milk producers, the term is incredibly accurate. I ate the greenest, most nutrient-dense foods I could get my hands on so that my milk would have the most bang for its buck. I like a good plan of action, so I methodically kept track of my babies' pees and poops to make sure I wasn't starving them.

Prior to Shepherd, in response to those well-intentioned people who would tell me, "Oh, you'll figure all that out," I would think, *No, I won't. But I'll know what my options are before he gets here.* I wasn't interested in multiple-choice motherhood: Will I choose A or B? And I'm not a big fan of surprises. (It would be very difficult to throw me a surprise party because I'd want to control everything and know in advance how it would turn out.)

As I've said, both my babies had their birth certificates, social insurance numbers and passports before they were three weeks old, and Sterling even had a Brazilian visa. I was quicker on the draw with Sterling than I had been with Shepherd because after Shepherd was born on August 20, I was supposed to fly to Berlin on Friday, September 8, to begin rehearsals with the Berlin Philharmonic for concert performances of *Porgy and Bess* with Sir Simon Rattle. It would have been our follow-up collaboration to the performances of *Carmen* I'd sang in Caracas. I didn't want to cancel and I didn't see why I should. Unfortunately, Shepherd's passport didn't arrive till Monday—three days too late. There was no way I was leaving without my Shepherd, whom I had committed to breast-feed exclusively for three months before supplementing with formula.

Children are so adaptable. Their home is where their parents are (at least until they're in school, when you have to release them to God knows who, to be taught God knows what). Having my boys only means that my life is made fuller . . . while my bank account gradually becomes emptier. But at this stage in my life, I don't see the point of making money at all if it isn't to spend on having a life where my boys and I can be together. Fortunately, I'm blessed with a good job, and though I do enjoy fine meals and great clothes, lustfully binging on that life is what I did in my twenties.

I struggle (daily) with leaving my kids to do my job. When I decided to have children, I made a commitment to being present with them. I know it's not enough to just be there. Your physical presence isn't the be all and end all. The fact is, there's not a lot of work to sustain the career of a classical singer in Falmouth, Nova Scotia. My job has to be done outside the home, and more often than not, outside the time zone.

After more than a few tearful conversations with my mother about how I feel guilty all the damn time, she asked me if I ever remembered her being away from me. She said to me, "Think back. Do you ever remember a time when I wasn't there?" The answer is no. My mother reminded me that she had a full-time job outside the home but that the time she had with me counted. She was present and she was mine. And I'm sure a lot of the satisfaction she got from being a mom had to do with her having her own career.

The best mother is a fulfilled mother. One of the most subversive forms of child abuse is an unhappy parent. Some sacrifice is necessary, but if I hope to be a worthwhile example for my kids, I can't put myself through the torture of pretending I'm someone I'm not. I'm teachable and I respect my elders, but I will never be pressured into having my gift of parenthood tainted by the judgment of strangers who don't know me or my boys.

I was disappointed to miss my concert with Sir Simon in Berlin, but I wasn't disappointed about spending an extra couple of weeks at home with my baby. Instead of going to Berlin, I did a thirty-day hot-yoga challenge to help me bounce back from sharing my body with another human. I figured if I didn't get some endorphins pulsing through my veins, I was at risk of post-partum depression, during which I might turn into one gigantic eating-and-feeding machine.

What surprised me most about becoming a mother was the bottomless depth of my love for my boys. There is nothing I won't do for these little meat sacks. I catch myself looking at them, admiring them, in awe at how connected I feel to them.

I'd never kept any kind of schedule before I had kids, because my days were my own and I organized them according to what needed to get done. You can't do that with kids. Not mine, any-way. Not if I want them to sleep. I put Shepherd on a schedule he could depend on, and by his third month he was sleeping six hours in a row. Like clockwork. While I say that about Shepherd, we hadn't yet made room in our lives for Sterling, and my young-est has proven to be quite the rascal.

Shepherd sleeps like the dead, while Sterling can be woken by the sound of me blinking. Shepherd can roll with the occa-sional disruption to his schedule, while Sterling? He'll make you pay for the tiniest hiccup (bless his heart). Sterling will tell you exactly what he wants and when he wants it (and he doesn't even speak!). Shepherd will make you work just a little bit harder and bargain so he can jostle for the upper hand. He's his mother's son . . . so he can also hold a grudge and be secretive. But he's four. So I'm usually onto him pretty quick.

People talk about a mother's intuition. This was something I'd always possessed, but it was a muscle I'd never flexed before.

The doctors were right to warn me that having babies would risk my life, but not for the reasons they were talking about. I never once doubted my physical abilities to produce them, but once my boys were outside the protected cocoon of my womb for all the world to see and influence, this is when the real danger to my health began. I have spiralled down the rabbit hole of hypothetical scenarios, potential misadventures and overkill against boo-boos. Don't even get me started on how I bolt out of bed if I suspect they're even having a whiff of a nightmare. I understand the importance of introducing risk into their (awake) playtime to expand their capacity for problem solving; but that they would have nestled into the tranquility of slumber only to be betrayed by the unconscious activity of their own brains literally keeps me up at night. Despite all that, if you saw my boys—or their dad with our boys—you'd understand why I'd do it a million times over for the same result. I have to believe this is a "parent thing," because I don't even recognize Mama Measha sometimes—she's sooo much more intense than the other Meashas.

The ungrudging adjustments of becoming a parent doesn't mean time stands still. Truer than ever to the title of this book, over the past year (within the span of eight months, in fact), I was dropped by both my agents—the one in New York and the one in London. You'll remember the first one, Bill Palant, whom I'd been with for over a decade, downsized his roster and I didn't make the cut. The other one retired from the business . . . in his forties. And I got the boot.

I wish both these guys all good things as they move forward in their lives and careers as best they know how, but WTF? I know it could not have been easy to look down the list of opera singers on your roster and know you would need to have a frank conversation with each one of them. I'm truly grateful to have at least gotten that courtesy, because not all artists do. But leaving an opera singer on her way to her forties, established or not, with the task of finding new management, the economy being what it is and classical music being the industry it is? That was tantamount to a nail in my professional coffin. I'm sure we've all heard the horror stories of agents and managers running off with their artists' money and prospects—but if the upside to my situation is that I didn't get robbed? That means the downside was that I found myself destitute—financially and professionally—with no managerial prospects. And it happened in laughably quick succession, too. One minute I had two large, reputable companies making my business happen and the next I was on my own.

I create this sense of high drama only to illustrate that a test can present itself as so *obviously* a test that you have no choice but to roll up your sleeves and give up sleep, because only *you* can pound the proverbial pavement to protect your bread and butter.

I took to the internet and worked my way backward. I looked at the singers whose careers I liked or revered. I saw where they were performing, who was representing them, and the repertoire that that orchestra, concert hall or opera house was prone to programming, and decided whether there could be a home for me amid them. Then I looked to see if those companies tended to prefer certain artist agencies over others—because it's no good to sign on to an agency with no hold in the market. I started my career seeking name recognition in my representation, but now that I'd made a name for myself, I was looking for a specific agent who was up for the challenge: representing the type of opera singer who has a good reputation, an impressive biography and discography, many fingers in many pies, and who is always on the lookout for more pies . . .

I'm not what you'd describe as "easily classifiable" and I don't see any reason to change that, because I'm having a fascinating career, by anyone's standards. I was searching for a classical agent who would take one look at my body of work and say, "How exciting!" not "Sorry, too difficult to categorize."

I spent countless hours researching, investigating and creating a road map for my way forward. To keep the panic at bay, I would remind myself of what I had built over my several-decades-long career. After I put the boys to bed, I would continue my due diligence, formulating my plan of attack and praying to God that I would find a home that would welcome what I had to offer with open arms. That my breath of fresh air would blow into the life of someone who was just waiting for me to arrive.

The God I pray to sent Alan Coates to take over my worldwide classical management. In hindsight—after all the bellyaching

I've done about being downsized—I actually needed a change in management because my priorities had changed. I now needed to use the currency of whatever influence and reputation I had built throughout my career to customize a team to represent my output as a creator, singer and performer.

In addition to Alan, I am immortalizing Steve Zsirai, Evan Newman and Tom Kemp in this memoir because I owe them big time for being the right fit at the right moment. I think history will show that they came from extremely good stock and had a hand in making the lives of many great artists manageable, fulfilling, lucrative and balanced. Managing me isn't easy. There's the classical (my bread and butter), the non-classical (my legacy projects), the crazy (my travels), the sane (my time alone), the time off (my non-singing appearances), the babies (my everything), the "I'm off the grid at a yoga retreat (or language course)," the "could you book this flight because I have no money," the hustle, the frank conversation about what this or that presenter said. The role of any artistic management team is to confront and comfort.

They aren't the only ones hustling. It's a two-way street. To any artist wondering why management isn't doing more for them, I would say that there are lazy managers out there to be sure, but this career doesn't just happen. It takes time to build new bridges and open doors—that goes double if you're new to your agency. Don't be an artist with unrealistic expectations attached to unrealistic timelines. But trust your instincts. If you see the signs and you can smell that something's off—you have no work; he won't return your calls; she's cagey when you ask for a progress report; you've heard cautionary tales from reputable sources—then do not forget that you're not helpless. You are not a name on a list. You are the president of your own company.

Have a well-defined list of what you bring to the table. If you've sat back and waited for your calendar to fill itself without knowing enough about the inner workings of your business to actively engage your management with potential solutions and opportunities that they could easily turn around and knock out of the park, then that's on you. Of course, your hustle is different from your agent's, but you are the voice (and face) of a mutually agreed upon plan for Total World Domination. You are the engine—and the financier!—of that plan.

Securing management is when the real work begins. You now have actual personnel to help define and facilitate your goals. Can you articulate what those goals are? Be specific. If I didn't know what I wanted out of this life and this job—and, more important, what I did not want—then the trusted custodians of my business would be left to guess if their efforts were bearing the kind of fruit I was hoping for. They'd be justified in their frustration when I wasn't grateful or enthusiastic about all the hours they'd put in to get me something I ultimately didn't want. If there's a gig for no money that they deem strategic, then I have to get on board and believe it's leading to bigger and better things. Meanwhile, if I wanna chase the rabbit and waste my time doing something for short-term gain, they have to put the brakes on and let me explain why. In a lot of ways, we're starting from scratch, because as far as I know, the career I want isn't one that currently exists.

At the end of the day, to anyone chasing the dream of self-sufficiency, the collaborative scheme you've concocted within your "team" has to make everyone accountable for (and excited about) his or her contribution . . . and fanning the flame of its execution is your job. You are the focus of the picture and the flash that lights it up. I'm not saying that everyone's a leader, but people won't know how they fit in my life if I don't know who I am and what I bring to the table. It's so much better if everyone can be on the same page and take equal credit when things work out—but I've also accepted that it's me who must bear the brunt of the load when they don't.

By the time this book is published, I'll be forty years old. By now I have a very clear idea of my worth. I've learned to list my strengths before my weaknesses. I've worked hard and have a strong social game: I am kind and work well with others. I am a Queen . . . with a team spirit. I'll listen to reason, but I know my own mind. I prefer to cultivate the tools to react to the unexpected and execute a strategy, not the other way around.

I'd say that in the classical music industry, I have a reputation for being willing to try just about anything. I maintain a healthy song recital schedule—a typical program might include a combination of Ravel, Chausson, Duparc, Mahler, Strauss or Schoenberg. At this point, encores are likely to be Barber, Bolcom, a traditional spiritual or an off-beat song by Tom Lehrer—depending on how the wind blows. My operatic roles range from Elettra in Mozart's *Idomeneo* to Madame Lidoine in Poulenc's *Les dialogues des Carmélites* to Jenny in Weill's *Rise and Fall of the City of Mahagonny*; Generally, I'm cast as a whore or a nun. But either way, I'm usually dead at the end. (Although Jenny doesn't physically die at the end of Mahagonny, she was dead inside from the beginning.)

Adjacent to the wacky list of misfits I've gotten to sing are the works whose births have been entrusted to me: The premieres. A new work (sung in Cantonese) by Chinese composer Xiaogang Ye, commissioned by the Detroit Symphony and premiered at Lincoln Center in New York. Also, in the spring of 2016, Michael Tilson Thomas (MTTizzle, as I affectionately refer to him) wrote a thirty-minute tour de force for me called *Four Preludes on Playthings of the Wind* (set to the poem of the same name by the American poet Carl Sandburg), which we premiered at Frank Gehry's concert hall creation, the New World Center, in Miami. Most recently, I sang Miroslav Srnka's new work *Make No Noise*, in a new production for the Bregenzer Festspiele in Austria.

This Srnka situation was no joke. How did I know it was destined to be amazing? Because my purse was stolen from my best friend's apartment in Toronto two days before I was to fly to Austria to start rehearsals. Keeping in mind that sometimes you are presented with a scenario that is so obviously a test (*and* that persecution breeds perseverance), everything I needed to work, travel and caffeinate was in that purse. In fact, I'd placed it by the door of my best friend's apartment with the full knowledge that in a fire it would be the only thing I would need. I woke up the next morning and it was gone. Turns out, placing it next to the door also made it the perfect thing for a thief to grab and leave. And the weird thing was, nothing else was stolen. For the petty criminal, it was like my purse was everything anyone could ever hope for in a robbery and exactly what the thief had come for. And rightly so. Cell phone, computer, passport, all my ID, even my AeroPress coffee maker and freshly roasted Jonnie Java coffee from Fredericton. All zipped up and neatly packaged. I made it so easy.

The thief also knew what he was doing. When I called Visa to cancel my credit cards (they were hopelessly overdrawn, anyway—suck it, thief!), the bank told me someone had already tried (unsuccessfully) to make a purchase at the grocery store down the road. The person had also turned off all my devices so I couldn't use the app to find him. Bastard. I had to replace everything and had no money to do it.

But I believe I said it was the best thing to happen to me? Maybe not the best thing ever, but because you need identification to get identification, after I tracked down my absolute favourite bank manager in the whole world at a CIBC in the west end of Toronto—the bank that gave me my first mortgage—I was able to replace my bank card, get access to my (limited) funds and begin the process of rebuilding.

It is amazing how God can send you little shreds of encouragement as He brings you out of the fire. Close to ten years later and this wonderful woman was still working at the same bank branch, in the same office. She heard my voice on the phone (a landline, since my cell phone was in my stolen purse) and I hadn't said two words before she screamed my name and asked me how I was doing. I've chosen to withhold her name but she knows who she is . . .

I realized the passport was the most pressing item since my flight to Austria was scheduled for the next day, but even with a twenty-four-hour rush put on replacing it, I couldn't produce the two pieces of government-issued photo ID required to process the application.

I don't think I exhaled all day. I felt mighty uncomfortable and exhausted (not to mention violated and betrayed), but through it all I could sense God's hand over everything that was happening, and believe it or not, I felt His peace. I had a dear friend stick with me and help me get from place to place when I had no money to do it. It even turned out that the person at the passport office was at my last concert in Toronto and did everything in his power to help me. And my dear friend in Halifax used his Air Miles to get me to Halifax when it became apparent that I would need to go back home to replace my identification because I wasn't in my province of residence when all my identification was stolen.

The worst part—the thing that reeeally hurt—was that the

thief, in addition to everything that could be wiped clean and resold, had also stolen my musical score. The hours of work I lost! I had explained my painstaking colour-coding process, along with the IPA symbols, the rhythmic transcription and all the accidentals, each handwritten beside every note. The technical cues, the little hints, the lines and connections drawn to melodies and pitches that would give me my entrance. All gone.

If you'll indulge me a teensy bit more—just to really drive it home how exceptionally bad it was to have this score taken from me—please allow me to do my best to describe the music of *Make No Noise* by Miroslav Srnka. Simply put, it was the hardest thing I'd had to learn in my career to date. Hands down. It could best be described as "word soup." And I say that with complete affection! I happen to find "word soup" mighty tasty. To understand what I mean, simply bring to mind the most outlandish piece of experimental twenty-first-century music imaginable. Then play it backward with thrasher metal and wind chimes blaring in the background. Now try and find your starting pitch. Or the touchstone enharmonic structure within any given phrase. Anything that would conventionally be seen as providing some recognizable framework. You don't get that from Srnka. Ever. And therein lies the genius.

Forget any semblance of conventional rhythm. It was all metre changes and polyrhythms. Under normal circumstances, the quarter note in a simple metre time signature might get subdivided into triplets or quintuplets and maybe the occasional septuplet. I had never actually seen a *sixteenth*let until this piece. There are markings that I still don't know what they mean. That would be like asking a deer in headlights to formulate a question before impact. There was so much black on the page I wasn't sure if I was coming or going. Oh! And it was meant to sound like talking! Eeeasy and non-operatic. (Even above the staff.) With opera singers? This was *Make No Noise*.

Miroslav Srnka is truly a great composer. He's inspired and, as he would describe it, if he didn't write it down—through the triumph of discomfort and hardship—it would drive him crazy until he did. And yes, he was regularly at rehearsals, in the flesh.

By the time I'd gotten my passport replaced and was on a plane to Austria, the cast had already had close to a week of rehearsals. The piece's first section (which I was still learning the notes for), had already been staged. Developing any level of comfort in a piece this impossible, and being a performer who does not like to be put through the humiliation and unprofessionalism of showing up less than prepared, I was sure this couldn't be happening. Remember the Verdi *Requiem* in Peterborough in 1999? This experience took me right back there—only this time it was 2016 on the international stage at a prestigious music festival.

Before I left Toronto for Bregenz, I had set up a pianist to work with me—sending her the score so she could get it under her fingers, because no one knew this piece since it had been written, like, five minutes ago. But none of my preparation happened, because my life blew up when my purse got stolen.

As if that wasn't enough pressure, this piece had been written for me and was meant to have been premiered by me a few years earlier, but I had been pregnant then and had had to cancel, so it got premiered with someone else. But it was always meant for me.

When I arrived at rehearsal, as much as I wanted to believe everything would work out, my stress level was at fever pitch. I had been to the Bregenzer Festspiele the year before, to great success, and they had programmed *Make No Noise* only once I confirmed that I could do it. I was working with cast, conductor and director all for the first time. The only thing I had going for me in terms of a first impression was my smile. My preparation had been sabotaged by the theft of my purse.

Every day I arrived at 7:00 a.m., two hours before everyone, and left at 9:00 p.m., after everyone. I worked and cried and sweated and practised. I knew in my gut that I would get there eventually, but I was genuinely scared. All. The. Time. Scared that I'd hold the production back, scared my colleagues would hate me, scared the conductor would yell at me, scared I'd be fired. Eventually, the conductor did yell at me, and it was singularly the worst moment of my professional life. I thought the ground would open and swallow me whole.

He really laid into me, yelling everything I would yell at me if I were in his position:

"This is unacceptable!"

"How can you not know this by now?"

"I'm doing everything in my power and you still can't get it right?"

Dude. Get out of my head.

Everything he said was spot on, but it wasn't who I was. I didn't take it personally, because he wasn't wrong. He was just responding to what was in front of him. He didn't know me. He didn't know the depth of my resolve. He didn't know I wasn't sleeping. What I didn't know at the time was that during rehearsals for this opera, every performer, in his or her own way, would take a turn at having a mini breakdown. And it was completely understandable. We were short on time, the score was impossibly dense and the staging was incredibly ambitious.

But in my heart of hearts I knew. I knew, I knew, I knew I would get this done. I was not going to be beaten by a stolen purse, an unlearnable score and an enraged conductor. This was *not* how my story ends. I felt this kind of force field around me keeping me on course and moving me forward. There was this reserve of energy that would kick in and wake me up around 6:00 a.m. and not deplete itself until 10:00 p.m., after I'd had a chance to decompress. The fear fell away and I had a mission. I was at war against myself and against the powers that would seek to destroy me and my reputation—the reputation I had worked close to two decades to build.

As I slaved away trying to memorize (even though I had barely learned the nonsensical jumble of pitches), I believed that it was only a matter of time before all those black dots would start to make sense. If I trusted, put in the work and stayed the course, I would come from behind and elevate this production to the high standard it deserved, given the renown of the festival and the faith the organizers had put in me. Despite how devastated I was by the conductor humiliating me the way he did, I know he was a mechanism to get me where I needed to go. The leadership of the festival always had my back, and I am forever indebted to Elisabeth Sobotka, Olaf Schmitt and Nina Wolf. They honestly did everything they could to support and encourage me.

Sure, it may not have been how I would have accomplished this goal, but I also understood that God needed to bring me out of a fire so intense that I would have no other recourse but to trust in Him and give Him the glory. I would be elevated from a professional disaster in order to breathe the fresh, rarified air on the mountaintop and give Him all the glory for it. To accomplish that, He needed for my purse to be stolen, my music not to be learned and the conductor to lose his s*** on me, in front of the whole cast and director.

And I can tell you this: It tasted so sweet to finally feel like I was contributing the way I'd hoped I would. The early mornings and sleepless nights spent in focused study paid off big time—just like I knew they would. The violent tornado of mystery notes and rhythms swirling in my head at last took shape, and there was no finer feeling than knowing what music was coming next and when I was supposed to come in. It felt heavenly to hear and recognize the pitch I was about to sing, where I was supposed to be onstage and how I was supposed to feel about it.

The new production of *Make No Noise* by Johannes Erath was breathtaking and I could finally enjoy it. It was staged in a basin of "oil"—a thick, gelatinous mix that got its deep, dark colour from coffee grinds—because the story took place on an oil rig, and figuratively, all the characters were toiling through their own traumas to somehow find each other through the thickness of their pasts. The metaphor of having to drag yourself through sludge to get where you need to go and become who you need to be was not lost on me. I enjoyed every single, solitary minute of that production, and it was the hardest professional experience of my life—mentally, musically and spiritually.

But who could be with me except Jesus? Who could possibly understand the whirlwind of stress and disappointment but an empathetic God who wants me to be victorious according to His plan for my life? I came out of that production coated in titanium and ready for battle. And I would need it, because I came home to a husband hell-bent on divorcing me and a financial crisis that I had hoped would magically find its own solution. I hadn't been in a hole this deep since I was in university when, with the last quarter to my name, I called my parents from a pay phone and asked them to please put five dollars into my account so I could withdraw it (when you could still withdraw five-dollar bills) and pay for the subway so I could get home from church. It was pretty dire.

Two decades later, the circumstances might be different, but it's still the same God.

Moving forward into the next forty years, I consider what's in front of me right now versus what I would like to see off in the distance. All the Meashas I have described in this memoir will continue their push-pull for supremacy. I want to continue to be grateful for all of it. To feel blessed in all things and perform every task—come what may—as unto the Lord. More specifically, I want to be healthy (as if anyone wants to be sick). I'd like to sing what I want with whomever I want, and I want to be able to live my faith without making people feel like I'm trying to convict or convert them. I don't have that kind of pull and I don't want the pressure of saving you. Plus, it's honestly not my job to save you. My job is to love you with the love of the living God. I won't always succeed, but I'm talking about goals here, not slam dunks.

I want to be a mother who is fully present and pursuing my dreams. I want my boys to grow up with a mother who is fulfilled by her work but is never happier than when she is holding them, helping them, cooking for them and listening to whatever it is they have to say.

Time, perspective and immeasurable joy are what helped me to recognize the loss of my babies, my aorta exploding, my marriage ending and my career flourishing as the broadening and deepening of my humanity and faith. All the major transitions in my life, qualified by sadness or not, are invaluable lessons that I couldn't trade, even if I wanted to. They certainly didn't feel that way at the time, I can tell you. But as I come up to the next decade having seen my discomforts directly correlated to something that made me better and expanded my territory, my knee-jerk reaction to feel like the world is against me (or that God has abandoned me) has been replaced by the assurance that I'm going to be brought through this fire, refined and strengthened. When the smoke clears, I will still be standing at the end, and so will *you*!

Whether the storms are here or their inevitable arrival is pending, some kind of hurricane, tornado, firestorm or angry mob will catch up with us all eventually. They may come for you by name, or they may come for your ideas or for what separates them from you. Your job is to develop a tolerance for the heat, and thus manage and control the temperature of your own life. Your job is to build that bridge that brings you together. Pressure, circumstance, livelihood, responsibility: all metaphors for the fires that burn in our lives. For the heat that threatens to consume us, but that also keeps us warm enough to survive. And if you want it to run hot, then you had better like to sweat. And if you like it on the cooler side, you had better get a thick skin. Even if what they say about you is true (indeed, especially if what they say about you is true), only you can decide which fires need tending and when.

I've used the analogy of a fire because of its purifying qualities. It is a rough, painstaking, agonizing process of elimination.

Its intensity sanitizes the blade and cauterizes the wound. It selects what stays by burning up what can't withstand the heat. The punishing fire of atonement leads to the refined steel of wisdom. And it's not for the faint of heart.

It's funny that I've always considered myself a water person, when it has been fire that has provided the most comfort, drama, excitement, celebration, refinement and romance in my life so far. Fireworks, a bonfire, stacking firewood, little scars from the oven, little nicks from the fireplace, second-degree burns, barbecue, gasoline, kindling, propane, firepit, a hearth and candles. There is a corresponding incendiary element to every fire, match, eruption, bomb, explosion, ember, simmer and spark in all our lives. Everything has to start somewhere, and for me, the element of fire being both a starter and a finisher, as well as a sustainer and a purifier, was the image that best illustrated the balancing act of first feeding yourself in order to maintain the heat (and intensity) of the fires within your realm of influence, while also being discerning enough to not throw yourself into any fire simply to keep it burning.

None of us can control anything, so I choose to be the Mother of Dragons, not Jeanne d'Arc. I can orchestrate a host of parameters that might/could lead to a desired outcome, but at some point, it's out of my hands. Discovering that helped me loosen the white-knuckled grip I had on aspects of my relationships, my finances and who I wanted the world to think I was. Since I have this one book in me, I wasn't going to squander my singular opportunity by not telling you the truth and then wishing I had. Because after a lifetime of lying, I know how good it feels to tell the truth, especially when it's hard. The stronger the expectation of ostracism, the more rewarding the lighthearted, self-made space of peace you get to live in, instead of the heavy shackles of lies that used to bind you. Living the truth is the most liberating weight-loss program you'll ever find.

It is not in our nature as humans to seek tribulation, but if we can take the heat, we can be a witness to that triumph for others. As a Christian, I give God the glory for the things He's done in my life, but if that is not your system of belief, then I would urge you to at least allow for the possibility that all things are as they're meant to be. Deeply consider the possibility that you're being groomed for greatness. I know that might ring a little hollow, which is why the boundless, all-powerful presence of God is so central to my life. Because if HE is the one readying you for your blessing, then hold on to your hat, because He says that He will supply every need of yours according to His riches in glory in Jesus Christ! (Philippians 4:19)

I am sure that there are no lengths to which the enemy will go to discourage me and render me ineffective for Christ. My impatience, my pride, my ego and my addiction to the creature comforts and trappings of this world keep me enslaved and blind to the will He wants to impose over my life, for His glory. But even as satan has an annoying fly buzzing around my head trying to distract me from finishing this sentence, I know that only

God can keep me from falling (Jude 1:24) and that no weapon against me shall prosper (Isaiah 54:17).

And I get it if all this "Jesus talk" doesn't apply to you. But I will be praying that you will come to faith. In the meantime, I hope we can at least agree that your life has a purpose, and the harder you seek it, the more difficult it will be to attain. All the odds will be stacked against you because you are precisely pursuing the only thing that for you is going to make you a powerful force for good in your own life and in the lives of those around you. We all experience the fiery daggers that are flung our way the minute we get on the right track. Choosing between the mortgage and the hydro bill. Getting more sleep or having "the talk" with a loved one. Writing one more page before turning on the TV. Going for a run instead of emptying the dishwasher. It's possible that all your options might just plain suck. But you are to wait on the Lord. Lean in to whatever new horror comes around the corner and stand your ground.

Adversity is an indication that you are on the right track. If this life comes too easy, with zero resistance, it won't fill you up how you thought it would. You have to work for it, lose sleep over it, sacrifice for it, even bleed for it. Let's get on with embracing the thrill of freedom that comes with rejecting the notion that our hardships have to intimidate or isolate us. You are not alone. Let's stop pursuing anything that remotely resembles perfection, actively forgive our inadequacies and find peace in the truth that something is always on fire.

To Him who is able to keep you from stumbling and to present you before His glorious presence without fault and with great joy—to the only God our Saviour be glory, majesty, power and authority, through Jesus Christ our Lord, before all ages, now and forevermore! Amen.

—JUDE 1:24-25

ACKNOWLEDGEMENTS

If you've made it all the way to the acknowledgements then you know already that I didn't get here alone. My parents, Sterling and Ann Gosman, have always said it's never too late to say thank you. I would not have had the courage or the vocabulary or the stamina to write a book if I hadn't been raised right, so thank you, Mom and Dad. Teah and Neville, tears come to my eyes as I think of the hard-working, protective, headstrong example you both have set for me as my older siblings and as parents. I pray my children will love each other as yours do.

The enlightened guidance shown to me by my editor, Jennifer Lambert, is something for which I shall be eternally grateful. She equipped me with courage. As did my faithful proofreaders, Jeff Embleton, Julie Beun, Megan MacDonald, Evan Newman, Jill Groom, Steve Zsirai and Alan Coates. They should start a commune for wayward souls in search of encouragement and reassurance. They would make a killing.

ACKNOWLEDGEMENTS

I started this process five years ago with a ghostwriter named Sylvia Fraser. She is a patient, long-suffering, incredibly tolerant angel of a woman who sat with me over months and months, only to have none of her words published in this book. But the material she succeeded in unlocking in me is the only reason this book exists in the form that it does. Thank you, Sylvia.

To the best human I know and the father of my children, Markus. Though we are no longer married, yours has been the greatest love I have ever known. I delight in seeing you in our boys' faces and welcome your voice in my head. Held in similar esteem is my dear friend Kristin Johnston, who was taken from us while I was writing.

To HarperCollins, the Leighton Artists' Colony at the Banff Centre for Arts and Creativity, Tamara Ross, Jim Fleck, Pastor Daniel Cormier, Heather Lohr and Shelley Fleckenstein. All of you have bent over backward, opened your doors and given me shelter in your own ways. You came into my life exactly at the right moment and our time together has shaped me, my faith and this book.

Finally, to my teachers and mentors: the cornerstones of my career. Every brick of my artistry and ambition has been laid by David Steeves, Dianne Wilkins, Mabel Doak, Wendy Nielsen, Edith Wiens, Bishop T. D. Jakes and the incomparable Mary Morrison.

THANK YOU.

MAR